CHINESE COSMOPOLITANISM

THE PRINCETON-CHINA SERIES

Daniel A. Bell, Series Editor

The Princeton-China Series aims to publish the works of contemporary Chinese scholars in the humanities, social sciences, and related fields. The goal is to bring the work of these important thinkers to a wider audience, foster an understanding of China on its own terms, and create new opportunities for cultural cross-pollination.

Chinese Cosmopolitanism

THE HISTORY AND PHILOSOPHY
OF AN IDEA

SHUCHEN XIANG

PRINCETON UNIVERSITY PRESS

PRINCETON & OXFORD

Copyright © 2023 by Princeton University Press

Princeton University Press is committed to the protection of copyright and the intellectual property our authors entrust to us. Copyright promotes the progress and integrity of knowledge. Thank you for supporting free speech and the global exchange of ideas by purchasing an authorized edition of this book. If you wish to reproduce or distribute any part of it in any form, please obtain permission.

Requests for permission to reproduce material from this work should be sent to permissions@press.princeton.edu

Published by Princeton University Press
41 William Street, Princeton, New Jersey 08540
99 Banbury Road, Oxford OX2 6JX

press.princeton.edu

All Rights Reserved

Library of Congress Control Number 2023938219
ISBN 978-0-691-24272-9
ISBN (e-book) 978-0-691-24271-2

British Library Cataloging-in-Publication Data is available

Editorial: Rob Tempio and Chloe Coy
Production Editorial: Jill Harris
Jacket Design: Heather Hansen
Production: Erin Suydam
Publicity: William Pagdatoon
Copyeditor: Cynthia Buck

Jacket image: *The Palaces and Gate Towers of Penglai,* by Zhu Dan. Ink, color, and gold on silk. Qing dynasty, 1683. Courtesy of Rawpixel.

This book has been composed in Arno

Printed on acid-free paper. ∞

Printed in the United States of America

10 9 8 7 6 5 4 3 2 1

Dedicated to the wretched of the earth

Rise! People who refuse to be slaves!

Qilai! Buyuan zuo nuli de renmen!

起来! 不愿做奴隶的人们!

CONTENTS

ACKNOWLEDGMENTS

FOREMOST, I would like to express my deepest gratitude to Daniel Bell for supporting me throughout the development and publication of this project. My thanks also to Rob Tempio and Chloe Coy at Princeton University Press for all their help, and to my mentors and friends Roger Ames and Martin Powers for their guidance and advice on aspects of this project. I am also extremely grateful to Cynthia Buck, whose editing helped clarify my writing and pushed me to be less complacent in some of my wording, and to Zhang Yixuan of Peking University, who helped me check some classical Chinese textual materials.

Finally, I am grateful to Jacob and my mum for always being there for me and encouraging me. A special note of thanks is due to Jacob, my husband and partner-in-crime, who read each chapter many times and then read through the whole manuscript (twice!) and offered me much-needed perspective. I am always grateful for the time, care, and attention he brings to helping me cultivate my work when he could be focused on his own projects. Jacob and I met at the University of Hawai'i in 2014, and our intellectual paths and ethical convictions have evolved in conjunction ever since. I have benefited much from his companionship throughout the years.

Parts of chapter 1 have been published as "Why the Confucians Had No Concept of Race (Part I): The Anti-Essentialist Cultural Understanding of Self" and "Why the Confucians Had No Concept of Race (Part II): Cultural Difference, Environment, and Achievement" in *Philosophy Compass*; parts of chapter 3 have been published as "Chinese Processual Holism and Its Attitude towards 'Barbarians' and Nonhumans" in *Sophia*. I thank both of these publications for permission to reuse this material.

CHINESE COSMOPOLITANISM

Introduction

HISTORICALLY, the Western encounter with difference has been cata-strophic. Europe's first encounter with significantly different peoples on a large scale—during its "Age of Discovery"—led to the decimation of 95 percent of the native Amerindian population in what one historian calls "the most massive act of genocide in the history of the world" (Stannard 1992: x). The European encounter with difference also gave rise to the trans-atlantic slave trade, which, according to demographers' estimates, may have halved Africa's population through deaths on the continent and exportation of its population (Bayley 2004: 409). The United States, Canada, Australia, New Zealand, Rhodesia, and South Africa were all founded on the extermi-nation, displacement, or herding onto reservations of aboriginal populations (Mills 1997: 28). By 1914 colonialism had brought 85 percent of the earth under European rule as colonies, protectorates, dependencies, dominions, and commonwealths (29).

This colonial world order is now being challenged by China, which has a different way of understanding difference. It is little realized in the West that China and Chinese culture have not been static throughout the coun-try's history. With a dynamic identity created out of difference, China has always been "cosmopolitan." Throughout history, the Chinese have dealt better with difference than have the Europeans, owing to fundamentally different philosophical and cultural assumptions. This study argues that Chinese philosophy has the conceptual resources to provide alternative paradigms for thinking about pluralism—which have never been more needed than in our current era.

1

The Chinese Tradition's Challenge
to Western Racism and Colonialism

I had several interconnected motivations for pursuing this project. One is the need to set the record straight about the nature of the Chinese tradition. At a time when China's global profile is rising, misunderstanding China is likely to have significant geopolitical consequences. It is thus imperative that the nature of Chinese self-identity, the Chinese worldview with regard to difference, and the Chinese historical view of the "other" be more clearly understood. Second, I believe it is important to correct a pervasive assumption in modern academia that colonialism, genocide, racial violence, and hatred of the other arise from universal and stable characteristics of human nature. Instead, as I argue here, these phenomena are culturally contingent. Third, it is my hope to correct the increasingly popular assumption among many contemporary Sinologists and Western academics, that the Western discourse of race is applicable to the Chinese tradition. As shown here, employing the Western discourse of race to frame the Chinese view toward non-Chinese is a category mistake, as well as irresponsible in that making this mistake can have grave consequences. Just as the Jesuits mistranslated *tian* as the Christian "heaven," so do many contemporary Sinologists mistranslate certain Chinese concepts as "race." Applying the concepts related to the ideological constellation of Western racism—such as referring to non-Greeks and non-Europeans as "barbarians" and viewing the European encounter with others as a "civilizing mission"—is problematic with respect to the Chinese relationship with its historic border peoples.

Finally, I hope to show here that Chinese philosophy is of relevance in thinking about contemporary issues related to pluralism; indeed, it has many valuable lessons to offer in this regard. Charles Mills puts it well: "How is cosmopolitanism to be realized on a globe shaped by hundreds of years of European expansionism?" (Mills 2005: 190). Chinese philosophy can help us rethink how to create a multipolar world, and it can make valuable contributions to contemporary discussions of the critical philosophy of race and decolonialism. If we are to think of serious alternatives to racial and colonial order, then Chinese philosophers, postcolonial scholars, decolonial scholars, and critical philosophers of race need to start engaging with each other's works.

Famously, the philosopher Zhao Tingyang gives an account of the Chinese tradition's notion of *tianxia*, or "all under heaven," as a borderless world. He contrasts it with the notion of the nation-state in Western history, which he considers to be the largest political entity in the Western political framework. Unexplored in Zhao's work is the issue of Western racism (Zhao 2021). Any notion of *tianxia* would have been metaphysically impossible in the Western tradition, which sees the world as populated only by those who embody civilization and those who embody barbarism. This Manichean division between ontologically distinct groups is perennial and irreconcilable in the Western tradition. Projecting the concept of the barbarian onto the racial other, the Spanish conquistadors understood colonialism as a holy war in which the native Americans, whom they viewed as barbarians and natural slaves as well as minions of the devil, had to be either converted or extinguished in order to secure humanity, Christendom, and civilization. Relatedly, Western metaphysics understood the world in terms of the ontological Great Chain of Being, no element of which had the same worth. In the natural order of things, according to this metaphysical view, different peoples are created unequal and "white" peoples or nations dominate racial others; hence the casual racial violence toward and genocide of nonwhite peoples during settler colonialism. The ontological dualism and Great Chain of Being intrinsic to Western metaphysics prevented the Western tradition from developing a notion of *tianxia*.

The history and nature of Western racism is not well known. In *The Racial Contract*, Charles Mills coined the term "the epistemology of ignorance" to refer to a systematic ignorance of how "race" epistemologically, materially, and historically shaped and continues to shape our world. Here, the "racial contract" is used as a theoretical concept for recognizing, describing, and understanding how racism *actually* structures the polities of the West and elsewhere. Under the two-tiered moral code of the racial contract, we have been living with one set of morals for whites and another for nonwhites (Mills 1997: 23). However, the architects and beneficiaries of this white, racialized world also benefit from obscuring how race (the system they created) works. The epistemology of ignorance is a framework that inculcates peoples with a self-deception that makes them blind to or denies the reality of how racial hierarchy materially and epistemically shapes our world. This ignorance is not accidental, but purposeful. Nonwhites are not immune to the epistemology of ignorance, or "white ignorance," or "white denial," since the power relations and patterns of ideological hegemony can inculcate such ignorance into them as well.

The "epistemology of ignorance," (Mills 1997: 18) pervading the Western academy about the West's racial violence and genocidal actions has combined with the Western academy's dominance in international academic discourse to keep this history from being well known. It is only when we place issues of race and racial hierarchy in the picture can we understand why the Western tradition has historically been so incapable of tolerating difference. It is my intention here to make clear the formative impact of concepts of the barbarian, race, and associated ideas on Western historical practice and to describe the positive impact of the absence of such ideas and the presence of alternatives on Chinese historical practice with regard to the embrace of difference. I begin by establishing what we mean when we speak of "racism."

The Singularity of (Western) Racism

As the editors of the collected volume *The Origins of Racism in the West* put it, "One often encounters a vague sense that racism is basically the same as ethnic prejudice and discrimination, but in a more malicious and serious form." This understanding of racism, however, is "an erroneous view" (Eliav-Feldon, Isaac, and Ziegler 2009: 5). Apprehension of different and unfamiliar things and peoples is a universal and instinctive human reaction. There is a difference between an initial mistrust of something unknown and the ideology of racism. The initial distrust of the unknown fulfills the practical purpose of preserving one's own well-being, the reification of this fear of the unknown turns it into the ideology of racism. In other words, the ideology of racism begins when a fear of foreigners is sustained after it has outlasted its practical purpose. As Miriam Eliav-Feldon, Benjamin Isaac, and Joseph Ziegler write:

> We do not assume that prejudice and bigotry were invented in the West; we claim rather that the specific form of rationalizing these prejudices and attempting to base them on systematic, abstract thought was developed in antiquity and taken over in early modern Europe. Racism, the nineteenth- and twentieth-century ideology familiar to us, developed in Europe, not in China, Japan or India. (Eliav-Feldon, Isaac, and Ziegler 2009: 9)

It is the ossification of the fear of difference into an ideology that is distinctive of racism. We can see this ideology structuring the European encounter with the Amerindians. "Despite increased contact with other continents during this part of the age of discovery," writes the American historian Paul Gordon Lauren, "Europeans' attitudes about race demonstrated little change at all. Growing familiarity did not result in greater toleration, compassion, or acceptance, and the old stereotyped images showed tenacious persistence" (Lauren 2018: 10).

Absent the ideology of race, greater interaction with initially different peoples would lead to the understanding that we are all human. It is only the presence of racial ideology that blinds us to this fact. This ideology is not universal but rather mainly, if not exclusively, Western. The classicist Benjamin Isaac, in *The Invention of Racism in Classical Antiquity*, notes that the Greeks and Romans "have given us, through their literature, many of the ideas of freedom, democracy, philosophy, novel artistic concepts and so much else that we regard as essential to our culture" (Isaac 2004: 516). If such foundational aspects of Western culture come from the Greeks and Romans, "can it be denied," he asks, "that they were instrumental in conveying the idea of racism?" (131). We must recognize racism as a legacy of Western culture.

As we will see, what sets (Western) racism apart from normal prejudice and bigotry is the idea that some people are (ontological) barbarians—quasi-human beings who are irredeemably other. Ever since ancient Greece, the essence of the barbarian and Manichean racial other has been seen as antithetical to Western civilization. There is no point in educating non-Greeks because no amount of education can rehabilitate them for civilization. Just as the philosopher Alfred North Whitehead famously characterized all of Western philosophy as a footnote to Plato, we could say that all of the West's later racial ideology and practice has been a footnote to Aristotle and his theory of natural slavery. Aristotle first formulated the consequential idea that non-Greeks are subhumans whose purpose (*telos*) is to be enslaved by the (white) Greek man. Natural slaves are those who, left on their own, are incapable of reason and must be subjugated by a rational (read: male, Greek) agent in order to partake of reason. For Aristotle, because non-Greeks are barbarians and barbarians are natural slaves, *all* non-Greeks are natural slaves. The status of barbarians is thus ontological. They have no way of improving their status and can never become non-barbarian, non-natural slaves. Just as it is in the nature of a dog to be a dog, the essence of the barbarian is to be a barbarian. A barbarian can never become properly human, just as a dog can never become human. By no means does the Greek concept of "barbarism" merely describe uncouthness. It carries the culturally specific meaning of the Manichean other who, being eternally (essentially) savage, is antithetical to civilization.

The record of the meaning of "barbarian" in the Western historical context and its association with the (genocidal) project of Western colonialism is the background and point of contrast for this study. The assumption underlying the Western project has been what Aimé Césaire calls a "dependency complex," that is, the assumption that natives, being irrational, are incapable of self-rule and so the white man must rule on their behalf *for their own good* (a literal reading of Aristotle's theory of natural slavery) (Césaire 2000). It is this assumption that precludes our equating Chinese attitudes toward non-Chinese with the Greek view toward non-Greeks. As this study will elucidate, the Chinese historically never had a conception of non-Chinese as unimprovable. By the time of the Qing dynasty, the Chinese accounted for about 40 percent of the world's population; only a history of intermarriage with all kinds of "foreigners" could produce so populous a people. Further, and this is the more crucial point, there is no *metaphysical* basis in the Chinese context for the thinking that underlies Aristotle's views about natural slavery. That thinking depends on a *substance ontology* in which the substance determines the being or becoming of the thing. As will be clarified in this study, Chinese metaphysics, by contrast, is *processual*. If, as the central tenet of Confucianism has it, one is not born human and one only *becomes* human through acculturation and practice, then no groups of peoples are ontologically superior and there can be no natural hierarchies as in the Platonic-Aristotelian conception (the different grades of soul and the hierarchy of Greek and barbarian) and later the Christian conception (the Great Chain of Being).

Signification must be understood in a structuralist manner; an isolated example is meaningful only within the context of the whole. Those who assume that Western concepts, phenomena, and behaviors have parallels in the Chinese tradition bear a burden of proof. Can they point to a broader meaning context in which certain Chinese ideas and practices can coherently be framed in terms of Western racism? Can this context be shown on a philosophical and mainly metaphysical level? My study argues that the nature of Western racial practice and the absence of such practice in the Chinese context are primarily explained by their differing metaphysics.[1]

The different metaphysical models underlying the Western and Chinese worldviews have practical implications for their understandings of what is efficacious and virtuous. In his paper "Devastation: The Destruction of Populations and Human Landscapes and the Roman Imperial Project," Myles Lavan observes that, throughout Roman rule, the image of devastation is the "single most common metaphor for empire as a relationship of power" (Lavan 2020: 179n2). Lavan notes the prominence of verbs such as *uasto* (devastate), *tollo* (remove, eliminate), *excido* (eradicate), and *deleo* (erase) in the lexicon of public service and aristocratic achievement. Lavan singles out *deleo*: intimating "total obliteration and the sense of creating a blank space to be filled by something else." This term, he argues, is most saliently associated with aristocratic achievement (189). "To claim to have erased a people or a city was to inscribe oneself into a long tradition of Roman excellence" (190). For example, one element of the "iconography of victory" is the image of desertification: "The desertification of Jerusalem's hinterland during the war seems to have been transformed into a central image of the awful outcome of the revolt against Rome" (181). Lavan finds it paradoxical that many of these terms connote ameliorative actions when the violence they describe was so horrific. The verb *excido*, for example, "is shared with technical discourses such as medicine which impart connotations of reasoned and ameliorative action" (198). As I show in discussing the Great Chain of Being (chapter 4), we can argue that imperial Roman discourse celebrated violence against barbarian tribes because, under the ontology of the Great Chain of Being, violence was a display of virtue. Interestingly, for Lavan, "Roman culture is in no way unusual in this respect." The images and texts he discusses "stand at the end of a long Near Eastern and Mediterranean discourse of state formation and empire, in which the capacity to destroy populations and landscapes was an important index of state power" (180). We can say that Roman culture shared with these Near Eastern and Mediterranean discourses the ontology of the Great Chain of Being.

A contemporary example of the Great Chain of Being psychology in action could be seen in the shock-and-awe tactic employed by the US Army in its 2003 invasion of Iraq. Nothing better captured domination through erasure than the US military camp built on the archaeological site of the Babylonians' famous Ishtar Gate south of Baghdad (built in 575 BC). Around three hundred thousand square meters were covered over with gravel; three areas were flattened to make a helicopter landing pad, a parking lot, and a site for portable toilets; and trenches were dug, dispersing brick fragments bearing cuneiform inscriptions (Sigal 2018). Arguably, the psychology that is informed by the ideology of the Great Chain of Being is not a mere historical curiosity but still shapes Western practice today. There is no place, however, for the Chinese tradition's understanding of efficacy within the (Western) framework of the Great Chain of Being, where the physical eradication of a people and place is a sign of virtue. The very different metaphysics of the Chinese tradition has helped to shape the noncolonial behavior of Chinese states throughout history.

Enrique Dussel is one of the foremost philosophers of the Latin Americas. Born in Argentina, he fled to Mexico in 1975 when socialist sympathizers were being hunted down and some thirty thousand civilians were "disappeared" during a period of US-backed state terrorism known as the "dirty war" (Feitlowitz 2011: ix). For Dussel, the Spanish conquistadors (symbolic of Western military aggression) and their missionaries (embodying Western ideologies and philosophy) during the conquest of the Americas reduced the Amerindian other to a mere object onto which could be imprinted the form of European civilization; the Amerindian was reduced to the same. This meant that these Europeans never arrived at the metaphilosophical position foundational for intercultural dialogue: an ability to assess their own presuppositions (Dussel 1995). The difference between cultural exchange and cultural appropriation is that, in the former, one learns the culture of the other in order to gain a metaphilosophical perspective on one's own culture—the double vision of which W.E.B. Du Bois spoke. A true comparative philosophy is an ongoing dialogue that cannot proceed without recognizing that one is making cultural assumptions.[2] In cultural appropriation, the culture of the other is reduced to a dead object from which one can learn nothing about oneself. Any knowledge of this object, like cultural objects in the British Museum, serves merely to consolidate one's own ego. Today examples of China being treated like a dead object to which theoretical paradigms can uncritically and arbitrarily be applied are ubiquitous, if not the norm.[3]

The West's current confrontation with China will be the biggest shock to the Eurocentric worldview since the Spaniards' confrontation with the differences of the other embodied by the Amerindian. The question is, how will the West cope with an other or a difference that cannot be reduced to the same in the way that many others throughout history were? This time, will the West finally learn the humility needed to assess its own assumptions and intellectually make room for the presence of strangers and their differences?

A Summary of the Chapters

Chapter 1, "A Brief History of Chinese Cosmopolitanism," establishes that historically China was both internally cosmopolitan, in that it incorporated an enormous number of originally distinct peoples and their cultures into a common identity, and externally cosmopolitan in that its extensive knowledge of faraway lands did not give rise to an ideology that required the subjugation of these lands. This chapter shows that this internal and external embrace of difference was indebted to both an ideal of "harmony" premised on the metaphysics of organic life and the (Confucian) "cultural" conception of personhood that was operative in Chinese history. After providing brief surveys of Chinese history focused on the issues of pluralism, the chapter ends by addressing some common fallacies in writings about China that reveal important unexamined assumptions and problematic motivations.

Chapter 2, "The Barbarian in the Western Imagination and History," describes the formative influence on Western practice throughout history of the idea of the barbarian. Crucially, the barbarian embodies two antithetical characteristics: formlessness, but also the form of evil. This chapter provides a historical survey of the European tradition's negative self-definition. Since its Greek inception, civilization and humanity were defined through an imagined barbarian who is the antipode of the Greeks' own espoused cultural values. This barbarian became the medieval "wild man" when inherited by the Christian consciousness. During the age of empire, the subliminal barbarian of the European subconscious was projected, with devastating consequences, onto the newly encountered peoples of the "New World," who were so physically and culturally different from the Europeans.

Chapter 3, "Chinese Processual Holism and Its Attitude toward 'Barbarians' and Nonhumans," describes the dynamic processual nature of Chinese metaphysics, especially with respect to its view of nonhumans, such as animals and demons. Key to Western colonialism's violence toward the native was its view of the "barbarian" other as merely nature and so beyond the pale of moral concern. The ideology informing Western colonialism provided a metaphysical framework where a preestablished ontological hierarchy did not grant to animals and nonwhite races the same moral status as whites. Since Chinese metaphysics, in contrast, never saw (certain) human beings as transcending nature, it also did not see nonhuman aspects of the natural continuum as "mere nature." Concomitantly, there was no place in such a metaphysics for the dualistic Western idea of the transcendent dominating mere nature because the latter had no moral status. The implication of the stark contrast between the Western view and the Chinese view of the relationship between the myriad things is that the Chinese saw their relationship to foreigners in very different terms.

Chapter 4, "Race, Metaphysical Determinism, and the Great Chain of Being," explores in more detail the assumption of racial hierarchy that underlies the colonial view of the world. From the view that difference must be situated in an ontological hierarchy, it follows that the white races bear an ontological mandate to subjugate the "lesser" races to safeguard the cosmic order.

Chapter 5, "The Metaphysics of Harmony and the Metaphysics of Colonialism," contrasts the Chinese understanding of efficacy, described as "harmony," with the Western understanding of efficacy, which, following the ontology of the Great Chain of Being, is described as imposing form upon matter.

Chapter 6, "The Metaphysics of Harmony in Practice," shows the practical implications of the Chinese (harmony) understanding of efficacy. The Chinese traditionally did not see imposing one's will on others—manifested in the international context as "colonialism"—as efficacious because they understood that this would lead only to the other's resentment of the colonizer. Instead, the Chinese sought to gain influence over others by noncoercively convincing them of the attractiveness of the Chinese position. In this worldview, the only way for the agent to sustain long-term influence over others was to persuade them to view the agent as a person whose abilities, qualities, and continued existence would ensure their collective flourishing. Furthermore, in the absence of the idea that the foreigner was a formless barbarian onto whom form should be imposed, the historical relationship between China and its neighbors was not one of unilinear domination but of attempts to harmonize—that is, mutual exchange.

A New Model of Comparative Philosophy

Today's dominant model of "comparative" philosophy cannot but affirm its detractors' opinion that introducing other philosophic traditions to the canon is a superficial exercise in political correctness. If "comparing" philosophies from different cultures only reveals that philosophies in the West find their commensurable counterparts in non-Western philosophies, then there is nothing of significance that other philosophies can add to the existing Western canon.[4] We need to discard this paradigm of (asymmetrically) comparing non-Western philosophy with Western philosophy and replace it with a paradigm that allows us to learn from each other's traditions.

In *Analects* 7.22, Confucius says, "When walking in the company of two others, I am bound to learn from them. The good points of the one I copy; the bad points of the other I correct in myself." Taking this attitude of humility and applying it to philosophy, we can envision comparative philosophy as a company of others in which—and only in which—we can fully understand and improve ourselves. In the words used by the decolonial scholar and revolutionary Frantz Fanon to describe his vision for a more inclusive humanity: "What we want to do is to go forward all the time, night and day, in the company of Man, in the company of all men" (Fanon 1963: 314–15). Nobody in Confucius's "company" of fellow travelers or Fanon's "caravan" can claim an exclusive monopoly on truth. Instead, both regard difference as enriching.

The image that Confucius paints of understanding oneself and improving oneself by being in *dialogue* with others is not so different from Goethe's idea of *Weltliteratur*, whereby the literatures of different nations form a symphonic whole: each instrumental note does not merely assert its own uniqueness but also understands its uniqueness in relation to the uniqueness of other notes and the *complementarity* of its own uniqueness with the uniqueness of others. In both Confucius's and Goethe's vision, none of us can be the best version of ourselves isolated from others. For Confucius, the isolated individual has no chance to improve himself. For Goethe, without other instrumental notes, one instrumental note cannot produce music. For Fanon, the future of humanity lies not in the "obscene caricature" of merely imitating any one member of humanity, but in a caravan whose members recognize each other, meet with each other, and talk to each other (Fanon 1963: 315). For philosophy, each tradition can only truly understand itself and what it offers the world in relation to other traditions. In my own version of comparative philosophy, (1) the uniqueness of each tradition is affirmed and respected; (2) the uniqueness of each tradition enriches other traditions; (3) difference is understood as enriching; and (4) an openness to change through engagement is maintained through an understanding that cultural traditions are dynamic and evolving.

Just as the previous generation asked the "Needham Question" of why modern science did not develop in China but did in Europe (posed by the British biochemist and historian of Chinese science Joseph Needham), it is now time to subject the Western tradition to similar scrutiny and ask: Why did racism become such a pernicious problem in the Western tradition? The old anthropological model of the West studying "the Rest" should be replaced by a more equal relationship whereby all traditions can be the subject of analysis. Western culture is just another world culture, not an Archimedean point, devoid of perspective, from which to study the (merely cultural) traditions of others.

Relatedly, we could ask a question just as important as the Needham Question: Why did racist ideology *not* develop in China? If the project launched by Needham's question is worth the gamut of an ever-expanding series and a Cambridge research institute, then the question of why racism did not develop in China is also a case study worthy of extensive scholarly engagement. One could even argue that this question has greater social repercussions than the Needham Question. If Niall Ferguson could famously offer, in *Civilization: The West and the Rest*, the six "killer apps" that explain why Western civilization came out on top, my project can respond by detailing the "killer apps" of Chinese cosmopolitanism and revealing, in stark contrast, the "kill apps" employed in Western racism. Comparative philosophy needs to question its *raison d'être* if it refuses to accept that there are in fact alternatives to the West as the end of human history. To explain this point I borrow from James Baldwin, who writes in *The Fire Next Time*:

> I cannot accept the proposition that the four-hundred-year travail of the American Negro should result merely in his attainment of the present level of American civilization. I am far from convinced that being released from the African witch doctor was worthwhile if I am now—in order to support the moral contradictions and the spiritual aridity of my life—expected to become dependent on the American psychiatrist. It is a bargain I refuse. The only thing white people have that black people need, or should want, is power—and no one holds power forever. White people cannot, in the generality, be taken as models of how to live. Rather, the white man is himself in sore need of new standards, which will release him from his confusion and place him once again in fruitful communion with the depths of his own being. (Baldwin 1998: 341–42)

It should be the work of comparative philosophy to find such "new standards."

What this book strives to do is to imagine the horizons of a "larger, freer, and more loving" humanity (Baldwin 1998: 314). No one holds on to power forever. When that power is gone, we cannot ignore the fact that we were always alone in a universe with nothing but each other. Comparative philosophy can either take the lead or be the Owl of Minerva who flies only after the battle is over.

This project is as much about understanding Western racism as it is about understanding Chinese pluralism. The Chinese tradition is not utopistic, and I do not mean to present historical China as such by highlighting certain aspects of Chinese culture for their contributions to a more cosmopolitan world. However, juxtaposing Chinese culture with the Western tradition around the issue of pluralism helps us understand why Western racism became so pernicious in human history. Some of the resistance to this thesis is grounded in the very Western chauvinism I critique. With Chinese history placed alongside Western history, we are able to see why Chinese history was *comparably* far more cosmopolitan than the Western tradition. What we will not see is historical China as a utopia (which, after all, means a "no-place"). Critics of this work should keep in mind that the epistemology of ignorance will be the Western audience's greatest obstacle in understanding the arguments in this book.[5]

The Epistemology of Ignorance and
the Universalization of Western Racism

There is a recent trend[6] among Western Sinologists of mapping the colonial paradigm of otherness and race relations onto the Chinese tradition (Nylan 2012).[7] These same Western Sinologists think they are scientists of primary texts who bring no *a priori* assumptions to the texts they are interpreting. Many of those who work on traditional Chinese relationships to the non-Chinese remain unaware of the voluminous work conducted in the critical philosophy of race, a field in which it is orthodoxy that racism was a Western invention. For instance, as stated in *Racism: A Short History*, a staple of undergraduate critical philosophy of race curricula, racism "is mainly, if not exclusively, a product of the West" (Fredrickson 2002: 6). The methodological ignorance of some Sinologists has allowed an uncritical uptake of common folk beliefs in Western societies. Given that, since World War II, Western societies and governments have made a concerted effort to whitewash the history of their racism, this folk belief amounts to amnesia about Western racism. In his novel *Fatherland*, Robert Harris depicts an alternative reality in which the Nazis won World War II and eradicated all the records of their genocide of the Jews, so that only scattered evidence remains. Such a reality is not altogether fictional: as Charles Mills writes, in certain respects we do in fact

> live in an actual, nonalternative world where the victors of racial killing really *did* win and have reconstructed and falsified the record accordingly. Holocaust denial and Holocaust apologia thus long precede the post-1945 period, going back all the way to the original response to the revelations of Las Casas's *Devastation of the Indies* in 1542. (Mills 1997: 104–5)

Amnesia about Western racism takes various forms. It is found in the assumption that colonialism, genocide, racial violence, and hatred of the other is a universal feature of human nature and human practice, as well as in the assumption that terms used in the Western discourse of race such as "barbarian" and "civilizing mission" are applicable to the Chinese context.[8] The folk beliefs that many Sinologists uncritically apply to their interpretations of Chinese texts arose from a careful process of censorship and vetting designed to legitimize and further the project of Western imperialism. For example, as Robert Bernasconi has shown, even after the idea of race lost its respectability in the post–World War II period, major international institutions, such as the United Nations and UNESCO, tended to equate racism with a fallacious biological understanding of race that was applied to Jews (Bernasconi 2019). This neat equation confined racism to fringe figures associated with the Nazi movement, thus avoiding any association with the genocidal history of European colonialism. The *cordon sanitaire* erected around the concept and history of "race" allowed most peoples of European descent to disassociate themselves from this purportedly anomalous history.

Bernasconi's account of racism being narrowly defined so as to save the West from moral damage shows us but a snippet of Western institutions' concerted campaign to suppress the West's history of racial violence. In *The Silent War*, the sociologist Frank Füredi describes the "compulsive [...] desire" of postwar Western governments and the Western academy to transform Western racism into a universal human trait (Füredi 1998: 229). In his account of the efforts of the postwar Western governments, institutions, and academy to reconstruct Western racism as "an attitude that characterizes the behaviour of all people" (225), Füredi writes:

> It is striking just how far the specialist academic literature echoed the official line that racism was not the monopoly of white people. There was something compulsive about this desire to transform racism into a transcendental curse that afflicted all societies throughout history. In the 1950s, even UNESCO publications adopted the perspective that Western racism was one among many examples of racism. (Füredi 1998: 228–29)

The willingness to equate Western racism with "literally all forms of group conflicts" led to it being "recast as a catch-all category that could be discovered in all cultures and was seen to define most relations of conflict" (Füredi 1998: 228). With racism reduced to a universal trait, Western societies were absolved of any greater responsibility for racism than others (229). "Diverse forms of human cruelty are abstractly compared, and not surprisingly, Western racism emerges with flying colours" (229). It was Western racism's exposure of "an important flaw in Western societies"—one that was difficult to refute (231)—that explains the efforts, both cynical and sincere, to discount the uniqueness of Western racism by painting it as universal. As Füredi writes, "The literature reflected an instinctive reaction against the moral damage which the accusation of racism imposed on the West" (230). To defend the universality of Western values and history, such a blatant historical failing was projected onto the global South—that is, those states that were victims of Western racism and colonialism.

Sinological works that argue for the existence of racism in the premodern Chinese tradition not only are a product of the epistemology of ignorance but further that project. The most prominent example is Frank Dikötter's[9] *The Discourse of Race in Modern China*, which attempts to prove the existence of race-consciousness in premodern and modern China.[10] Seeking to overturn the measured consensus of a previous generation, Dikötter concludes, within the space of ten pages, that "race" or "racism" existed in early China, and within thirty pages he establishes that "race" or "racism" existed during the whole span of Chinese history until 1793. By attempting to prove that proto-racism existed in China prior to the introduction of such concepts by the West, Dikötter's work plays into the narrative of apologia for Western racism, both historic and contemporary.[11] The paucity of scholarship that Dikötter marshals to support his thesis, along with the incommensurable alacrity with which it was greeted by the Western academy,[12] speaks volumes about how much the West wants to believe that China is just as guilty of racism as the West.[13] A more recent instance of this epistemology of ignorance is Odd Arne Westad's foreword to Zhao Tingyang's *All under Heaven*, in which Westad translates *yi* (夷) as "barbarian" and casually writes of "durable traditions of Chinese exceptionalism and preoccupations with race" (Zhao 2021: xxi).

This book challenges China scholars to do better. There is nothing innocent about perpetuating the amnesia of the West's historic racism. As Linda Martín Alcoff puts it, "Eurocentrism has a need *not to know*, a motivation *not to learn*, in the service of its material and discursive conquests"[14] (Alcoff 2017: 402, emphasis in original). As a result of this ignorance about the nature and scale of Western racism, some Sinologists and Western scholars regard their attempts to find historical instances of "racism" in the Chinese tradition as particularly virtuous. Automatically assuming that Chinese civilization is just as racist as Western civilization, these academics cannot countenance the alternative: that the Chinese tradition is morally superior to the Western tradition in this one regard of *not* being racist.

It should be acknowledged, however, that confronting the Western academy's amnesia about the nature of Western racism and ignorance of the colonial geopolitics under which Sinologists work is exhausting. As Lewis Gordon puts it:

> A great deal of the effort to study racism is marred by the core problem of self-evasion. This is partly because the study of racism is dirty business. It

unveils things about ourselves that we may prefer not to know. If racism emerges out of an evasive spirit, it is hardly the case that it would stand still and permit itself to be unmasked. Race theorists theorize in a racist world. The degree to which that world is made evident will have an impact on the question of whether the theorist not only sees, but also admits what is seen. The same applies to the society in which the theorist theorizes. (Gordon 1995: ix)

In 2017, Reni Eddo-Lodge, a British writer of Nigerian descent, wrote a book entitled *Why I'm No Longer Talking to White People about Race*. Eddo-Lodge writes of her utter exhaustion in trying to educate white people on how the Western world earns its continued moral authority through an institutional forgetting, repressing, and suppressing of the history of murderous white supremacy that accompanied its ascent. The West, she writes, has "rewritte[n] history" to "make the lies the truth" (Eddo-Lodge 2017: xi), and its "white denial" follows a well-worn circuit: "Their mouths start twitching as they get defensive. Their throats open up as they try to interrupt, itching to talk over you but not really listen, because they need to let you know that you've got it wrong" (x). Eddo-Lodge gave up on talking to whites about race "because of the consequent denials, awkward cartwheels and mental acrobatics that they display when this is brought to their attention" (x–xi). The same issues that frustrate Eddo-Lodge were already described by James Baldwin in 1965. Half a century has passed, and not much has changed since Baldwin wrote in an essay entitled "The White Man's Guilt":

They [white Americans] *do* see what they see [the color of Baldwin's skin]. And what they see is an appallingly oppressive and bloody history, known all over the world. What they see is a disastrous, continuing, present condition which menaces them, and for which they bear an inescapable responsibility. But since, in the main, they seem to lack the energy to change this condition, they would rather not be reminded of it. [. . .] And to have to deal with such people can be unutterably exhausting, for they, with a really dazzling ingenuity, a tireless agility, are perpetually defending themselves against charges which one, disagreeable mirror though one may be, has not, really, for the moment, made. One does not *have* to make them. The record is there for all to read. It resounds all over the world. It might as well be written in the sky. One wishes that Americans, white Americans, would read, for their own sakes, this record, and stop defending themselves against it. Only then will they be enabled to change their lives. The fact that they have not yet been able to do this—to face their history, to change their lives—hideously menaces this country. Indeed, it menaces the entire world. (Baldwin 1998: 722)

Applying Baldwin's sentiments to those Western Sinologists and academics working on traditional China's relationship with the non-Chinese who are wont to uncritically apply Western concepts of race and its associated history to the Chinese context, these Sinologists should read, for their own sakes, the record of Western colonial aggression. They should recall the genocide, violence, and oppression behind the West's arrival at geopolitical preeminence through which Western ideas became the standard by which all other thinking is judged. Only if we learn this history can we change our lives and work. My conjecture is that there are four nonmutually exclusive explanations for why so many Western Sinologists lack the energy to truly learn about the history of Western racism and its relationship to colonial aggression. First, the culture of imperialism has informed their scholarly orientation in the sense that they are either unwilling to acknowledge the atrocities and violent practices that have helped the rise of Western powers, or they believe that this violent behavior was for a "greater good." Acknowledging this bloody history does not help their arguments that Western values produce better civilization. Nor is there any willingness on their part to acknowledge modern forms of (violent) Western oppression as a continuation of the same project. Second, paternalistic attitudes toward the cultural other have been normalized in Western academia and normal society. Orientalism, a cultural framework that normalizes these aggressive and paternalistic attitudes toward the cultural other, helps to make the very domination or subservience of the other seem reasonable and "moral." Third, there is, on some level, a subconscious awareness of how bad Western colonialism was historically. The desire to make racism both a naturally occurring phenomenon and a practice that anyone could be guilty of committing speaks to a desire to sweep Western responsibility under the rug. Making such behaviors simply "natural" excuses those who are responsible. The West simply did what any other cultural tradition would do if given the same power and technology. Finally, all of these issues and more are aspects of the "epistemology of ignorance." To all these points, Baldwin's voice is once again hauntingly relevant:

And I know, which is much worse, and this is the crime of which I accuse my country and my countrymen, and for which neither I nor time nor history will ever forgive them, that they have destroyed and are destroying hundreds of thousands of lives and do not know it and do not want to know it. (Baldwin 1998: 292)

Our continuing inability to face this history hideously menaces the possibility of East-West dialogue; indeed it menaces the entire world. Much of the Western academy suffers from an inertia that prevents any recognition that China, or the non-West in general, could have historically been Europe's moral superior in certain respects—or, to be blunt, just not as perverse. (It's a *very* low bar.) Certain Sinologists and a not insignificant demographic of the Western academy *tout court* need to ask themselves why they so automatically assume that the Chinese tradition was just as guilty of Western-style racism as the West. When they finally work up the courage to look, what they will find, I hazard, is an ugly and uncomfortable truth.

As an "other" in the view of the Western academy, the Chinese tradition has suffered the same demonization under racist ideology as many other traditions throughout colonial history. Historically, the pervasive tendency to characterize another culture (including aspects of Chinese culture) as illegitimate and morally suspect preceded colonial takeover. The phrase "Yellow Peril" (*Gelbe Gefahr*), for instance, was coined at the end of the century by Kaiser Wilhelm of Germany to justify Germany's grab for concessions in China. To illustrate his point, in 1895 the Kaiser commissioned a painting of the nations of Europe dressed as female warriors and defending Christendom from the Yellow Peril (Lee 1999: 246n4). However, Yellow Peril racism preceded the invention of the term. As the "great" idealist philosopher Ernst Renan (1823–1892) wrote, "Nature has made a race of workers, the Chinese race, who have wonderful manual dexterity and almost no sense of honor." The Chinese were thus, he declared, "crying aloud for foreign conquest" (quoted in Césaire 2000: 38).

Yellow Peril racism or Sinophobia is normalized today in a way similar to the normalization of Islamophobia, especially in the post-9/11 period; indeed, much of current Western Sinological and academic work on China's historic relationship to non-Chinese peoples is an exercise in Yellow Peril racism. A veritable cottage industry is dedicated to demonizing the Chinese tradition as racist. This cottage industry is part of an even larger industry that manufactures consent in the American and other Western populations. Once the Chinese have been well and truly demonized as the worst racists of them all, then the military-industrial-capitalist state can legitimately step in and make yet another windfall selling weapons to subjugate China (or any other enemy of the state) without the Western public identifying said subjugation as a moral transgression.[15] The subjugated are architects of their own oppression for being so morally reprehensible to begin with.

As we will see in greater detail, portraying the racial other as immoral—or victim blaming—is one of the oldest tricks in the racist handbook for legitimizing colonial takeover of non-Western land. Before so painstakingly detecting the faintest traces that might be construed as "racism" in the Chinese tradition, the virtue-signaling Western Sinologist or scholar should critically ask themselves three questions: (1) Why is it always states that pose a threat to Western hegemony that are simultaneously portrayed as moral transgressors and subjected to the greatest moral scrutiny by the Western academy, the media, and the public? (2) Why is there no dearth of works on "racism" and "perceptions of otherness" in China when critical philosophers of race, especially those of color, working on Western racism are marginalized and struggle to gain visibility for their own works, especially from the most respected publishers and journals?[16] (3) Is the Sinological class, which is overwhelmingly white, middle-class, and from the heart of the Anglo-American empire, culturally (mis)appropriating the discourse of African-Americans (the "critical philosophy of race"), whose original purpose was to critically assess structures of white-supremacist oppression toward nonwhites within their *own* (American) society and internationally? Further, in so doing, are these Sinologists helping to diminish the capacity of a discourse that was one of the few ways in which the global South could understand and critique the racist hegemony of the West? They should ask if they themselves have not become enablers of a narrative that justifies Western aggression.

As is well known, America was founded on an imagined moral superiority and purity, but Europe too still believes in its own (equally imagined) mythic innocence. According to this myth, colonial Europeans, the "gentle civilizers"[17] of the world, were kind enough to bring civilization to the primitive peoples of the world.[18] Europe's current global eminence, in this construction, is only a result of its own virtues. The myth of its own innocence is an almost impregnable fortress that renders its host psychologically unassailable by empirical facts about its actual historical conduct. The West's inability to take responsibility for its historic actions creates a perverse psychosis in which its own guilt is projected onto the racial other. Chris Hedges eloquently summarizes Baldwin's social critique of this white denial:

> The steadfast failure to face the truth, Baldwin warned, perpetuates a kind of collective psychosis. Unable to face the truth, white Americans stunt and

destroy their capacity for self-reflection and self-criticism. They construct a world of self-serving fantasy. Those who imbibe the myth of whiteness externalize evil—their own evil—onto their victims. (Hedges 2019: 54)

Those Sinologists and Western academics who depict China as historically racist need to remember that the racist actions of the West have all but wiped out the entire peoples of three of the earth's six inhabitable continents (North and South America and Australia), enslaved and killed half the population of a fourth (Africa), and, in Aimé Césaire's words, "defiled and perverted" one of the remaining ones (Asia) (Césaire 2000: 74). Just as white people have projected their guilt onto the African-American so as to avoid facing their trespasses, so has the Western academy projected its racism onto China. "Such is the 'East,'" writes François Jullien, "or rather its mirage, the eternal, exotic East that the 'West' has chosen to represent as its polar opposite that so conveniently fuels its own fantasies and that it constantly exploits to compensate for its own failings" (Jullien 2004: 84–5).

Before so quickly calling out the perceived shortcomings of others, some Western academics need to remember that it was the West, and no one else, that committed genocide and pursued colonialism on so global a scale. They need to remember that the status of the Western academy was won and has been sustained through violence and genocidal suppression of other peoples and their cultures.[19] There is very little in the history of Western engagement with the non-West that warrants the moral authority that Western academia arrogates to itself for judging others. By so enthusiastically framing another culture with the original sin that led to white peoples' domination of the globe, certain Sinologists and Western academics have forgotten that "all of the Western nations have been caught in a lie, the lie of their pretended humanism; this means that their history has no moral justification, and that the West has no moral authority" (Baldwin 1998: 404).

Although much of the West lives by the myth of its own innocence, "the Rest" of the world will never forget that, as Césaire wrote in *Discourse on Colonialism*, the West "is responsible before the human community for the highest heap of corpses in history" (Césaire 2000: 45). In this respect, the "wretched of the earth" possess a marked epistemological advantage over those who suffer under the illusions of exceptionalism. In *Anti-Semite and Jew*, Sartre describes the classic behavior of a racist: "demand[ing] rigorous order for others, and for himself disorder without responsibility" (Sartre 1995: 31).

What Sartre says about the hypocrisy of the racist corresponds with what he calls the "racist humanism" of the West:

> Chatter, chatter: liberty, equality, fraternity, love, honour, patriotism and what have you. All this did not prevent us from making anti-racial speeches about dirty niggers, dirty Jews and dirty Arabs. High-minded people, liberal or just soft-hearted, protest that they were shocked by such inconsistency; but they were either mistaken or dishonest, for with us there is nothing more consistent than a racist humanism since the European has only been able to become a man through creating slaves and monsters. (Fanon 1963: 22)

We can say that part of the racist or racist-humanist agenda of a representative proportion of the Western academy is to legitimize and academically normalize its asymmetrical expectations for others. It is only through demonizing the other in this way that the racist-humanist can live with the record of what they themselves have done.

In a 1965 speech entitled "The American Dream and the American Negro." James Baldwin said, "What we are not facing is the result of what we've done. What one begs the American people to do for all our sakes is simply to accept our history" (Baldwin 1998: 716–17). Relatedly, Baldwin also said, in *The Fire Next Time*, "People who cannot suffer can never grow up, can never discover who they are" (343). Some intellectual opinion-makers in the West need to face the reality of what the West has done. "People pay for what they do," Baldwin wrote, "and, still more, for what they have allowed themselves to become. And they pay for it very simply: by the lives they lead. The crucial thing, here, is that the sum of these individual abdications menaces life all over the world" (386).

I have few illusions that important sections of the Western academy will ever undertake the necessary self-critique, owing to the moral apathy that I have already mentioned. Nevertheless, I would urge certain Sinologists and Western academics to make some changes. First, Sinology cannot persist in using the terms "barbarian" and "race" and their cognates to describe the relationship between "the Chinese" and China's neighbors throughout history without first establishing the necessary frameworks. There are many historical works by Western scholars, from the earliest writings of the Greek tradition and throughout Western history, on the history of the (Greek) "barbarian" as a Manichean other antithetically opposed to civilization. These "barbarians" tend to be animalistic, passion-driven others who cannot be assimilated into civilization because, having been metaphysically determined to be ontologically other, they are dualistically opposed to civilization. The Western tradition then identified these "barbarians" with the Persians and subsequently with all non-Europeans.[20] Sinologists need to establish whether the Chinese have subscribed to a similarly dualistic ontology or whether, as I argue in chapter 3, the processual nature of Chinese metaphysics in fact enables a different understanding of ontological otherness.

Second, the notion of the barbarian and the related ideas of natural slavery and oriental despotism as formulated by Aristotle in the *Politics* and elsewhere became instrumental in the project of Western colonialism and racial genocide. Indeed, Europeans legitimated their depopulation of the Americas and colonial takeover on the basis of Aristotle's theory of natural slavery. Such ideas about race and their later formulations by Enlightenment philosophers during the age of empire are implicated in Europe's responsibility before the human community for committing racial genocide on an unprecedented scale around the world. Sinologists therefore need to ask if it is intellectually sound to use terms like "race" for other cultures that have not committed mass killings or undertaken projects to dominate the globe on the basis of the ideology of race supremacy.

Third, racism is neither purely ideology nor purely practice; racism is simultaneously a theory and a practice. If Sinologists want to argue for the existence of racism in premodern China, they must provide evidence on both an ideological level and a material level. Further, they must be able to find coherence between the ideological and material, between the cultural and practical spheres of human life. Pointing to a few instances of either the theory or the practice and isolating them from the larger cultural framework is not sufficient evidence. Scholars must be able to find systematic coherence among the different theories and practices of the culture they analyze for any claim of racism to be instantiated.

Fourth, Sinologists who use Western paradigms of race and barbarism need to describe how they will avoid what Füredi called the post–World War II compulsion on the part of Western political elites and the Western academy to transform Western racism into a universal condition that afflicts all humankind. That is, these academics need to explain how, in using terms such as "barbarian" and "racism," they do not further the West's project of universalizing its own historic racism and so become court-rationalists for Western imperialism, both contemporary and historic. Can they argue that applying Western paradigms as consequential as "race" and its related idea of "barbarism" is truly critical work and academically acceptable on philosophical, historical, and political grounds?

Finally, Sinologists need to remember what Edward Said wrote in his 2003 preface to *Orientalism* about Orientalists who "betrayed their calling as scholars" by justifying the American invasion of Iraq in 2003:

> What I do argue also is that there is a difference between knowledge of other peoples and other times that is the result of understanding, compassion, careful study and analysis for their own sakes, and on the other hand *knowledge—if that is what it is—that is part of an overall campaign of self-affirmation, belligerency and outright war. There is, after all, a profound difference between the will to understand for purposes of co-existence and humanistic enlargement of horizons, and the will to dominate for the purposes of control and external dominion.* It is surely one of the intellectual catastrophes of history that an imperialist war confected by a small group of unelected US officials (they've been called chickenhawks, since none of them ever served in the military) was waged against a devastated Third World dictatorship on thoroughly ideological grounds having to do with world dominance, security control, and scarce resources, *but disguised for its true intent, hastened and reasoned for by Orientalists who betrayed their calling as scholars.* (Said 2003: xiv–xv, emphasis added)

Imperialism, as Said reminds us, is not simply the political and physical domination of one group of peoples by another. Imperialism relies on a discursive, symbolic, philosophical infrastructure, an entire mode of knowledge production whose violence is epistemic as well as physical. Making imperialism appear reasonable and even *moral* to its citizens requires a sophisticated cultural and ideological infrastructure. A culture of exceptionalism is integral to this ideological infrastructure in America, where an entire population has been systematically convinced of its exceptionalism. The Chinese cosmopolitan ideal explored in this book is offered not only as an alternative ideal but as a critical response to exceptionalism and the attendant moral obtuseness that dominates much of cultural, political, and academic life in the West, where, in the words of Pankaj Mishra, "self-congratulation" is used as an "analytical framework" (Mishra 2021: 15). Bearing the material and social costs of this exceptionalism are those whom Frantz Fanon has called the "wretched of the earth." In this respect, the "wretched of the earth" possess a marked epistemological advantage over those who suffer under the illusions of exceptionalism in that they see beyond the rhetoric of imperialism as they endure its material consequences.

One defining feature of Western exceptionalism has been the willingness of academics to participate in manufacturing master "narratives" that defend the imperial status quo. Sinologists will increasingly find themselves in the limelight in the coming years. Whether they betray their calling as scholars, as did many Western scholars of the Islamic-Arabic world early in the twenty-first century, will be the measure of their integrity.

Clarification of Terms

The terms "cosmopolitanism" and "racism" are umbrella terms that are used loosely in the English language. To avoid misunderstanding, I specify here the senses in which I employ these terms throughout the book; I define the terms "barbarism/barbarian," "China/Chinese," "colonization/colonialism," and "the West/Westerner" in the glossary.

Cosmopolitanism

I use the term "cosmopolitan" to describe the view that difference is enriching. I do not use it in the sense of those who coined the term, the fourth-century BCE cynics for whom a cosmopolitan was a citizen of the cosmos and thus not a citizen grounded in a particular culture and community. This universalistic sense of cosmopolitanism underlay some of the great moral landmarks of the Enlightenment, such as the 1789 "Declaration of the Rights of Man." Relatedly, I also do not use the term as it is used by current moral and political philosophy to refer to a global justice owed to individuals directly, rather than indirectly as members of different states. I also do not use "cosmopolitan" in the superficial way it is understood by the liberal left. As I use it, "cosmopolitanism" is not a vacuous buzzword signaling a safe space in which one can be conversant with the merely decorative and thus non-offensive aspects of foreign cultures, such as their art and food, while never seriously engaging with the perspectives of others and thus challenging one's own.

I use "cosmopolitanism" in the same way that the Chinese use "harmony," and as Césaire conceives of a universal:

> I'm not burying myself in a narrow particularism. But neither do I want to lose myself in an emaciated universalism. There are two ways to lose

oneself: walled segregation in the particular or dilution in the "universal."
My conception of the universal is that of a universal enriched by all that is
particular, a universal enriched by every particular: the deepening and coexistence of all particulars. (Césaire 2010: 152)

I too use "cosmopolitanism" to refer to a "universal enriched by every particular: the deepening and coexistence of all particulars." The universal is not a
static, eternal ideal that is merely imprinted onto the docile matter of the particular. Rather, the universal is the result of interactive engagement between
all the particulars, which are in turn constantly changing because they are interacting with and being enriched by each other.[21]

Racism

I take the idea of "race" to mean that a group of people have inborn characteristics that define them and that cannot be changed through the actions or
acculturation of the group or of individuals in the group. Race is the substantial and unchangeable *essence* of a person. The essences of peoples are
furthermore understood hierarchically, such that those with higher essences
legitimately dominate those with inferior essences. Racism as an ideology
is inextricable from its practice (Fredrickson 2002: 6). Ideas about race are
manifested in social, cultural, economic, and institutional practice. The
geopolitical manifestation of racism is colonialism. I do not take the materialist position that racial ideology is merely an outcome of historical capitalist expansion.

The academic philosophical discourse of race and racism adheres to the
opinion that racism did not exist prior to the invention of the concept.[22]
The accepted wisdom is that "racist" practice waited upon systematic racist
theory, that is, the "scientific" ideology of racism that rationalized Western
imperialism and colonization. Under this view, systematic European intolerance of the other emerged from a historical vacuum sometime around the
Enlightenment owing to the confluence of the rise of the biological sciences and
the growth of colonialism. I think this view, which makes racism a strictly modern phenomenon, is mistaken. It does little to explain why Aristotle, back in antiquity, regarded all non-Greeks as barbarians and thus natural slaves. Nor does
it account for the ostracization of Jews and Muslims through medieval purity-of-
blood laws, or for what David Stannard has termed the "American
Holocaust"—the near-annihilation by the European elite of the population of

the American continent in *good conscience* because they understood the Amerindians to be naturally inferior savages (Stannard 1992).

My argument emphasizes the strong connection between Western racism and its metaphysics. As I have said, the *locus classicus* of racism is Aristotle's theory of natural slavery. Therefore, I take racism to be a practice that preceded its naming and theorization; racism existed *avant la lettre*. I define racism in such a way as to avoid a definition that relies on the espousal of the term by racism's practitioners before their actions and motives can be characterized as such. Broadly, I am in agreement with the likes of Benjamin Isaac and George Fredrickson, who argue that racism is a Western phenomenon (Isaac 2004; Fredrickson 2002). Although being wary of unknown individuals serves a pragmatic function and so may be a universal characteristic, racism differs in that it reifies this fear of difference into a systematic worldview even after the fear has outlasted its practical purpose. To fear the foreigner for ideological reasons rather than out of pragmatic need is racism.[23]

This book limits its scope to showing that traditional China did not have a concept of "race." Although there may be other, premodern, non-Western cultural traditions that harbor something akin to the Western notion of race, their existence needs to be established in a separate work; it is outside my present purview. Following previous scholars, I understand racial metaphysics as a culturally specific ideology, and a specifically Western one. China, as I show, did not theorize about difference; nor did it, in practice, oppress and destroy encountered difference to nearly the same level and degree as the West did.

I also reject the dominant tendency today to understand "racism" as intrinsic to human nature. Much of this argument speciously conflates the ability to recognize difference and a pathological hatred of difference. All humans recognize human difference; it is only under certain forms of cultural conditioning that this recognition leads to racist behaviors. The desire to dominate humans perceived to be different is not a stable feature of human nature, but rather a learned behavior that makes sense only in certain cultural environments enabled by certain philosophical assumptions.

One final note: The question of whether "racism" is a stable feature of human nature is relevant to how we understand modern China and the drastic changes to its habits wrought by globalization. Readers are probably aware of the current situation with the Uyghurs in the Xinjiang region and might wonder if the ethnic tensions there present a challenge to the idea of a Chinese cosmopolitanism that I defend here. Providing an account of it that does justice to that complexity would deflect from the main purpose of this project: to present a cosmopolitan ideal found in China's history and to show the relation between this cosmopolitanism and the Chinese philosophical worldview. Suffice to say here that the very complex history of the Xinjiang issue is intimately tied to America's "Global War on Terror," and that the situation has been very politicized in both China and the West. Not only is doing it academic justice beyond the scope of this book, but any such effort will become possible only when the issue is less politicized. Thankfully, a recent publication has already rigorously and charitably examined the causes and conditions giving rise to recent ethnic tensions in the Xinjiang region, Yan Sun's *From Empire to Nation State*.[24] As Sun notes, premodern China (consistent with the thesis of this book) interpreted differences among peoples as cultural and not as essentially or ontologically unbridgeable. Globalization, colonialism, and the Chinese state's use of the Soviet model of ethnic classification led the CPC to adopt institutions that were foreign to the traditional Chinese way of thinking about cultural difference. Further, being unfamiliar with Western ideas and models for dealing with difference, party leaders were unable to anticipate the problems that such institutions would produce.

In sum, racism cannot be defined simply as any form of intergroup tensions. Further, this study argues only for the nonexistence of racism in premodern China and does not widen the lens to look at racism in the modern world. All of the cultural interaction and spread of practices and ideas in the modern era—including both modern science and modern philosophies—put doing justice to the complexity of modern racist ideology beyond the scope of this book.

1

A Brief History of Chinese Cosmopolitanism

THIS CHAPTER SKETCHES the main outlines of Chinese history while paying attention to issues of cosmopolitanism and pluralism. It shows that the synthesis between peoples and cultures that constitutes what emerged as "the Chinese" and as "China" is indebted to a *cultural* rather than a *racial* understanding of human difference. Relatedly, the historical process of amalgamation is indebted to the Chinese tradition's assumption that order is a dynamic, emergent function of diverse particulars and thus that the order that is "Chinese-ness" is subject to change. That being the case, the Chinese tradition understood that there can be no order without difference. It is through this understanding of "Chinese-ness" as an emergent function constituted by ever-changing particulars that this chapter narrates the story of "China."

Overcoming (False) Dualisms: The Hybrid Nature of Chinese Identity

There is a persistent shibboleth in the West that China has always been homogeneously "Chinese." What makes this idea of an "unchanging China" (Mote 2003: 376) a myth is the fact that throughout Chinese history China "always comprised groups of more or less unassimilated minorities" and that "even the so-called 'Han' 汉 people appear much less homogenous than it is often imagined" (Pines 2009: 223n4). The "Han" epithet, with which around 90 percent of mainland "Chinese" people identify, is not what the West understands by the concept of "race"—a biological descriptor of a group of persons related by common descent or heredity. A comparison with the other most populous countries of the world makes this point clear. India, the United States, Indonesia, and Brazil are all highly multiracial. By its very definition, "race" is highly exclusionary. A race stops being a race as soon as the boundaries of its class membership are broadened. Yet the boundaries of "Chinese" class membership were ceaselessly broadened throughout history, resulting in the "Chinese" becoming one-fifth of the world's population today: China currently accounts for about 20 percent of the world's population, and this number excludes the sizable Chinese diaspora.[1]

"Chinese" describes the hybrid product of a long mingling of different groups of peoples.[2] Historically, the Turkish, Mongol, Tungus, Korean, Tibeto-Burman, Thai, Miao, Yao, and Mon-khmer strains, as well as those of distant peoples from the borders of India, Iran, and Southeast Asia, all contributed to the formation of the Han peoples. From the north of China, Altaic-speaking peoples from the steppes and northern Manchuria added their share to the "Chinese" identity, as did, from the west, the mountaineers of the Himalaya and the Tibetan plateau and the semi-nomadic inhabitants of Qinghai. In the southwestern provinces of Guizhou, Yunnan, Hunan, Sichuan, Guangxi, and Guangdong, there are still numerous non-Han elements (Gernet 1982: 9–12). The hybridity of the "Han-Chinese" people dispels the myth that the Chinese are a single race of people.

Related to this myth of Chinese racial homogeneity is the related myth of China as a "Walled Kingdom" (Rodzinski 1984) that had little to no connection with the outside world prior to its "discovery" by Europe. As Nicola Di Cosmo and Don Wyatt explain: "Indeed, perhaps the most ingrained and resistant stereotype we hold of China throughout its traditional epochs is that of an isolated and xenophobic monolith, a static empire mostly turned inward upon itself against the outside world" (Cosmo and Wyatt 2003: 2). The myths of Chinese racial homogeneity, historical stasis, and inwardness reflect three methodological fallacies committed by the Western academy that are, in turn, characteristic assumptions of Western metaphysics.

There are three enduring misconceptions about Chinese history in the Western academy. The first is that the "Chinese" people have always been Chinese. The second is that "Sinicization" has been a one-way influence from the center to the periphery. Both of these (mistaken) paradigms are used to explain the longevity and success of China as an entity. Relatedly but antithetically, the third misconception is that historically there never was a "China" in the sense of an overarching identity, but only local identities.[3] These misconstructions of Chinese history persist because key aspects of the Western

worldview, reflected in its methodological practices, are informed by ontologically bivalent dualisms that prevent the Western academy from grasping the
nondualistic Chinese worldview. Suffice it to say that none of the Western
academy's three paradigms accurately describes China or its people. Instead,
the very nature of China as both heterogeneous and blessed with historical
longevity and unity remains a paradox or a mystery to most Western observers.
Let us consider each of these misconceptions in turn.

The fallacy that the "Chinese" people have always been Chinese. A conventional
expression of the persistent stereotype of China as a land that has always been
homogeneously "Chinese" was expressed by the Sinologist Olga Lang when
she wrote that "imperial China was a static civilization" characterized by a "stagnant character" (Lang 1946: 10–11, 333). This pervasive (Western) conception
of China as a homogeneous entity, landlocked and stagnating in the eternal
return of (Mircea Eliade's) primitive man before its "discovery" by the West, is
a racist myth (Eliade 1971). This stereotype is also voiced by Hegel: "China,
India, and Babylon [. . .] have remained enclosed within themselves." As such,
"the only connection they could have with later developments in history was
through being visited and explored by other nations" (Hegel 1975: 194).

The idea that China has always been homogeneously Chinese is also indebted to another widely held assumption that is foundational to the Western
tradition: that humanity is constituted by originally distinct "races" that only
later interbred. Implicit in this assumption is the further idea that interbreed-
ing between discrete races is a perversion of the original state of humanity
(pure, separate races) and leads to their decline. The biological anthropologist
Jonathan Marks explains the fallacy of this assumption:

> Racial analyses have generally proceeded with a flawed conception of
> human history: that in the obscure past, a few small homogeneous groups
> of people settled and proliferated, to become large identifiable races, grada-
> tion coming as the result of subsequent interbreeding at their margins.
> There was probably never a time, however, in which the human species
> existed as a few, small, biologically divergent groups that only later began
> to interbreed, for this has probably always been occurring. (Marks 1995: 115)

Although fallacious, the myth that the original humans were members "of a
few, small, biologically divergent groups" and only later began to interbreed
has become accepted folk wisdom. This folk wisdom has been taken up by academic researchers with the result that, for example, "conventional area studies
scholarship" assumes that there are immutable major divisions between

historical peoples and cultures. Under this assumption, we have been encouraged by conventional scholarship to "regard China—the so-called 'Sinic' zone—as just one of several discrete and self-contained compartments into which we can neatly divide the world" (Cosmo and Wyatt 2003: 2–3). This assumption, indebted to the Greek tradition—which placed a premium on autochthony, as it was understood to ensure the longevity and unity of a people—makes Western audiences unable to grasp the Chinese identity's ideal of coherence among diverse things (harmony) and clouds their view of China as a geographic entity.[4]

The fallacy of "Sinicization" flowing only one way. Another way the unity of China has been explained is through the paradigm of "Sinicization." With its implication that influence flows only one way, from the center to the periphery, "Sinicization" is an inaccurate way to describe the formation of "China" and its history. China never merely made those that it drew into its orbit identical to itself—the (Chinese) center itself changed as identities were reciprocally exchanged between the center and the periphery (Bauer 1980: 7–8; Gernet 1982: 12). While it is impossible to map out all the cross-fertilizations of history, we know that China was enriched by cultures—ancient Mesopotamia, pre-Islamic Iran, India, Islam, the Christian West—that "were profoundly alien to it by their very nature" (Gernet 1982: 20), and we can be sure that throughout China's history contributions to its culture from foreign cultures were "considerable" (175). The fact is that the history of the Chinese world took place in a vast and heterogenous geographic region extending from Siberia to the Equator and from the Pacific Ocean to the heart of the Eurasian continent, which "more than any other" had always "been in contact and maintained permanent relations with peoples whose modes of life and culture were very different from its own" (20).[5]

The fallacy that there never was a unified "China." The third misconception falls on the other side of the dualistic understanding of historical China: it posits that there never was any unity there. In recent decades, some scholars have tended to "deconstruct" China as an entity, using local identities, margins, identity shifting, and other such postmodernist vocabularies to challenge the idea that there ever was a "China."

The epistemological error underlying all three paradigms in explaining the nature of Chinese identity is a deeply engrained mode of thinking in Western philosophy and culture under which unity and longevity can result *only* from substance metaphysics, i.e., something that is self-identical with itself; thus, either "China" was a static, homogeneous entity throughout history, with all its parts uniformly bearing the essence of "Chinese-ness" or "China" was a mere aggregate of heterogeneous particulars and *ipso facto* did not exist at all. The conceptual stumbling block preventing much of the Western academy from understanding China as a coherence among diverse entities stems from this prevailing metaphysics of substance, whereby either there is a single order or identity or there is chaos. Under this dualistic paradigm, the *only* explanation for the unity and longevity of the Chinese tradition is that there has always been the single order or identity of "Chinese-ness." Under this dualistic assumption, only by being homogenous could China have existed as an entity throughout millennia. There are only two explanations, in this view, for why China has endured: the "Chinese" shared from their inception the property of "Chinese-ness" and did not change through the millennia, or the Chinese imposed Chinese-ness on that which was heterogeneous (non-Chinese). Since this view identifies heterogeneity with chaos, China's stability could only be due to homogeneity and unity.

Since its vast geography made China enormously diverse in population, "the durability of the Chinese empire defies easy explanation" for Western audiences, mired as they are in deep-seated substance ontology (Pines 2009: 1).[6] Under a substance monist explanation, China seems to paradoxically embody two antithetical characteristics: it is empirically heterogeneous, yet has been blessed with historical longevity and integrity.

The Fallacy of Racial Purity

Before we introduce an alternative paradigm that resolves this paradox, it is worth briefly stressing just how unempirical the idea of racial purity is, especially with regard to the proposition that the Chinese are a single race of people. Beginning in the post–World War II period, many anthropologists, biologists, and geneticists have contributed to the enormous amount of evidence establishing that biological race in humans is nonexistent. Today, according to the anthropologist Robert Wald Sussman, the "vast majority of those involved in research on human variation would agree that biological races do not exist among humans," and that "this scientific fact is as valid and true as the fact that the earth is round and revolves around the sun" (Sussman 2014: 1). Much of the consensus that race is not biologically real follows Richard Lewontin's (1972) claim that there is more genetic variation within socially constructed racial groups than between "races." Today we know that the genetic difference between individual humans is minuscule—about 0.1 percent on average.[7] Since the "ancient DNA revolution"[8] enabled geneticists to conduct whole-genome analysis of ancient DNA, we now know that "present-day populations are blends of past populations, which were blends themselves" (Reich 2018: xxiv).[9]

In short, there are no grounds to believe that there are biologically discrete groups among human beings that follow the lines of socially constructed racial groups. As the anonymous author of an article on seeking genetic definitions of race writes, "The process of using genetics to define 'race' is like slicing soup. You can cut where you want, but the soup stays mixed" ("Slicing Soup," 2002: 637). Contra Kant, who once said, "Instead of assimilation, which was intended by the melting together of the various races, Nature has here made a law of just the opposite," it would appear that assimilation and melting together of human populations is precisely what nature intends (quoted in Mills 2005: 175). Race is not biologically real, and we are only one race: the human race.

Of course, while all of the world's inhabitants are intermixtures of many waves of historic human migrations, the Chinese tradition was arguably more empirical in that it recognized and accepted this. The European tradition, on the other hand, even though it was empirically the result of many blends of past populations, held fast to the unempirical idea of discrete human races and the importance of "racial purity." Up until the nineteenth century, no European questioned the *fact* of racial hierarchies (Gould 1996: 63–64); moreover, until very recently, race was a central category in international relations and a positive ideal in the self-image of the West, and race relations were "central to the outlook of the Western ruling classes" (Füredi 1998: 4):

> Until the late 1930s, racial thinking was an accepted part of the intellectual climate. Important characteristics were attached to racial differences and the view that some races were superior assumed the status of self-evident truth. These sentiments permeated academic communities. They were part of the self-knowledge of the Anglo-American political elites and were strongly absorbed into what passed for common sense. (Füredi 1998: 5)

That race and racism were, until very recently, commonsense assumptions of civilizations can be seen in the attitude of Thomas Jefferson. In his *Notes on the State of Virginia*, Jefferson casually writes that the incorporation of blacks into the state is inhibited in part by "the real distinctions which Nature has made [. . .] which will probably never end but in the extermination of the one or the other race" (Jefferson 1853: 149). It is deep-seated assumptions of the reality of racial division such as Jefferson's that explain why Western academics have relied for so long on the idea of Chinese racial purity as the reason for China's longevity as a political-cultural entity.[10] As this book argues, however, the traditional Chinese metaphysical system was radically different from the metaphysics of Western racial ideology.

Equilibrium and Exchange: Harmony Out of Diversity

Both the fallacy that the Chinese have always been one people and the fallacy of Sinicization flowing only one way purport to explain Chinese longevity by resorting to the substance ontology explanation of the Greeks: China has endured because of its sameness. Either China was always self-identical with itself, or it eradicated what difference it encountered throughout history and replaced it with sameness ("Chinese-ness"). This view of identity, however, is antithetical to the Chinese understanding of longevity. In the Chinese tradition, pluralism is the condition for longevity. Contrary to the assumption of sameness in both of these Western fallacies, the stability and durability of the Chinese empire are due to its heterogeneity and thus lack of homogeneous unity, both in theory and in practice.

The pluralism that the Chinese tradition identifies with longevity is not, however, a chaos of radical particulars; it is not simply the heterogeneity side of the dualism (as in, for example, the fallacy that there never was a unified "China"). Instead, longevity stems from coherence among diverse things—that is, from harmony. As understood by the Chinese tradition, harmony is an order or coherence marked by differentiation and inner multiplicity. We see many examples in the Chinese classics of this idea of harmony as a coherence among diverse things as a precondition for flourishing. In *Discourses of the States*, Shi Bo, in conversation with Duke Huan of the state of Zheng, explains the importance of harmony—the lack of which led to the decline of the Zhou dynasty:

> Harmony [*he*, 和] indeed leads to fecundity [*shengwu*, 生物], identity [*tong*, 同] means barrenness. Things accommodating each other on equal terms [*ping*, 平] is called harmony, and in so doing they are able to flourish and grow, and other things are drawn to them. If identical things [*tong*, 同] are used to supplement identical things then, once they are used up, nothing will remain. (Chen 2013: 573; my translation based on Ames 1993: 60–61, my modifications)

Shi Bo's counsel continues as he explains that the former kings attained the utmost harmony by harmonizing the five phases, the five flavors, and the six musical notes, taking consorts from different clans, and allowing for a plurality of different opinions. The passage ends with the injunction, "There is no music in a single note, no refinement/culture-civilization [*wen*, 文] in a single item, and no taste in a single flavor, no comparison with/reconciliation [*jiang*, 讲] in a single thing" (Chen 2013: 573; my translation based on Ames 1993: 61, my modifications). The practical, historical implication of this conception of harmony is that overall, even considering the periods of chaos and disunity in the country, the Chinese people have exemplified this harmony or coherence among diverse things.

If we understand the Chinese ideal of harmony as putting a premium on creatively realizing coherence out of diversity, then we can explain away the seeming paradox of both Chinese heterogeneity and China's longevity and unity. Through the idea of harmony, we can let the fly out of the bottle. The seeming paradox of China—its simultaneous ethnic diversity and longevity—is a false one, for it is its very diversity that has determined its longevity. To understand the reason for Chinese longevity, we can borrow a sentiment from Aimé Césaire: "Whatever its own particular genius may be, a civilisation that withdraws into itself atrophies; [. . .] for civilizations, exchange is oxygen" (Césaire 2000: 33). Because Chinese history has heeded a similar idea and historically replenished itself with the oxygen of diversity, it has been able to endure. No one has expressed this all-embracing nature of Chinese history better than the New Confucians, who explained in their manifesto that

> throughout its history, whatever alien cultural elements were acceptable to our human moral nature [*xinxing*, 心性] were tolerated and assimilated. [. . .] It is because of this that Chinese culture was endowed with magnanimity, which is also the root cause of its longevity. (Quoted in Bresciani 2001: 45, modified).

China has endured because of its ability to draw diversity and difference into a harmonious whole. "Harmony" is here understood as a creative organizing function that brings differences into complementary and productive relationship with one another. Underlying this function is the assumption that difference enriches that which is doing the harmonizing. Thus, bringing particulars into productive relationship enriches (changes) the harmonizer. Conversely, the particulars are enriched as well. In the Chinese tradition, harmony is not mere (passive) toleration. To bring different particulars into a resonant relationship requires great vision, insight, and creativity, and the ability to harmonize is a sign of great agency.

The "Chinese" people are not a single stock of people, but a hybrid people produced by the coalescing of originally different peoples and their cultures from the geographical region of present-day China and its environs (Fairbank and Goldman 2006: 25; Ge 2018: 25). Contra the pervasive stereotype of Chinese history, China's heterogeneity itself, and thus lack of homogeneity, is the reason for its stability and durability. The Chinese became such a populous people only because "Chinese" is not a racial (and thus a deterministic and exclusionary) definition, but rather a cultural identity. The process of becoming "Chinese" evidences "China's 'culturalism'—that is, the devotion of the Chinese people to their way of life" (Fairbank and Goldman 2006: 25).

As quoted earlier from *Discourse on Colonialism*, Césaire describes civilizations metaphorically as organisms. An organism is a living thing in constant exchange with its environment; as soon as this exchange stops it is dead. The same logic of the biological organism underlies the Chinese valorization of harmony.[11] Key to the concept of harmony is the insight that it is only difference that brings forth meaning and value. Sameness, in the sense of being, is tantamount to death and nullity. In the Chinese worldview, the first truth is the continuation of (organic) life itself. The metaphysical basis of the Chinese conception of civilization is the metaphysics of procreativity of the *Yijing* encapsulated by the phrase "let all beings be in their becoming" *(sheng sheng,* 生生). The central metaphor behind such a metaphysics is the fecundity of nature itself, the measure of which is its dynamic ability to support increasing diversity and growth. The Chinese view is that the self, like an organism, always exists in a relationship with the myriad things of the world. The self is simultaneously the nonself, in the sense that the self depends on the environment in order to exist. For example, materially I depend on water, food, and air and socially I depend on human relationships in order to sustain my existence. This understanding that an organism depends for its existence on exchange with difference is encapsulated by *Xici* 1.5: "In its capacity to produce and reproduce, we call it change" (生生之谓易; Lynn 1994: 54, my modifications). Change is not a threat to life, but rather its very source.

The concept of harmony is the ideal of Chinese metaphysics. The harmony model, which is reflected in "China" and the Chinese people is best understood in analogy with the organic. An organism maintains coherence among a heterogeneity of parts. Since the parts of an organism are constantly changing (through exchange with its environment), the whole changes in correspondence with changes in the parts. In our own bodies, the highly diverse parts and substances that make up who we are continuously being replaced. The self is not a thing, but a process of maintaining equilibrium and harmony with the environment. An organism persists because it is *actively maintained,* not because of what it is passively given or because of a property that it always possesses. Stasis, for an organism, is death.

Organic life is characterized by metabolism, that is, by the "exchange of matter with the surroundings." This means that the organism is "never the same materially and yet persists as its same self, by not remaining the same matter." If two different moments in the life of the organism fully coincide, then that organism is dead (Jonas 2001: 76). There is no persistent, eternal core in a living thing that stands apart from its metabolizing activity. The organism is "wholly and continuously a result of its metabolizing activity"; moreover, "none of the 'result' ceases to be an object of metabolism while it is also an agent of it" (76n13). The organic order continuously creates harmony out of diversity, and order out of plurality. The "whole" is understood as the *functional* law derived from the spontaneous arising of novelty as the parts interact. It is this logic of the organism that underlies the Chinese concept of harmony.

In contrast to the Greek view of self-identity, or persistence, which require that nothing changes, the Chinese concept of harmony understands self-identity as the maintenance of harmony or equilibrium throughout change. The Greek view of self-identity as a self that is identical with itself is premised on a metaphysics of being that values completeness, independence, and non-change. For example, in Plato's *Timaeus* (33–34) Timaeus describes the demiurge's creation of the cosmic body. Because the cosmic body is complete—in both the sense of perfect and the sense of self-sufficient—it is spherical, as this is the shape most like itself and thus most complete. It would have no sense organs or appendages since, being complete, it would have no need to interact or engage with its environment. The only movement that the cosmic body makes is around itself, turning "in a circle, a single solitary universe, whose very existence enables it to keep its own company without requiring anything else. For its knowledge of and friendship with itself is enough" (34b; Plato 1997: 1238–39). What Timaeus describes is something that is already dead. Only a non-organic thing can be truly identical with itself.

The Chinese tradition did not share this view of identity. Instead, it understood identity as the ability to keep equilibrium or harmony through exchange with the environment. As a result, the Chinese view of self-identity is not characterized by the exclusivity that characterizes the Greek conception of self-identity.

Addressing Common Fallacies about Chinese Cosmopolitanism

So far, we have addressed three fallacious paradigms common in conventional Western understandings of "China," all of which rest on an inability to understand the metaphysics of harmony. This section describes three more misapplications of the Western experience to China: the misidentification of Chinese historical expansion with "colonialism," the misidentification of the Chinese "tributary" system with the relationship between European empires and their colonies, and the assumption that China has been the only political entity in the region with agency throughout the millennia.

The Misidentification of Chinese Historical Expansion with "Colonialism"

A common rebuke to narratives of cosmopolitanism such as mine is that the southward and westward expansion throughout its history of the "principalities of the center," or the later unified China, is evidence of "colonialism." We can direct objections of this kind to Albert Memmi, who points out the difference between "colonization" and "assimilation." The latter, he maintains, is "the opposite of colonization. [Assimilation] tends to eliminate the distinctions between the colonizers and the colonized, and thereby eliminates the colonial relationship" (Memmi 2003: 194).

The relationship between colonizer and colonized under colonialism is a very particular one that perpetuates the status of the colonizer and colonized. In the preface to *The Wretched of the Earth*, Jean-Paul Sartre, echoing Memmi, refers to the colonial relationship between the colonizer and the native as that of "domesticat[ing] a member of our own species" (Fanon 1963: 16). Under colonialism, "there is no claim or pretense that the subject peoples will ever be incorporated into an integrated empire. There is only the theory of mutual benefit on an unequal footing" (Isaac 2004: 181)[12] Anthony Pagden notes that the European empires initiated since the "Age of Discovery" "did not, in general, conceive of their subject peoples as 'fellow citizens.'" The Europeans had "a far starker conception of what divided the civilized European world from the world beyond, and a far more instrumental view of how the one should govern the other" (Pagden 2015: 27). Frantz Fanon famously characterized the colonial world of these new empires as "Manichean," in that "the totalitarian character of colonial exploitation" went beyond physical apartheid between colonizer and colonized and allowed the colonizer to paint the colonized as "a sort of quintessence of evil" (Fanon 1963: 41).

As these scholars have noted, the colonial relationship between colonizer and colonized is one that maintains the distinction between them. By contrast, "Chinese" expansion always assimilated the diverse peoples thus encountered, and the distinctions blurred between what would previously have been differentiated groups. One manifestation of this integration, as Roy Bin Wong notes, was an economic relationship between the center and the periphery in the Chinese historical experience completely *opposite* to the European experience. Rather than extracting resources from the peripheries, the Chinese state has been more likely to invest in them, and so political expansion has required that the government shift resources to the peripheries, rather than move them in the opposite direction (Wong 1997: 148). As Giovanni Arrighi remarks with regard to Wong's observation, the "logic of political economy" associated with the kind of competition that prevailed during European colonialism "had little in common with China's practices" (Arrighi 2007: 318). Although expansion is arguably a necessary characteristic of colonialism, it is not colonialism per se, as most political entities in history have pursued expansion.

Colonialism may be more accurately defined in terms of the following four interrelated characteristics: (1) conquering a subject people with no intention or practice of letting the conquered peoples become equals; (2) intentionally maintaining an unequal relationship between the colonizer and the colonized so that the colonized are hereditarily exploited for the benefit of the colonizer; (3) justifying this colonizing practice with a philosophy of ontological superiority; and (4) including in this philosophy of ontological superiority of the right to overwhelm the entire earth (one expression of which is the idea of "manifest destiny"). Expanding on this last point, Wong points to the fundamental difference between Chinese expansion and European expansion: the former had no such vision of owning the earth:

China expanded its empire through a combination of moral, material, and coercive means with a principal goal of achieving security and stability. As a territorial empire, the government recognized spheres of influence. While not borders in the modern geographical sense, the Chinese state nevertheless imagined spatially defined zones contiguous to each other. European

empires of the early modern period were, of course, fundamentally different. The mercantilist goal was to amass as great a portion of the more or less
fixed wealth in the world as possible. (Wong 1997: 148)

Defined in this way, the term "colonialism" is not an apt description of Chinese
historical expansion. As I have defined it, colonialism is not mere expansion,
as this activity characterizes most political entities throughout human history.
Although I cannot go into this it in detail here, suffice to say that the "mercantilist
goal" that Wong describes of extracting wealth from the whole extent of the
earth is based on a metaphysical worldview that did not exist in the Chinese
context. The desire to "own the earth" is also indebted to the same metaphysical
bifurcation of nature that underlies western racism: certain races are understood
as formless "mere nature" and thus to be subjugated by the races that embody
form.[13]

Traditional China's lack of an aggressive ideology of expansion can be seen
in what happened when China did expand. Two of the largest historical episodes of Chinese territorial expansion were the Han expansion toward the
northwest and the Ming expansion toward the southwest. As we will see, both
expansions were motivated by pragmatic concerns about defense rather than
by a desire for domination.

The purpose of the northern expansion of "Chinese" territory under the
Han was to deter invasion and prevent the formation of nomadic coalitions.
As the historian Zheng Yangwen writes, "Had the Koreans, the Filipinos or
the Indonesians challenged her [China] as they did the nomads from the
north and west, China may well have fought back and dominated the seas,
rather than the landmass of Asia" (Zheng 2012: 7). The expansion of Han
China into the western regions was a reaction to the threat of the Xiongnu, a
tribal confederation of nomadic pastoral people who dominated much of
Central Asia from the third century BCE to the second century CE (Yü 1967:
2; Yü 1986: 405–7). China aimed to prevent the Xiongnu from forming a large
steppe empire after their conquest of several smaller Central Asian peoples.
The Han had sent envoys to many states in Central Asia (around the upper
valley of Syr-Darya) in order to make military alliances, including the famous
mission of Zhang Qian in 138 BCE (Yü 1986: 407). It was through Zhang's
mission that the Han established contacts with Ferghana (in modern-day
Tajikistan), Sogdiana (an ancient Iranian civilization), Bactriana (the area
north of the Hindu Kush), and Khotan (an ancient Iranic Saka Buddhist kingdom) (408) and later brought them into the Han tribute system (416). It

could therefore be said that the "whole policy of the First Han emperors was dominated and directed by the problems of the steppe" (Gernet 1982: 117).

To help stem Xiongnu aggression, a policy of marriage alliances (*heqin*, 和亲) between the Han and the Xiongnu was in place for seventy years. It has been estimated that the Han dynasty used 30 to 40 percent of imperial revenue as gifts to its neighbors (Gernet 1982: 132). These gifts functioned, in effect, as expensive appeasement—basically a "tribute in reverse" (Yang 1968: 21)—in order to buy a non-aggression promise from the Xiongnu. The dominant policy of the early Han period was thus "one of appeasement and accommodation in which China became a virtual tributary of the Hsiung-nu [Xiongnu]" (Cosmo 2002: 9). The celebrated historian Yü Ying-shih has argued that this appeasement policy was a forerunner of the unequal treaties of the Song and late Qing periods, which acknowledged China's military weakness (Fairbank and Goldman 2006: 61). It was the failure of this policy in stemming Xiongnu aggression that motivated Zhang Qian's missions to the west and thus the beginnings of the Silk Road.

Official expeditions to the south can be traced to the Han period. In the fight against the Xiongnu, the Han emperor Wudi tried to find an alternative route through the territory of the southwest so that Han forces could complete a siege attack from the right side of the Xiongnu (Yang 2008: 3, 13). Large-scale migration south gained momentum, however, after what is famously known as "the uprising of the five barbarians" (五胡乱华), when the "five Hu" peoples began marauding across the Central Plain during the Yongjia (永嘉) era (307–313 CE).[14] After the fall of the Eastern Han dynasty, three kingdoms— Wei (魏), Shu (蜀), and Wu (吴)—dominated China. Following a brief period of unification in the Western Jin dynasty (西晋), the country entered an era marked by coexisting multiethnic regimes. By 311 CE, the Hu had captured the capital of the Western Jin, Luoyang, in what is called the Yongjia Disturbance (永嘉之乱). By 317 CE, the Hu had chased the remnants of the Western Jin government south of the Yangzi River (江南). The *Jinshu* (晋书), the official history of the Jin dynasty, estimates that 80 to 90 percent of the Western Jin officials either died or fled into exile during this time (Holcombe 1994: 27). It has been estimated that more than nine hundred thousand people were permanently displaced. The Yongjia Disturbance initiated what Herold Wiens has termed "China's March towards the Tropics" (Zheng 2012: 26, 208–209). Migration continued in the Tang era, during which the Chinese people filled out the Yangzi River drainage basin and continued into southeast China coastal regions as far as present-day Guangdong and Vietnam. It is significant that "the centuries-long process of Chinese southward migration seldom involved large-scale military confrontation, even though it was not always peaceable" (Mote 2003: 6). Immigrants continued pressing south in the Song period (960–1279) as North China faced foreign occupation at the hands of the Jurchens and then the Mongols (Herman 2007: 3).

Another great wave of official expansion southward was the Ming dynasty invasion of Yunnan, which was motivated by the threat and danger historically posed by the region to the security of the kingdom. Immigrants continued pressing south in the Song period (960–1279) as North China faced foreign occupation at the hands of the Jurchens and then the Mongols. (Herman 2007: 3) A key element in the Mongol success in overwhelming the Southern Song and conquering all of China was their ability to launch a two-front attack from the north and the south (made possible after they took over the Dali kingdom in Yunnan). After the founding Ming emperor pushed the Mongols back to the grasslands, the Mongols still retained control of Yunnan. Emissaries were repeatedly sent to persuade the Mongols to surrender Yunnan (in 1369, 1370, 1372, 1374, and 1375) but met with no success, and in fact several emissaries were killed. Only then did the Ming emperor resort to force (Mote 2003: 711). What steeled the emperor's resolve was the historical experience of the two-front war that led to the fall of the Song: "The familiarity of the situation pushed the Ming ruler to launch a campaign against Yunnan in order to avoid the fate of the Southern Song" (Yang 2008: 3, 75).

As with the history of Chinese expansion in general, the historic expansion of Chinese frontiers was not motivated by a desire to own the earth. Arrighi describes the main purpose of military activity during the end of the Ming and the beginning of the Qing (which was a "conquest dynasty") as defensive:

> Their main purpose was the transformation of a hard-to-defend frontier into a pacified periphery and a buffer against raiders and conquerors from Inner Asia. Once the objective had been attained, as it was by the 1760s, territorial expansion ceased and military activities turned into police activities aimed at consolidating the monopoly of the Chinese state over the use of violence within the newly established boundaries. Although quite substantial, this territorial expansion paled in comparison with the successive waves of European expansion—the earlier Iberian expansion in the Americas and Southeast Asia; the contemporary Russian expansion in North Asia, and Dutch expansion in Southeast Asia; not to speak of the later expansion of Britain in South Asia and Africa and of its offsprings in North America and

Australia. Unlike these successive waves, the Qing expansion was strictly limited in space and time by its boundary-drawing objectives, rather than a link in an "endless" chain of connected expansions. (Arrighi 2007: 317–18)

The quest for infinite expansion is an ideology. Just as the historic Chinese attitude toward the other was based on pragmatic advantage rather than ideology, overwhelming the earth was not relevant to the traditional Chinese worldview.

The Misidentification of the Chinese "Tributary" System with the Relationship between European Empires and Their Colonies

Another related paradigm that is often misapplied to Chinese history is the idea that China dominated its neighbors through the "tributary system." As Ji-Young Lee writes, this pervasive view of China as a hegemon that exercised its power through the tributary system "rests on a misunderstanding of the tribute system" as it "rests on a mistaken belief that the tribute system was imperial China's tool for projecting its power or culture onto others in the East Asian states system" (Lee 2016: 2). The persistent stereotype of an oriental despot subjugating an East Asia devoid of its own agency needs to be reassessed.[15] The stereotype of China's historic neighbors as passive agents devoid of initiative is offensive to both China and its neighbors.

One of the earliest formulations of this particular trope of oriental despotism can be found in Aristotle's *Politics*.[16] For Aristotle, tyranny as a political form exists among non-Greeks but not among Greeks, because non-Greeks are servile in nature and thus do not revolt against tyranny. Further, since all non-Greeks are natural slaves, tyranny is a legitimate form of government for them.

> There is another sort of monarchy not uncommon among foreigners, which nearly resembles tyranny. But this is both legal and hereditary. For foreigners, being more servile in character than Hellenes, and Asiatics than Europeans, do not rebel against a despotic government. Such kingships have the nature of tyrannies because the people are by nature slaves; but there is no danger of their being overthrown, for they are hereditary and legal. For the same reason, their guards are such as a king and not such as a tyrant would employ, that is to say, they are composed of citizens, whereas the guards of tyrants are mercenaries. For kings rule according to law over voluntary subjects, but tyrants over involuntary; and the one are guarded by their fellow-citizens, the others are guarded against them. (*Pol.* 1285a18–28; Aristotle 2007: 2039)

The idea that China was an oriental despot tyrannically lording over the servile peoples of its sphere of influence is racist because it assumes that the Chinese despot was able to maintain rule over his subject peoples for such extended periods of time because "Asiatics" were more servile in character and so did not revolt.

The Fallacy of China as the Only Regional Actor with Agency

Of course, the reality is very different from the orientalizing stereotype that underlies Western accounts of the relationship between China and its neighbors. To maintain peace on the frontier, for example, the Han and Tang dynasties married daughters of the ruling family to neighboring tribal chiefs (Yang 1968: 20). In a vivid example, Empress Dowager Lü (241–180 BCE), the widow of the Han dynasty's founder, who acted as regent and was effectively the de facto successor, was asked for her hand in marriage by the Xiongnu leader. China was clearly weak enough (in relation to their northern neighbor), and therefore exposed to further military attack, that the Xiongnu leader felt comfortable asking the widow of the former emperor and mother of the current emperor for her hand in marriage. Although insulted, the empress dowager was forced to send back a conciliatory note; in it she declined his offer on the grounds that she was too old and ugly to be married. This episode shows how vulnerable the early Han dynasty was in comparison with its northern neighbor, which remained aggressive throughout China's history.

It should be borne in mind that, throughout history, such was the threat of China's northern neighbors that China often had a systematic policy of buying them off with gifts. The Han and the Song sent what was nominally economic aid to their neighbors but in fact was "tributes in reverse." As mentioned earlier, the Han dynasty between the first century BCE and 150 CE sent a high percentage of annual revenues to foreign peoples as gifts—a kind of ransom for their non-aggression (Gernet 1982: 132). During the Khaghan's reign (553–72), the Northern Zhou court (which was itself founded by a Xianbei warrior) made an annual gift of 100,000 rolls of silk to the Khaghan, and the Northern Zhou court was compelled to lavishly entertain Turkic visitors in the capital (Barisitz 2017: 55). As Jacques Gernet summarizes, "Probably no other country in the world has ever made such an effort to supply its neighbours with presents" (Gernet 1982: 132).

The founder of the Tang, Emperor Gaozu (566 CE–635 CE), followed an appeasement policy toward the Eastern Turks, treating them as "an equal adversary" and paying them tribute (Pan 1997: 171–72). Nevertheless, the Khaganate began a campaign of pillaging incursions into Tang territory, effectively asserting authority over Tang territory while also supporting anti-Tang forces. The Khaganate incursions were causing so many problems for the Tang that Emperor Gaozu even considered burning the capital, Chang'an, to the ground and moving his seat elsewhere (172–74; Hung 2013: 118). In 630, Gaozu's successor, the emperor Taizong (598–649 CE), defeated the Eastern Khaganate (183). When we fast-forward to the Song dynasty (960–1279 CE), we see that during the tenth to thirteenth centuries, "China did not dogmatically enforce its system of foreign relations." Instead, the Song "was flexible in its dealing with foreigners" and "generally adopted a realistic foreign policy" (Rossabi 1983: 4).[17] In the Song dynasty, the Liao, Xixia, Jurchens, and Mongolians forced the Song into the role of one state among many. By 1005, the Song and Liao dynasties had already begun to refer to each other as the "Northern and Southern Dynasties," and their rulers referred to each other as "emperor" (Ge 2018: 56). To make peace with the Jin (金) in 1138, the founder of the Southern Song dynasty even accepted the status of vassal (臣) to the Jin (Yang 1968: 20).

Since many of China's historic northern nomadic neighbors no longer exist as the entities they once were, it is easy to forget what an existential threat they were for China throughout most of Chinese history. Invasion from the north hung over China as "a permanent threat," since "any barbarian nation that could guard its own rear and flanks against other barbarians could set out confidently to invade China" (Lattimore 1934: 22). During much of China's history, the nomads of the periphery were better armed and more mobile than the Chinese. To China's north and west were the Manchus, Mongols, Uyghurs, and Tibetans, and later the expansionist Russian empire. As Frederick Mote writes, the martial tribal peoples of inner Asia "were always potential raiders, invaders, conquerors, and rulers" (Mote 2003: 5). Throughout the whole span of Chinese history, "when the inner Asian chieftains scanned their horizons, there were many targets of military expansion to tempt their ambitious warriors. But beyond all the others, China was the great prize, for plunder and for more long-range exploitation" (29).

The Chinese did not go to such extraordinary lengths as building the Great Wall of China because they had an irrational fear of the "other." The peoples of the northern steppes who historically were military threats to China included the Xiongnu (third to first centuries BCE), the Xianbei (third to sixth centuries CE), the Turks (sixth to eighth centuries CE), and the Uyghurs (eighth to ninth centuries CE). The peoples of the northern steppes who actually conquered and established empires in China include the Khitan (Liao dynasty, tenth to twelfth centuries CE); the Jurchen (Jin dynasty, twelfth to thirteenth centuries CE); the Mongols (Yuan dynasty, thirteenth to fourteenth centuries CE), and the Manchu (Qing, the last Chinese dynasty, seventeenth century to 1911). Should any reader be skeptical about who was historically the more aggressive neighbor, China or the northern steppe tribes, they should recall the visceral (and racist) fear that the notorious Hun and later the Mongol army evoked in the minds of Europeans.[18]

In the Western imagination, Attila the Hun is synonymous with fearsome hordes who tear down the doors of civilization. The thought of Mongols at the gates of Vienna still makes the European imagination shudder. It bears stressing that the Huns claimed they were the descendants of the Xiongnu (Vaissière 2015: 190), and modern scholarship has confirmed that the "Huns are beyond doubt the political and ethnic inheritors of the Xiongnu empire" (Vaissière 2012: 146). Where the Chinese and European experiences differed was that these northern steppe tribes were not a continent away from China; they were a permanent threat, not just a threat once every few generations. Again, we should not fall into the fallacy of thinking China's historic neighbors lacked agency. Arguably, it was the nomadic tribes to China's north who were the imperialistic forces.

Another point worth stressing is that after pacifying (to some extent) its fierce northern neighbors in the early part of its history, China's later relationships with its neighboring states was remarkably peaceful. Compared with Europe, which was constantly at war, the Sino-sphere was markedly more peaceful. As David Kang notes, from the founding of the Ming dynasty to the opium wars—that is, from 1368 to 1841—there were only two wars between China, Korea, Vietnam, and Japan. These were China's invasion of Vietnam (1407–1428) and Japan's invasion of Korea (1592–1598). Apart from these two episodes, "these four major territorial and centralized states developed and maintained peaceful and long-lasting relations with one another" (Kang 2010: 2). Furthermore, contrary to the metaphysical assumption of the Great Chain of Being that "might makes right"—and so the stronger one's (Hobbesian) conatus the more one wishes to overwhelm the weak—in the Sino-sphere the more powerful these states became the more stable were their relations. Although China was clearly the dominant military, cultural, and economic power among these players, Kang writes, "its goals did not include expansion against its established neighboring states" (2). Despite "having the military and technological capability to wage war on a massive scale," China, Korea, Japan, and other countries in the tribute system coexisted peacefully for extended spans of time (1). Similarly, Arrighi notes that, in sharp contrast to the "incessant military competition and geographical expansion of European powers," "the East Asia system of national states stood out for the near absence of intra-systemic military competition and extra-systemic geographical expansion."

> Thus, with the exception of China's frontier wars [. . .], prior to their subordinate incorporation in the European system the national states of the East Asian system were almost uninterruptedly at peace with one another, not for one hundred, but for three hundred years. The three hundred years' peace was bracketed by two Japanese invasions of Korea, both of which precipitated a war with China—the Sino-Japanese wars of 1592–98 and 1894–95. Between 1598 and 1894 there were only three brief wars that involved China—the 1659–60 and the 1767–71 wars with Burma, and the 1788–89 war with Vietnam—and two wars that did not involve China—the Siamese-Burmese wars of 1607–18 and 1660–62. Indeed, insofar as China is concerned, we should speak of a five hundred years' peace, since in the two hundred years preceding the 1592 Japanese invasion of Korea China was at war with other East Asian states only during the invasion of Vietnam in 1406–28 to restore the Tran dynasty. (Arrighi 2007: 316)

In sum, China treated its neighboring states, though historically not its military, economic, or (arguably) cultural equals, as sovereign. Despite having the capacity to overwhelm their territories, China steadfastly maintained a relationship of peaceful coexistence with these neighbors.

Here we have looked more closely at three conventionally used explanations for the longevity and success of China as a cultural-political entity—the misidentification of Chinese historical expansion with "colonialism," the misidentification of the Chinese tributary system with the relationship between European empires and their colonies, and the assumption that for millennia China has been the only political entity in the region with agency—and seen that each is fallacious.

"The Pliant and the Supple Overcomes the Hard and the Strong"

A fatal mistake that the Western academy makes in trying to understand the source of Chinese longevity is applying the historical experience of the West to the Chinese experience. According to this view, China became the most successful entity in the region, because, like Europe, it must have violently dominated all other competing entities. As we will see in chapter 4, the idea that "might makes right" is deeply entrenched in the Western ontological worldview. What the Western academy has not understood is that at the heart of the Chinese worldview is the (Daoist) idea that "the pliant and the supple overcomes the hard and the strong" (柔弱胜刚强, *Daodejing* 36), and indeed, that strength resides in being pliant (守柔曰强, *Daodejing* 52).

Although maintaining a competent military to deter invasion and disempower competitors was a necessary condition of its success, this was not the fundamental reason why China was the most successful and long-lasting political entity in the region. Historically, China outcompeted its innumerable political rivals precisely because it was supple. As this section shows, being supple requires an understanding that:

1. *Dominating others is not the only kind of strength.* Yielding to others often is more beneficial in the long term. Efficacy is displayed not only when the stronger overcomes the weaker, but when the bird hermeneutically reads the way the wind is blowing in order not to go against it but to make effective use of it.
2. *The supple can embrace difference.* China has been pliant and supple enough—cosmopolitan enough—to embrace and synthesize many originally distinct identities. China imaginatively synthesized the identities of other originally distinct peoples, allowing them to see their own image in the "Chinese" identity and readily tie their identity to this hybrid whole.

If Chinese identity had not been accommodating, supple, and dynamic enough to evolve in tandem with the identities of the peoples it absorbed, it could not have achieved its longevity. Political entities that are rigid and unable to successfully integrate difference will fracture. As we have seen, very early on in its history the Chinese tradition identified longevity with the ability to harmonize difference and saw difference as enriching. This idea of harmony as coherence among diverse things as the source of longevity is related to the idea of suppleness as strength. An example of suppleness as strength can be seen in *Daodejing* chapter 76:

> While living, people are supple and soft,
> But once dead, they become hard and rigid cadavers.
> While living, the things of this world and its grasses and trees are
>   pliant and fragile,
> But once dead, they become withered and dry.

Thus it is said: Things that are hard and rigid are the companions of
   death;
Things that are supple and soft are the companions of life.
For this reason,
If a weapon is rigid it will not prevail;
If a tree is rigid it will snap. (Ames and Hall 2003: 195)

The bamboo is so admired in the Chinese tradition because it embodies this
strength through pliancy. With its tensile strength and versatility, bamboo can
yield to the wind but not break. It can maintain equilibrium *because* it is supple
enough to yield to the wind—or the force of the situation.

Maintaining integrity in the long term requires being accommodating to
the particularity of a situation. An identity that is flexible and dynamic enough
to accommodate change is the real source of a long-term, sustainable integrity
(in the related senses of wholeness and consistency). China was able to endure
because its identity was not rigid but instead supple, soft, and accommodating. In chapters 5 and 6, we explore the Chinese view of efficacy as the non-
assertive ability to accommodate existing particulars. For now, let us look at
this suppleness in action in the historical process of synthesis that created the
Chinese identity.

Amalgamation, Acculturation, and Assimilation

The amalgamation of different peoples and their cultures and the acculturation
of foreign peoples into Chinese culture would enable the historical assimilation of vast swathes of peoples into the "Chinese" identity. We can see this
process from the formative period of Chinese culture and identity, the Zhou
period (1046–256 BCE).

From its inception, Chinese civilization was a hybrid product. According
to the Sinologist Herrlee G. Creel, "it was the process of acculturation, transforming barbarians into Chinese, that created the great bulk of the Chinese
people. The barbarians of Western Chou [Zhou] times were, for the most part,
future Chinese, or the ancestors of future Chinese" (Creel 1970: 197). An example of this hybridity is the founder of the Zhou dynasty himself. Situated
outside the Shang domain, the Zhou state was in "permanent contact" with
the tribes of the western regions (Gernet 1982: 51), and throughout Chinese
history it was common knowledge that the Zhou royal house was descended
from the Rong "barbarians." In fact, intermarriage with a member of one of

the Rong tribes constituted incest (Creel 1970: 196), and *Mencius* (4B1) talks of King Wen, the founder of the Zhou dynasty, as a man of the Western Yi (西夷; Mencius 2009: 86).[19]

The area that the Western Zhou ruled over was home to diverse peoples and far from homogeneous, but they were able to effectively bring these peoples into a political and cultural whole (Creel 1970: 204) because, "having intermingled with non-Chinese-speaking peoples on China's north and west peripheries, [they] were adept at tolerating cultural differences" (Fairbank and Goldman 2006: 44). In the Spring and Autumn Period (770–476 BCE), the people of the Central Plain called themselves the Zhuxia (诸夏, "the various principalities"), while those on the peripheries were referred to as the Man (蛮), the Yi (夷), the Rong (戎), and the Di (狄). As communication between the people of the Central Plain and neighboring groups increased during the late Spring and Autumn Period and the early Warring States Period, most of the Man, Yi, Rong, and Di peoples gradually mixed with the Zhuxia. This intermixing continued into the Han period (202 BCE–220 CE). After their military defeat by the Han army, huge numbers of people from the northern tribes were resettled within the borders of "China." Yü Ying-shih gives an indication of the scale of Han resettlement of the pacified Qiang, Wuhuan, and Xianbei peoples (Yü 1986: 425–46). In 94 CE, for example, more than half a million of the "Ts'ang-i tribe [*zangyi*, 牂夷]" surrendered to the Han as "inner subjects." In 107 and 108 CE, fourteen Qiang tribes totaling 55,180 individuals followed suit. In 108 CE, 2,400 members of the "Ts'an-lang tribe [*qianglong*, 羌龙]" were also admitted as inner subjects. As Yü writes, "It is clear that in the Later Han period [. . .] a large-scale movement of Ch'iang [Qiang] populations was taking place from points all along the western border into China proper" (Yü 1986: 429; Fan 1965: 2898–99). These resettled tribes were allowed to follow their own social customs and ways of life (Yü 1986: 383). The hybridity of the Chinese peoples is such that, as the Sinologist John Fairbank has written, the "inhabitants of the Middle Kingdom" were "themselves largely descendants of barbarians" (Fairbank 1942: 130).

An example of Chinese cultural identity as an amalgamation of differences from early on can be seen in the synthesis of northern and southern cultures during the formative Zhou period. During the Zhou dynasty, the southern kingdoms of Wu (吴), Yue (越), and Chu (楚) had cultures very different from those of the "principalities of the centre" based around the Yellow River region (Gernet 1982: 60). The most "striking illustration" of the Chinese identity as a fusion of diverse peoples, cultures, and traditions is the assimilation of the state of Chu into the Chinese identity (Creel 1970: 217). The Chu kingdom was a vast territory inhabited by aboriginal tribes who spoke a language that belonged to a different linguistic group from Chinese (Gernet 1982: 60). The cultural difference between Chu and the northern states is evident in its literary culture, which shows a marked difference in style, for example, between the *Songs of Chu* and the *Book of Odes*. The differences between Daoist texts, such as the *Zhuangzi*, and their northern counterparts, such as the *Analects*, are also appreciable. That today we consider these texts "Chinese" is a testament to the amalgamation that wove these various strands together into a coherent identity. (Relatedly, we should recall that Neo-Confucianism, constituting one of the golden ages of Chinese philosophy, is highly syncretic, as is Chinese philosophy in general.)

It would be a mistake, however, to think that the creation of a united whole is a one-way process of making the assimilated become the same as the assimilator. The Chu government, for example, appeared to be more advanced than its northern counterparts in a number of respects, and in the eventual amalgamation "it seems likely that Ch'u [Chu] contributed quite as much as it received" (Creel 1970: 219). The Chu, however, also admired the central states' culture. High officers from Chu quoted from the *Book of Odes* and the *Book of Documents* and cited King Wen and Wu as exemplars (220). The great king of Chu, Xiang Yu (项羽) (232–202 BCE), has long played a role in the Chinese imagination and is a fixture of Chinese lore.

After the fall of the Qin dynasty (221–206 BCE), Xiang Yu and Liu Bang, founder of the Han dynasty, vied with each other to become emperor of China. At the battle of Gaixia (202 BCE), Xiang Yu was finally defeated by Liu Bang, and with what remained of his men, he retreated to the banks of the Wu River. Ashamed, Xiang Yu refused to cross the river back to the safety of his own state. Instead, he made a last heroic stand before committing suicide. In 1127, when the Northern Song dynasty was about to collapse after the invasion of the Jin (金) army, the foremost female poet of the Chinese tradition, Li Qingzhao (李清照), frustrated at the Song government and her husband's cowardice, wrote a paean to Xiang Yu's courage:

> In life, [one] should be outstanding among men,
> In death [one] should also be a hero among ghosts
> Even today [we] think of Xiang Yu
> Who refused to cross east of the river.

The same process that assimilated Xiang Yu into the tapestry of Chinese history also produced the "Chinese" people. Indeed, I have the same surname as Xiang Yu, and my patriline is from the region of Xiang Yu's birth.

As Creel writes, when the narrative of early Chinese history was constructed in the late Spring and Autumn Period, "the reputed progenitors of a very large number of groups were worked into the tapestry." It was "this interweaving of genealogies" that "produced a united people with a sense of solidarity that could, perhaps, have been brought about in no other way" (Creel 1970: 226).[20]

Following the Zhou dynasty, the Qin royal house was also widely known to be Rong in origin (Pines 2005/2006: 15n15). Indeed, many of the most formative and subsequently celebrated dynasties were "foreign" in origin. The Northern (386–534), Western (535–556), and Eastern Wei dynasties (534–550), the Northern Qi (550–559), the Northern Zhou (557–581) of the Southern and Northern dynasties (南北朝), and the later Sui, Tang, Liao, Western Xia, Jin, Yuan, and Qing dynasties were all "foreign" or ruled by a clan with members who had foreign blood. During the Northern dynasties, non-Chinese rulers were Sinicized, but they also introduced new perspectives that enriched the Chinese tradition. This can be seen in, for example, the Sui's constitutional order (Pan 1997: 32).

Finally, we should not forget that the Manchus who conquered China and established the last dynasty are now so thoroughly assimilated that their descendants no longer speak their ancestral tongue but only Chinese. Conversely, popular entertainment today is dominated by dramatic reimagining of the court lives of the Manchu emperor and his courtesans. "Manchu" and "Han-Chinese" have mutually assimilated each other's identities such that they have adopted each other's culture and history as their own.

When thinking about Chinese identity, it is important not to fall afoul of what John Dewey described as the "philosophical fallacy," that is, "the abstracting of some one element from the organism which gives it meaning, and setting it up as absolute," then proceeding to revere this one element "as the cause and ground of all reality and knowledge" (Dewey 1969: 162). "China" is an emergent, dynamic function of a continuing historical process, not a preconceived form or universal that has teleologically used historical processes as the mere means to enact this preconceived identity.

The Confucian Cultural Conception of Humanness

One of the contributing factors to Chinese amalgamation, acculturation, and assimilation is the Chinese understanding that culture is constitutive of an individual's identity.[21] As Benjamin Schwartz has remarked:

A random perusal of discussions of barbarians in the various [Chinese] encyclopedias and other sources reveals again and again the degree of emphasis on the five relationships, the "three bonds" [the most important human relationships] [...] and the whole body of *li* [ritual] as providing the absolute criteria dividing barbarians from the men of the Middle Kingdom. (Schwartz 1968: 277–78)

Since the Chinese tradition had a cultural understanding of identity or personhood, it was possible for foreigners to acculturate into Chinese culture and so become "Chinese." Indeed, acculturation was the process that created the Chinese people, as testified to firsthand by an English army officer's account of Yunnan in 1909. Major H. R. Davis (1865–1950) wrote that once the indigenous tribes of Yunnan learned to speak the Chinese language and adopted "to some extent Chinese customs," an "idea gets hold of them" whereby they were "Chinamen." "A race of Chinese thus grows up who have really no Chinese blood in them" (Davis 1909: 367–68). Davis concluded that the ability to speak Chinese bore no correlation with "race," and so "the Chinaman of the present day has grown up out of a gradual welding into one empire of [...] races who were in original occupation of the country which has grown into China" (368–69). Davis's account testifies to "Chinese" being a *cultural* identity, not a racial identity, and to the "Chinese people" being the amalgamation of many different peoples who came to identify with and allowed into the cultural identity of "Chinese."

Chinese processual metaphysics leads to a very different conception of personhood from that arising from the Western tradition (see chapter 3). The absence of an assumption of metaphysical determinism results in a view of the human being as creatively indeterminate, as a potential to be formed. Instead of a *being*, the human is understood as a *becoming*. As I have discussed elsewhere, Confucianism had an anti-essentialist conception of selfhood that precluded any concept of "race" in the sense of an individual's essence determining their becoming. In that earlier work, I introduced the idea that race is the biological interpretation of the concept of substance (Xiang 2019b, 2019c).[22] Substance explains causality through hypostatization (or reductionism), determinism, and reification. Under a substance (racial) ontology, the human being's whole becoming is hypostatized (reduced) to a predetermined, reified substance (essence). Under this ontology, individuals' secondary, observable properties—the *work* they manifest—are of no consequence for their intrinsic, unobservable substance; their essence is assumed to be a priori, and their empirical manifestations, such as cultural competence and moral actions, are subordinated to this essence. The substance (racial) view allows its proponents to dogmatically assert that their superior essence is a truth requiring no empirical demonstration. Like the idea of substance, the idea of race cannot be refuted through empirical evidence in the way that a scientific theory can be if it encounters enough anomalies. Substance is instead taken a priori and so takes precedence over empirical reality.[23]

The Confucian-Chinese Conception of the Human:
Environment, Becoming, and Acculturation

For Confucianism, since the proof of a person's humanity lies in the empirical proof of evidencing culture, humanness is not an unobservable quality prior to its physical manifestation (in culture). Under this view, there is no substance behind appearance; there is only appearance. The truth about the self is not some hidden essence behind the welter of its expressions; the expression of the self (through cultural media) is the truth about the self. In existentialist terms, the self is not defined ontologically; it is not *being*. The self as a human *becoming* is always a work in progress that is the creative result of the human's choices and actions. The self is manifested in her effects, because she is what she is by virtue of her activity.

Given its empiricism, which makes no statements about qualities prior to their manifestation, this philosophy assumes the equal potential of all human beings for taking up culture. The Confucian canon holds that embodying culture in the performance of actions according to social norms is constitutive of the self. Humanness is thus a (moral) category to be achieved, not a natural category into which one is born. In defining humanness as the embodiment of cultural norms and the performance of culturally appropriate actions, the Confucians had a cultural conception of self.[24] Under a racial ontology—that is, under the assumption that there are immutable major divisions of humankind, each with a particular set of traits that are passed on genetically—humans' only agency over their becomings is the practice of a eugenics program under which only those with the best essence breed.[25] Under this racial determinism, the lawfulness of the self can be understood only when its individuality is subsumed by the rational law of the universe. This universal law distinguishes each individual as a member of a race that definitionally bears a relationship to others races. In contrast, the Confucian view is that who a person becomes is not predetermined by a (racial) essence but is almost completely determined by the sociocultural environment.

The Confucians argue that humans are what they are owing to contingent factors such as the environment in which they were raised. In the Confucian conception, what most defines humans is their having no fixed essence. Intrinsic to a person are her a posteriori, extrinsic actions and behaviors, which cannot be determined a priori. All that can be defined a priori about human beings is their potential for becoming human through acculturation. Humanness understood as embodying culture and moral behavior through acculturation is thus not a given, but rather a potential that requires formation to be realized. Humans' transformation through cultural education, or acculturation, takes ontological primacy before any substance or fixed essence that can be assigned to them. In the Confucian tradition, humans do not speculate about a final essence that determines what they are, but instead concentrate merely on the process of learning and thus on growth itself. They do not focus on some reality behind the appearance, but on the phenomenon itself. Conversely, we could say that it is because Confucians assume that acculturation plays the decisive role in determining who a person becomes that they see natural endowments as playing a negligible part and so assume the same natural potentiality in all peoples. To assume the equal potentiality of all peoples is just another way of saying that culture has causal efficacy in determining who we become. The self has potential for growth through participation in culture and is therefore perfectible. It is this assumption that culture is constitutive of the self that allows the Confucians to be so optimistic about the commensurability between all peoples.

The Confucian view of selfhood as a potential to be realized and thus as subject to change is another example of the philosophy of the organism, in which change and embrace of difference are the sources of creative growth. It is exchange with one's environment, both physical and social, that determines what one becomes. The human being is not determined by a nonchanging essence. Relatedly, the Chinese attitude tends not to think of the "bad" as ontological. Non-optimal people and actions are understood as the symptoms of a bad environment, such as a bad upbringing. Social ills have material causes and are not the result of some ontological property in people. The Chinese view, most famously espoused in Mencius 1A, is "materialist" in that crime is understood as a result of poverty. Mencius asserts that if people commit crimes owing to the sovereign's inability to provide them with a constant livelihood, this is entrapment. If a person who never had the right environment to predispose them toward making the right decisions subsequently falls into error, then it is their environment that is implicated in their failures, not some putative essence. To a large extent, the onus of making sure a population does not fall into error falls on the ruler responsible for ensuring that the population is materially satisfied. A harmonious society is created by providing adequate material circumstances, education, and avenues for self-cultivation. Human beings have a collective responsibility to provide an environment amenable to the growth of future generations.

Conversely, it was the pervasive substance ontology governing Western culture that made it difficult for the Jewish people to assimilate into Europe. Under this (racial) ontological view, no matter how much the Jew tried to acculturate, he never became "one of us" because his "essence" determined that he was forever a Jew. This substance ontology explains the paradoxical increase in Judeophobia in proportion to the success of Jewish assimilation into European society. For contemporary scholars such as Alain Finkielkraut, the genocide during the Second World War was "not imposed on the Jews in spite of their efforts to assimilate, but *in response* to this very attempt." The more they tried to assimilate and "hide their Jewishness, the more terrifying they became to others" (Finkielkraut 1994: 69).

It is because the "eternal Jew" (*ewige Jude*) is essentially and eternally a Jew that Jews' great ability to acculturate and assimilate into non-Jewish culture is so frightening to the Gentile. For the Gentile, the governing substance ontology marks the Jew as forever an unassimilable other, despite all appearances to the contrary. With Jews' acculturation and assimilation into European culture, the Gentile, trying to apply the logic of substance ontology, cannot tell Jew from Gentile and the now-invisible Jew is rendered even more horrifying, since the Gentile *knows* that the Jew is still a Jew. The proverbial "uncanniness" attributed to the Jew stems from his ability to appear in every way a European in manners, dress, and language (in sum, in culture) while still, according to the substance ontology underlying racial thinking, being *essentially* a Jew. In his unsettling ability to "fulfill the role of French writer or philosopher, or that of German industrialist or politician, without being either *really* French or German" (Friedländer 1999: 213, emphasis added), the Jew seems to schizophrenically unite, as if by some dark magic, two different things—Jew and Gentile—in one body. The Judeophobia of those who feel menaced arises from their conviction that Jews, as "protean carriers of an evil essence," meld *essential* difference (the essence of Jewishness) with sameness in appearance (the appearance and secondary properties of the Gentile) (216). The source of Judeophobia is thus a philosophy of substance that is badly equipped to explain empirical phenomena. Under a substance ontology view of personhood, one's essence (or race) eternally defines who one is, and acculturation cannot change it.

The acculturation and assimilation that took place in Chinese history and created the Chinese people could never have happened in the West, owing to its substance ontological understanding of selfhood. Further, the Chinese conception of cultural selfhood—that one essentially is the culture that one displays, not a putative essence that cannot be demonstrated—is more empirical than the view of selfhood that has dominated Western history. Unlike the eugenicist programs throughout Western history, the Confucian solution to social problems is not based in biological determinism, it being understood that an ordered society cannot be achieved by simply excising what are deemed bad substances (racial others, sociopaths, those with low IQs, and so on). The Confucian view understands that the issues that most trouble our lives resist reduction to a simple (biological) essence that can be located and then purged.

Given the Confucian assumption that humans *become* human, the onus for realizing humanness falls on those responsible for providing a constructive environment in which humans can be acculturated: shaping contingent factors to support their growth. Under the Confucian view, humans have such a large measure of control over their own becoming that factors such as genetic inheritance are negligible in comparison. The same optimism is seen in the Confucian view that humans have positive personal agency in determining their self, as it is their achievements that determine who they are. In short, Confucianism sees human beings as having positive agency, both personally and collectively, to determine human becoming.

The assumption of human agency implicit in Confucian ideas about determining humanness (embodying cultural acts and providing the right environment for acculturation) makes the Confucian understanding of hierarchy social as opposed to ontological. A person performs actions—such as the duties of a minister—to establish his position in a social hierarchy. His position in this hierarchy is contingent upon his own merit, not on the elevation of his birth. This view of hierarchy as social rather than ontological is a key reason why the Confucian-Chinese ideal of hierarchy is defensible in relation to the Western view of hierarchy, and indeed it is currently the subject of much interest in relation to Confucian meritocracy (Bai 2020; Bell and Wang 2020).

Sociopolitical Hierarchy, Not Ontological Hierarchy

What the Confucians and Plato had in common was a belief that hierarchy is integral to social stability. They differed, however, with regard to the nature of this hierarchy. Whereas Plato's hierarchy is ontological, with one's position on it determined from birth (a view taken to an extreme with Aristotle's theory of natural slavery), for Confucians the hierarchy is sociocultural and one's position in it is achieved through moral endeavors and competence in fulfilling the demands of a particular role. A father, for example, is higher in the social hierarchy than a son, but the determination of "father" rests on whether he fulfills his social obligations as a father. A father is not a father simply by virtue of being the biological progenitor of his children. A person's status—father, king, sage—must be embodied or merited; it is not ontologically (and so eternally) possessed already. Under the ontological Greek view, a person's embodiment of virtuous actions cannot change his place in the hierarchy, but under the Confucian view, his virtuous actions determine his place in the hierarchy. Intrinsic to the Confucian tradition is a meritocracy in which no one has a birthright to their place in a hierarchy. The sovereign is a sovereign only because he fulfills his duties as such. If he neglects those duties, he is no longer considered a sovereign, despite his birth into the ruling family.

The Platonic idea that a person's position in a hierarchy is not established through their own agency but ontologically predetermined also explains the persistent and pervasive Western idea that a person's virtue deteriorates in proportion to his distance from the (perceived) civilizational center. The civilizational center is not created by individuals' virtuous action but is ontologically predetermined: the civilizational center itself creates individuals' virtuous actions. And just as there is an ontological hierarchy within one's society, there is a hierarchy among the different peoples of the world. In Plato's dialogue *Protagoras*, for example, the ordering principles of cities, such as justice, reverence, the art of politics, and the bonds of friendship, were a gift from Zeus (*Protagoras* 322c; Plato 1997: 757–58). The implication of this gift of civilization from Zeus to the Greeks is that non-Greeks received no such gift and so cannot have civilization. This dialogue underscores "the fundamental irreconcilability of savagery and civilization by assigning divine origins to the establishment of the imperial polis" (Williams 2012: 71). As the historian of European colonialism Anthony Pagden explains,

> The *oikumene* was, of course, a closed world, access to which was, in reality, only by accident of birth; but for the Greeks, for whom birth could never be a matter of accident, it was a superior world, the only world, indeed, in which it was possible to be truly human. (Pagden 1982: 16)

It is because civilization was not seen as the work of human agency, of their achievements, but as ontologically predetermined that from the time of the Roman empire the idea that emigration away from Rome led to deterioration was so pervasive, as in the reports "again and again that [the troops] in Syria deteriorated" (Isaac 2004: 308). The American historian David Stannard explains:

> Whether Greeks, Romans, or medieval Christians, moreover, the Europeans of all eras considered themselves to be "chosen" people, the inhabitants of the center and most civil domain of human life. The further removed from that center anything in nature was, the further it was removed from God, from virtue, and from the highest essence of humanity. (Stannard 1992: 167–68)

The most representative example of this trope that civilization is geographically predetermined, making people's virtue dependent upon geography, is Joseph Conrad's *Heart of Darkness*. Conrad's theme of civilized man being unable to maintain his morality in a primitive milieu is an *idée fixe* and long-running neurosis in Western culture. Aristotle argues that the farther away from Greece a person travels the more likely he is to encounter peoples who lack rationality and live by sensation alone, like nonhuman animals (*Nicomachean Ethics*, 1149a 9–12; Aristotle 2007: 1815). Such geographical determinism, like racial determinism, is a species of the metaphysical determinism that declares hierarchy to be ontological.

Human Agency and Difference as Emergent, Not Ontological

In the Confucian view, civilization is not predetermined by geography but instead is created through human agency, and specifically through virtuous human actions. Just as a person's place in a social hierarchy is determined by their achievements, the hierarchy among civilizations is established through the achievements of peoples. Confucius insists that the mere presence of a moral exemplar will transform the conduct of those on the margins of civilization (*Analects* 9.14) and urges that virtuous conduct not be abandoned, even among the Yi, Di, Man, and Mo tribes (13.19, 15.6). Confucians believe that truly virtuous behavior has an affective dimension to it. The civilizational center is established by the spread of human virtue, with which all persons will naturally resonate. This view explains the numerous accounts in the classics of civilizational centers that are not located in the central states (*zhongguo*, 中国). In *Analects* 5.7, Confucius famously says, "If the Way [*Dao*] is not put into practice, I will set off upon the sea [that is, beyond the confines of 'China'] in a small raft" (Slingerland 2003: 41); the implication is that a geographically foreign place need not inhibit the realization of Confucius's ideal of civilization and morality. This view is antithetical to the Western view so canonically expressed in Conrad's *Heart of Darkness*.

In the Confucian view, the civilizational center is dependent on virtue, not vice versa. Virtue *causes* the civilizational center to exist, as opposed to the Platonic idea that the civilizational center causes virtue to exist. This logic is found in *Zuo Zhuan*, "Lord Zhao 17th Year," where Confucius is recorded as saying, "I have heard that 'when the Son of Heaven has lost his officials, then we must learn from the tribes from the four regions . . . learning is preserved in the tribes from the four regions [四夷]" (Durrant, Li, and Schaberg 2016: 1545, my modifications). It is for this reason that the revered founders of the Zhou were not from the central states. *Mencius* 4B1 attests to the received wisdom that the founding fathers of "Chinese" civilization were "foreigners": "Shun was born in Zhufeng, moved to Fuxia, and died in Mingtiao—a man of the Eastern Yi. King Wen was born at Mount Qi, in Zhou, and died at Biying—a man of the Western Yi" (Mencius 2009: 86). All of these founders, despite being born in regions peripheral to the central states, became the progenitors of Chinese civilization. Similarly, it is recorded in the "Excellent Persuasions" (善说) chapter of the *Garden of Persuasions* (说苑) that a certain Lin Jin tells Duke Jing of Qi that accomplished ministers emerged from peripheral regions:

> In Yue, they tattoo their bodies and cut their hair short, yet [the Grand Master 大夫] Fan Li and Wen Zhong came from there. The Western Rong fasten their garments on the left [a sign of uncivility] and wear cone-shaped buns, yet You Yu [a high minister in the state of Qin during the late Spring and Autumn Period] came from there. (Liu 1987: 275)

Neither a person's birth nor his birthplace is a determiner of his ability or virtue. It is also because the civilizational center is established through human virtue and not geographically predetermined that, unlike the Western conception, Confucius's virtue does not degenerate with increasing distance from the geographic center; virtuous conduct alone is sufficient to establish new civilizational centers, and geography does not determine the possibility of virtue. Further, the Confucian assumption that the acculturation environments thought to be formative for human becoming are shaped through human agency precludes any understanding of differences among peoples as ontological. As a result, there is no tendency to parse cultural differences as racial differences. Differences between peoples are understood to arise, not from racial differences, but from variations in cultures and customs. Under this view, humans differ in customs, ability, and temperament for socioeconomic and cultural reasons; in other words, difference is emergent, not ontological.

This view of the divergence of different human cultures and customs stands in marked contrast to the Western tradition, which from its Greek foundations up until the days of empire held fast to the idea that difference is essential. That certain "races" of people are ontologically determined and therefore unimprovable is an explanation of human divergence that is unavailable to the Chinese tradition. It bears stressing that the Confucian cultural understanding of personhood[26]—that we are principally defined by our culture and that our environment has the decisive role in determining who we become—is far more empirical than the Western tradition's essentialist model of personhood (Xiang 2021b). For the Confucian, a virtuous person who goes to another place ameliorates it and in doing so predisposes its inhabitants to become better moral agents. As the evolutionary biologist Stephen Jay Gould writes in his impassioned work against biological determinism, *The Mismeasure of Man*, "The adult being is an emergent entity who must be understood at his own level and in his own totality. The truly salient issues are malleability and flexibility" (Gould 1996: 34). The Confucians would agree with Gould and add that what allows the adult human being to emerge are social, economic, and cultural factors over which humans have collective agency and for which they are responsible.

For those with a racial identity (that is essentially superior to others), any admixture of their racial essence is seen as a corruption of that identity. By contrast, since Chinese culture *is* the Chinese identity, and since Chinese culture has continuously existed throughout millennia, the Chinese unproblematically think of themselves as having had a continuous identity. This view of identity as cultural is expressed in *Analects* 9.5:

> The Master was surrounded in Kuang. He said, "Now that King Wen [文] is gone, is not culture [Wen 文] now invested here in me? If heaven intended this culture to perish, it would not have given it to those of us who live after King Wen's death. Since heaven did not intend that this culture should perish, what can the people of Kuang do to me? (Slingerland 2003: 87, my modifications)

The continuing existence of Chinese civilization does not depend on the continued existence of specific peoples. The Zhou, or China, exists if its cultures exist. As long as the culture of the Zhou dynasty is practiced, then whether the emperors of the Zhou—such as King Wen—are still alive or not is inconsequential. The Zhou exists when its culture persists.

Cultural Syncretism

Like the Chinese people, Chinese culture is continuously evolving and amalgamating. Perhaps the most representative example is the emergence of the Chinese Buddhist traditions. Buddhism entered China via the Silk Road and Indian and Central Asian missionaries in the first century of the Common Era. Daoist Xuanxue of the Six Dynasties (222–589 CE) overlapped with and facilitated the introduction and spread of Buddhism in China; in the process Daoism influenced the emergence of distinctively Chinese forms of Buddhism, such as Chan (Zen). Chan Buddhism blended Neo-Daoism and Mahāyāna Buddhism so seamlessly that the later Neo-Confucians took them to be essentially similar religious-metaphysical outlooks.[27]

Another important school of Chinese Buddhism is Tiantai (天台). Founded in the fifth century CE, Tiantai was the earliest attempt at a systematic Sinitic reinterpretation of the Indian Buddhist tradition. In what Brook Ziporyn describes as a feat of "supreme intellectual effort," Tiantai Buddhism forged a vocabulary that brought the Indian and Chinese worlds of thought into "creative dialogue." The product of this dialogue was a synthesis that simultaneously satisfied the very divergent demands of Chinese and Indian Buddhism. In so doing, Tiantai produced "an entirely new vision of Buddhism and indeed of the human condition." Tiantai Buddhism testifies to the creative possibilities of the human spirit enabled through cultural engagement. By working through the worldview of another tradition, Tiantai created a theoretical edifice that used Indian Buddhism's style of argumentation and praxis, but in the "service of ideals and metaphysical conclusions that are rooted deeply in the indigenous philosophical traditions" (Ziporyn 2016: ix–x).[28]

The indigenization of Buddhism is justly famous as a paradigm of innovation through cross-cultural fertilization, but the indigenization of Islam and Muslims is another great success story. Muslims have lived in China since the eighth century and today live everywhere in China, with the densest concentrations in Beijing and Tianjing (Lipman 1997: xvii, 3). Muslims in China were never subject to specific legal discrimination (30). They retained their native dress, language, lifestyle, and customs, and by the Southern Song (1127–1279) they were allowed to take official positions and to marry an imperial princess if their family had lived in China for three generations and a household member possessed an official title (29). The Song history *Zizhi tongjian* (*Comprehensive Mirror for Aid in Government*) tells of foreigners, possibly Muslims, who had lived in Chang'an for forty years, married the local women, and did not wish to return to their native countries (29). The Muslim Semu and Ortaq of the Yuan dynasty remained in China and became well-known literati in the Chinese style.[29] Muslim poets, painters, and civil officials who attained a high level of Confucian learning are found in the cultural history from the mid to late Yuan dynasty (34). By the late Ming, Muslim families were writing Confucian-style clan genealogies (46). During the Yuan dynasty, the *Islamic Encyclopedia of Medicine* (回回药方) was translated into Chinese and came to have a profound influence on traditional Chinese medicine (Zheng 2012: 47).[28]

Since its arrival in China in the Tang dynasty, Islam and its traditions have long been inextricably woven into the fabric of the Chinese tradition. In a fascinating study, *The Dao of Muhammad: A Cultural History of Muslims in Late Imperial China*, Zvi Ben-Dor Benite shows how Chinese Muslims claimed an identity as simultaneously Muslim and Confucian-Chinese by defining their tradition as "our Dao" (吾道) (Benite 2005: 165) and Mohammad as a sage rather than a prophet (231–32). "The scholars of the *Han Kitab* [汉克塔布, a collection of Chinese Islamic texts written by Chinese Muslims that synthesized Islam and Confucianism] hinged their unique self-understanding on a vision in which they fully inhabited two worlds rather than being exiles from one and anomalous visitors in the other" (233). The thought was that the "Dao" of Islam was one Dao among many. This meant that

> we—we cultured Chinese—we are all Confucians. Some Confucians have a Dao that is Confucianism; some have in addition a Dao that is called Islam. Either way, we all are as good Confucians allowed to follow and respect our Dao. Thus we Confucians who are Muslims also follow the Dao that is Islam, and you Confucians who are only Confucians follow the Dao that is Confucianism. (Benite 2005: 194)

Understanding Islam as an intellectual-ethical tradition that contributed to the Dao made it compatible with the larger Confucian-Chinese way (181–85) and an essential part of the larger tradition (167).[30]

The historian Guotong Li gives a vivid example of the lives of Muslims in imperial China in an account of the reconstruction of the Great Mosque of Quanzhou. Built by the Persian missionary Ibn Muhammed al-Quds of Shiraz in 1310, the Great Mosque was rebuilt in 1609 under the supervision of a Confucian scholar named Li Guangjin (李光缙, 1549–1623). According to Guotong

Li, Li Guangjin was part of a local literati fellowship that included two other well-known Confucian scholars—Li Zhi (李贽, 1527–1602) and He Qiaoyuan (何乔远, 1557–1633). Of these scholars, the most famous is Li Zhi, a Neo-Confucian philosopher and the scion of a Muslim merchant family who traded in the Persian Gulf (Li 2016: 390). Li Zhi was one of the most central figures in the late Ming "cult of feelings" (Lee 2012: 1–2) and he had met in 1599 with the Jesuit missionary Matteo Ricci. Following the conventional course of most Chinese Muslim elite families, Li Zhi studied the Confucian teachings in order to pass the civil examinations (Li 2016: 380). After holding government posts for a time, he retired from service and in 1588 became a Buddhist monk. He subsequently wrote many critiques of Neo-Confucianism (380–381) but also expounded on his view that Confucianism, Daoism, and Buddhism all inherited the way and had a common origin (381). In his will, Li Zhi arranged to have a Muslim burial when he died (382).

He Qiaoyuan was a local historian who wrote what would become a well-known local history entitled *Minshu* (*Book of Fujian*), in which is included a biography of Li Zhi. In He Qiaoyuan's account, Li Zhi's lectures greatly influenced peoples across the Yangzi region, inspiring donors to contribute large sums of money to Buddhist temples (382). He Qiaoyuan placed Li Zhi's biography in the category of *Xude* (蓄德, "moral cultivation"), indicating that Li Zhi was considered a scholar of morals (382). He Qiaoyuan's *Minshu* also contains a careful tracing of the history of Chinese Islam (383). Li Guangjin was himself a contemporary of He Qiaoyuan and participated in the rebuilding of the Great Mosque in 1609. In his own writings, he notes that "this [rebuilding] matters for the survival of Islamic religion, as well as for Our Culture's [Confucian culture's] flourishing" (quoted in Li 2016: 386). As Guotong Li explains, "He was obviously trying to show that an Islamic mosque was part of the local heritage, in harmony with 'Our Culture'" (386).

By the time of the Ming dynasty, Chinese Islam had evolved its own indigenous identity, and by the seventeenth century specifically Chinese formulations of Islamic teachings had begun to emerge. We see this Islam with Chinese characteristics in Wang Daiyu (王岱與, 1584–1670), who published the first book of Islamic-Confucian synthesis, *The Real Commentary on the True Teachings* (政教真诠, 1642), Wu Zixian (伍子先, ca. 1598–1678), and Ma Zhu (马注, 1640–1711). The figure who gave the most mature expression to this Islamic-Confucian synthesis was Liu Zhi (刘智, ca. 1670–1724). Liu's *Nature and Principle in Islam* (天方性理) detailed the basic principles of Islamic philosophy through Neo-Confucian terminology and categories. Liu Yihong, a scholar of Islamic philosophy, argues that the precondition for the emergence of Chinese Islamic philosophy—that is, Chinese formulations of Islamic thought—was Neo-Confucianism, which is itself Confucianism synthesized with foreign heterogeneous cultures and other local religions and thoughts (Liu 2005). It was the metaphysical concepts found in Neo-Confucianism that enabled Chinese philosophy to engage with Islamic thought. Chinese-Islamic philosophy, which, in the absence of Neo-Confucianism, would not have been possible (43), is built on layers and layers of historic cultural synthesis.

Chinese culture is not static but dynamic, and like the Chinese people, it is an amalgamation. An example can be seen in the historical assimilation of Jews into China. As Tongdong Bai notes, Chinese history offers a rare example of the peaceful assimilation of Jews (Bai 2020: 205). From the ninth century on, there was an indigenous Jewish community in the city of Kaifeng, China. The Israeli historian Menashe Har-El notes that "the Tang dynasty in China was receptive to foreign religions and invited the Jews to settle in the country. [...] During this period, the Chinese used bilingual coins with Chinese inscriptions on one side and Semitic letters on the other" (quoted in Xu 2003: 8–9). Gradually adopting Chinese customs, the Kaifeng Jews developed a distinctive culture. The "greatest problem" for the Jews who came to China, writes Xin Xu, "was not separation from other Jews so much as the openness and tolerance of Chinese society." With frequent intermarriage and the full acceptance of Jews as merchants, government officials, and neighbors, over time they became completely assimilated, and because of how fully they were assimilated, Jews in China were losing the memory of their ancestry and becoming physically indistinguishable from the Chinese. In fact, they became so completely assimilated that few of their descendants carry any memory of Jewish ancestry and physically look much like other Chinese (Xu 2003: book blurb; see also Shapiro 1984 and Pollak 1998). The problem for the Chinese Jews was not any need to hide their difference to gain acceptance, but the difficulty of preserving their difference.

That the Chinese tradition had a cultural conception of Chinese identity explains its embrace of different traditions and peoples and its longevity. The Chinese anti-representationalist, humanistic conception of culture as a product of human activity (more on this in chapter 4) predisposes it toward accepting that culture changes and that there is more than one culture. As a consequence, a Chinese person is simply one who embraces Chinese culture, which is constantly evolving and amalgamating with foreign traditions. It is this conception of cultural identity that explains why, in spite of having consistently intermixed with foreigners throughout its history and in many periods of that history not having been continuously ruled by Han peoples, the Chinese people nevertheless think of their civilization as continuous.

Another example of the amalgamation behind Chinese identity is the historical encounter between northerners and their southern neighbors and the cultural exchanges that took place in what is contemporary Yunnan. Historic migration between the north and the south led to encounters here between very different cultures, and these encounters contributed to the hybridization of the Chinese identity as the different cultures responded to and interacted with each other, creating new forms and orders.

In Yunnan, order was not externally imposed but grew out of the interaction of particulars. As early as the Western Han, the conflict with the Nanzhao drew many Han military forces south. By the sixteenth century, scholars have estimated, Yunnan was home to over two million Han, or around one-third of the total population (Yang 2008: 5, 25). The southern cultures contrasted sharply with Han Chinese culture in crucial respects. As a historian of Yunnan puts it, "These social customs, especially the status of women, reveal the fact that Yunnan in general was more Southeast Asian than Chinese" (5, 10). Over time, however, these differences were mutually accommodated so harmoniously that, "by the late Ming period, a hybrid, plural cultural system had evolved, inaugurating the use of Yunnannese (*yunnanren*)."[31]

Yunnan's experience exemplifies the kind of stimulus and response that have been ubiquitous throughout Chinese history and in all regions of China and have created the Chinese identity. Chinese identity is merely a snapshot at one particular point in history of a continuously evolving, emergent, functional order.

Tang Cosmopolitanism

There is perhaps no better example of China as a product of historical synthesis than the Tang dynasty. Today the Chinese are proud of the Tang's might, its cultural confidence and embrace of all under heaven. "The Great Tang," as it is known and cherished in the Chinese imagination today, is celebrated precisely for its openness to foreign cultures, and this embrace of foreign peoples extended to the ruling class itself.

That the imperial clan that ruled during the Tang dynasty was genealogically connected to the Tuoba (拓拔) and other non-Chinese families was an open secret (Chen 2012: 5; Mote 2003: 5). The founder of the Tang dynasty,

Emperor Gaozu's (566–635) mother, was a Xianbei, and Gaozu himself married a Xianbei (Togan 2011: 177). Sanping Chen suggests that "the first half of the Tang might be more aptly called a Särbo-Chinese (or Xianbei-Chinese) regime" (Chen 2012: 8). As recorded in "Genealogies of the Counselors-in-Chief" (宰相世系表) of the *New Book of Tang*, there were 369 grand chancellors (宰相), who were the highest-ranked officials (Ouyang and Song 1975: 2179–3466). Of these, Zhou Weizhou (周伟洲) has calculated that 33 were from bordering tribes, such as the Xiongnu and Xianbei, and that they belonged to 11 different tribes (*zu*, 族). Thus, 9 percent of the officials in the highest echelons of power were non-Chinese "foreigners" (Zhou 1991: 119). Another source puts the number of "traceably nomadic" grand chancellors at 43 (Holcombe 2002: 71). Sources suggest that at least 2,536 foreigners (*fan*, 蕃) served as officers in the Tang army (72). One of these foreign peoples who lived in the Tang that we know of was an immigrant monk from northern India named Amoghavajra (不空三藏) (705–774). Amoghavajra served as preceptor of state for three Tang dynasty emperors, held ministerial rank, and was gifted with lavish honors (71). Another example of an elevated descendant of the Xiongnu is the great Tang poet Liu Yuxi (刘禹锡) (Zhou 1991: 118). As Jonathan Skaff writes, the Tang was a pluralistic realm "containing tens of millions of people who had different ethnicities, regional traditions, status rankings, and religions" (Skaff 2012: 10).

In 631 CE, after the Eastern Turks surrendered to the Tang, nearly ten thousand households, amounting to around one hundred thousand people, were moved to Chang'an (Hansen 2012: 149; Jeong 2016: 945; Pan 1997: 183). The migrants intermarried with the Han population and adopted surnames in the Chinese style.[32] Unsurprisingly, it even became fashionable to adopt a Hu (Central Asian) lifestyle (Zheng 2012: 37).[33] Before the monk Xuanzang set off for India, he visited Chang'an's Western market, home to many Sogdians, for advice on his journey (Hansen 2012: 141). The product of Xuanzang's journey, *The Great Tang Dynasty Records of the Western Regions* (大唐西域记), is today a substantial reference for medieval India.[34] As is well known, the Sogdian An Lushan (703–757 CE) rose to the highest ranks of the Tang military. These foreign guests left marks that remain to this day. The epitaph for a general of Sogdian descent reads: "It is always said that, in antiquity, among gentlemen there was no division between Chinese and barbarian. When we examine later eras, heroes were no different in China or abroad" (quoted in Holcombe 2002: 72). The tombs of assimilated Sogdians excavated in Xi'an show the extent of the cross-fertilization of cultures: "These tombs show how immigrants to China, mostly Sogdian, adjusted to—and modified—Chinese cultural practices" (Hansen 2012: 143–46, 143; see also Holcombe 2002: 72).

During the three centuries of the Tang, China was visited by natives from almost every nation in Asia (Schafer 1963: 10). The famous poet Bai Juyi, who was himself of Kucha descent (Jeong 2016: 946), describes one such visit in the poem "Biao Orchestra" (骠国乐), including the impressive performance of a musical troupe in Chang'an led by Prince Shwenadaw (舒难陀) from the Pyu Kingdom in 801. Another notable visitor was Peroz III (زوریپ, "the Victor," 卑路斯, 636–677), the son of the last Sasanian king of Persia (Yazdegerd III). After the death of his father, Peroz found refuge in Tang China. According to the *Book of Former Tang*, Peroz asked for military help from Tang China against the Arabs in 661 (龙朔元年). The Tang court replied by creating the Persian military post (波斯都督府) in what is now Zaranj, Afghanistan, with Peroz as commander-in-chief. Between 670 and 674 (咸亨中), Peroz arrived at the Tang court and was given the title of "Martial General of the Right [Flank] Guards" (右武卫将军). Later Peroz established a Persian temple in Liquan (Liu 1975: 5312–13; Jeong 2016: 655).

One indication of the depth of the royal ties between the Tang and the fallen Sasanian ruling house is that two statues of Sasanian Persian royals stand at the mausoleum of Emperor Gaozong and Empress Wu (Godwin 2018: 78). Less illustrious visitors than the descendant of the last Sasanian king of Persia were the many Arab traders who lived in Guangzhou, Yangzhou and Hangzhou (Chen 2020: 113), the Zoroastrians from Persia, the Manicheans, and the Jews who lived in Chang'an. At least five and maybe six Zoroastrian temples stood in the city (Hansen 2012: 149). When a delegation of Nestorians arrived at the city gate after traversing the Silk Road, they were formally greeted and respectfully given an audience with the emperor (Bays 2012: 9). The emperor Taizong then ordered that the Christian scriptures, which the Nestorians had brought, be translated. Three years later, in 638, after familiarizing himself with the Christian doctrine, Taizong issued an edict of approbation for Christianity, which is recorded on the Nestorian stele in Xi'an (known as Chang'an in the Tang dynasty):

In the kingdom of Da Qin[35] there was a man of the highest virtue called Alopen. Guiding himself by the azure clouds, he carried with him the True Scriptures. Watching the laws of the winds, he made his way through difficulties and perils. In the ninth year of the period of Zhengguan (635 CE), he arrived at Chang'an. The emperor sent his minister, duke Fang Xuanling

[房玄龄], bearing the staff of office, to the western suburb, there to receive the visitor, and conduct him to the palace. The Scriptures were translated in the Library. (His Majesty) questioned him about his system in his own forbidden apartments, became deeply convinced of its correctness and truth, and gave special orders for its propagation. In the twelfth Zhengguan year (638 CE), in autumn, in the seventh month, the following proclamation was issued: "Systems have not always the same name; sages have not always the same personality. Every region has its appropriate doctrines, which by their imperceptible influence benefit the inhabitants. The greatly virtuous Alopen of the kingdom of Da Qin, bringing his scriptures and images from afar, has come and presented them at our High Capital. Having carefully examined the scope of his doctrines, we find them to be mysterious, admirable, and requiring nothing special to be done; having looked at the principal and most honoured points in them, they are intended for the establishment of what is most important. Their language is free from troublesome verbosity; their principles remain when the immediate occasion for their delivery is forgotten; (the system) is helpful to (all) creatures, and profitable for men:—let it have free course through the empire. (Legge 1888: 9–11, my modifications)

From several early Nestorian documents found in a cache of manuscripts that had been sealed since 1005 and were discovered at Dunhuang, "we can see the remarkable combination of Christian ideas and concepts mixed with Daoist and Buddhist terms that constituted Nestorianism in China" (Bays 2012: 10).

Perhaps nothing captures more beautifully the cosmopolitanism of the Tang than the biography of one of the most celebrated poets of the High Tang, Li Bai, who, along with Du Fu, is commonly considered one of the two greatest poets in Chinese history. Li Bai is honored as the "poetry god" whereas Du Fu is honored as the "poetry sage." As Li Bai himself recounted toward the end of his life, he was born in a part of the western regions that scholars today identify as present-day Tokmok in northeastern Krygyzstan (Snodgrass 2010: 184). In Li Bai's own account, and with characteristic flamboyance, he asserts that his ancestors had originally been banished there for "some groundless accusation" (quoted in Jin 2019: 55–56). Some of Li Bai's letters, as he claims in his poetry, are written in Tocharian script, a now-extinct language of the Indo-European peoples of Xinjiang. According to Ha Jin, "it is entirely reasonable to assume that he was originally from Central Asia" and may even have been "half Chinese" (Jin 2019: 56). According to Su-il Jeong, Li Bai was a descendant of

Central Asian *huke* (胡客, "foreign guest") (Jeong 2016: 946). Li Bai, arguably China's most celebrated poet, whose life and poetry so perfectly epitomized the unrestrained passion for life that symbolized the height of the Tang, was a man from Central Asia.

Conclusion

This chapter has attempted to correct many long-standing orientalizing misconceptions about the Chinese tradition by showing that:

- China was never a static entity.
- The Chinese people are not a race but an amalgamation over millennia of what were once distinct groups of people.
- Chinese identity is *not racial.*
- Chinese expansion cannot be equated with Western colonialism, as discussed in more detail in chapters 5 and 6.
- The Chinese people were not created in a one-way process where other peoples were merely covered over and made identical with "Chinese-ness," but instead through an interactive process of mutual influence. China is the end result of a cosmopolitan melting together of innumerable elements.
- From its inception and throughout its history, China has been surrounded by foreigners whose practices and physical appearances were markedly different from those of the Han peoples. The presence of foreigners decisively shaped the course of Chinese history and China as a geopolitical entity.
- Throughout all periods of Chinese history, great numbers of foreigners were included in Chinese society and some achieved elevated status within it.

In the following chapter, we explore in more detail the absence in China of the Western idea of the "barbarian"—a key reason why China was able to be created out of difference and why it never espoused an aggressive ideology to justify trying to overwhelm the earth.

2

The Barbarian in the Western Imagination and History

FOUNDATIONAL TO THE Greco-Christian tradition is a dualistic ontology, a bifurcation of reality manifested as the dualism between good and evil, spirit and flesh, mind and body, reason and the passions, human (rationality) and animal (nature), form and matter, freedom and determinism. The same dualisms characterize Western racism. From Aristotle's statements on non-Greeks to medieval Christian representations of the Jew, European portrayals of the Amerindians, Enlightenment and post-Enlightenment philosophers' opinions on non-Europeans, and media portrayals of the non-West today, a consistent motif is the non-West's representation as the negative side of a dualism.

This chapter provides a historical survey of the European tradition, since its Greek inception, of defining civilization and humanity negatively through a Manichean, imagined barbarian. The barbarian was the antipode of the Greeks' espoused cultural values, and when inherited by the Christian consciousness, this figure became the medieval "wild man." During the age of colonialism, the barbarian of the European subconscious was projected onto the newly encountered peoples of the "New World." That is, the barbarian of the Western imagination came to be identified with the non-European racial other. As will be seen here, the barbarian-cum-racial-other paradoxically embodies two key characteristics. On the one hand, he is mere matter without form, and so is driven by passion and an animalic nature. On the other hand, he has the form of evil, which compels him by a perverse telos to overthrow form and order. If this sounds contradictory—that a formless, orderless thing is driven by a telos (which defines form) to subvert form (and so order)—we need to remember that "racism essentially is a form of rationalization and systematization of the irrational" (Eliav-Feldon, Isaac, and Ziegler 2009: 4).

For the Western tradition under survey, "barbarian" and "barbarism" are not merely pejorative terms intended to castigate perceived uncouthness. Instead, they signify the Manichean other who, antithetical to civilization, is eternally savage and cannot be assimilated through acculturation. "Barbarian" derives from the Greek *barbaros*, "someone who cannot speak Greek." Owing to the semantic connection between reason (*logos*) and speech (also *logos*), those who could not speak Greek were seen as devoid of reason. For Aristotle, the inability of animals to form civic society is due to their incapacity for the rational activity of speech (*Pol.* 1.2, 1253a8–18; Aristotle 2007: 1988; Sorabji 1993: 15). In Greek thought, the barbarian is like the animal in that he also has no capacity for reason, language, and correct political organization. Representative depictions of the non-Greek (and later non-European) as barbarians appear in Aristotle's writings:

> A bestial character is rare among human beings; it is found most frequently among barbarians, and some cases also occur (among Greeks) as a result of disease or arrested development. We sometimes also use "bestial" as a term of opprobrium for a surpassing degree of human vice. (Aristotle, *Eth. Nic.* 1145a 29–33; quoted in Isaac 2004: 199)
>
> People irrational by nature and living solely by sensation, like certain remote tribes of barbarians, belong to the bestial class, others who lose their reason because of a disease or insanity, belong to the diseased. (Aristotle *Eth. Nic.* 1149a 9–12; quoted in Isaac 2004: 199)

Aristotle points to two causes of a bestial nature: disease of some kind, or innate nature. In these passages we can also discern another pervasive Greek idea: that the Greeks were the chosen ones born within the *oikumene*—that is, the known, inhabited, or habitable world—and that it is only within the *oikumene* that a person can be truly human (Pagden 1982: 16). Because non-Greek speakers lived, by definition, outside of the *oikumene*, they were often understood to be less than human.[1] According to Aristotle, therefore, the birds that watch over the temple on the island of Diomedia are able to distinguish between Greek and barbarians: "If Greeks land at the place, [they] keep quiet; but if any of the barbarians who live around them approach, they fly up, and soaring in the air swoop down upon their heads, and, wounding them with their beaks, kill them" (Aristotle *De mir. aus.* 836a 10–15; Aristotle 2007: 1281).

From the end of the twelfth century to the beginning of the sixteenth century, the term "barbarous" had two meanings: (1) non-Christian, and (2) savage and uncivil. In both senses, it described imperfect humans, that is, non-Europeans and non-Christians (Pagden 1982: 24). Europeans subscribed to this idea of the barbarous before they ever encountered radically different peoples. "Long before they ever set foot in any significant way on other continents or met other peoples," writes the historian Paul Gordon Lauren, "Europeans possessed an extensive tradition of certain negative images, attitudes, and practices towards other races of the world" (Lauren 2018: 8–9). Likewise, the authors of the manifesto *Barbaric Others: A Manifesto on Western Racism* note that "it was the ideas and reflexes of the old world that crossed the Atlantic with Columbus and settled the fate of the enterprise of the Indies" (Sardar, Nandy, and Davies 1993: 1). Preexisting ideas and characteristics associated with the barbarian shaped Europeans' expectations and experiences when they encountered non-Europeans. We assess this extensive tradition of negative imagery of the other and the barbarian in what follows.

The History of the Civilization-Barbarism Dualism

As early as the writings of Homer and of others dating back to at least the eighth century BCE—including Ctesias (born fifth century BCE) and Megasthenes (born ca. 350 BCE–died ca. 290 BCE), Greeks wrote of "monstrous races" from distant lands (Stannard 1992: 167). In Book I of the *Iliad*, Western civilization's first great work of literature, Nestor, king of Pylos, tells the story of the immortal Greek warrior-heroes who defeated the half-human, half-horse centaurs, the Centauromachy. The centaurs were long represented in Greek mythology as mountain-dwelling, lawless, and hypersexualized, driven by bestial passions and irrational urges to violate the laws of civilization. According to one myth, the ancestor of the centaurs was born deformed and mated with the wild mares of Thessaly (Williams 2012: 19–20). The defeat of the centaurs by the earliest Greek heroes thus represents the victory of law and civilization against the lawless, irrational, animalistic savages and serves as the origin myth for the founding of civilization.

From this myth we can see that the Greeks defined civilization negatively. Civilization is established through the destruction of what is perceived as antithetical to it. Civilization as lawful and reason-guided is thus built upon the destruction of its antithesis, the chaos and lawlessness of the natural world. For the Greeks and, as we will see, for later Western civilization, civilization exists in a negative, dialectical relationship with a dualistically perceived other. In fact, under this view, it could be said that civilization derives from the destruction of barbarism—that is, barbarism is the precondition for civilization, since civilization comes into existence through the vanquishing of barbarism. The bivalent values of good (civilization) and bad (barbarism) are preexisting ontological properties of the world, such that the (Greek) agent promotes the good (civilization) to the extent that he destroys the bad (barbarism). As such, the barbarian *necessarily* needs either to exist or to be invented and then destroyed if civilization is to exist. The only role that human agency can play in achieving order and civilization is thus the negative one of removing the source of the bad that is the barbaric other. It is in this sense that Robert Williams writes: "Without the idea of the savage[2] to understand what it [Western civilization] is, what it was, and what it could be, Western civilization, as we know it, would never have been able to invent itself" (Williams 2012: 1). Here we explore in more detail Williams's claim that Western civilization needed to invent the barbarian in order to construct its own identity.

After the Greek victory against the Persian empire in the Persian Wars (fifth century BCE), relief sculptures of the legendary victory against the Centauromachy were chiseled onto the south metopes of the Parthenon in Athens. This relief has been interpreted by scholars as symbolizing the Greek triumph over the Persians (Castriota 1992: 152). "The battles of the wars against Persia," writes the classicist Edith Hall,

> were assimilated to the mythical archetypes of the Amazonomachy and Centauromachy, and began to appear alongside them in the self-confident art of fifth-century Athens as symbols of the victory of democracy, reason, and Greek culture over tyranny, irrationality, and barbarism. (Hall 1989: 102)

Thus, like the mythical Greek heroes' victory against the Centauromachy who were expelled from Thessaly, the Greek victory expelled Persians from Europe (the civilized lands). During this classical age of Greece in the fifth and fourth centuries BCE, tropes previously associated with mythical subhuman monsters were now used to depict existing non-Greek peoples (Williams 2012: 49).

We can see the non-Greek being used to represent the antithesis of civilization in the works of Herodotus, the first historian of the Western tradition. As the historian J. B. Bury notes:

> [Herodotus's] theme, the struggle of Greece with the Orient—possessed for him a deeper meaning than the political result of the Persian war. It was the contact and collision of two different types of civilisation; of peoples of

two different characters and different political institutions. In the last division of his work, where the final struggle of Persia and Greece is narrated, this contrast between the slavery of the barbarian and the liberty of the Greek, between oriental autocracy and Hellenic constitutionalism, is ever present and is forcibly brought out. But the contrast of Hellenic with Oriental culture pervades the whole work; it informs the unity of the external theme with the deeper unity of an inner meaning. It is the keynote of the history of Herodotus. (Bury 1909: 44)

The hermeneutic paradigm framing Herodotus's account of the Persian Wars is the dualism between civilization and barbarism. Herodotus did not think that the Persians were the only people antithetical to Greece and thus humanity. Herodotus writes of the "despotic" Egyptians: "Not only is the climate different from that of the rest of the world, and the rivers unlike any other rivers, but the people also, in most of their manners and customs, exactly reverse the common practice of mankind" (quoted in Isaac 2004: 58). For Herodotus, the Egyptians are the antithesis of what is human in all regards. His comments on the Egyptians show this rigid dichotomy between civilization and barbarism being taken to an extreme and all other dichotomies being arbitrarily mapped onto it. Williams observes that the exotic stories about faraway peoples in Herodotus's *Histories* pivot around the idea of the savage "as the most extreme form of the difference from the Greeks." Further, in using stereotypical markers of the savage to describe faraway actual peoples, Herodotus "confirmed the ancient mythic belief that the most extreme forms of human difference from the norms and values of civilization are to be found on the remote edges of the world" (Williams 2012: 63). These descriptions of existing ethnic groups through tropes previously associated with the mythic monsters of Greek lore now identify them with those monsters. Fantastical imaginings have been made geographical facts.

Aristotle's *Nicomachean Ethics* and *Politics* include fantastic stories about foreign peoples practicing cannibalism.[3] As Benjamin Isaac notes, such stories were not original with Aristotle; he was merely generalizing from established public opinion (Isaac 2004: 207).[4] Such was the Greek obsession with the barbarian other that nearly half of the three hundred tragedies known to classicists portray foreign peoples, were set in non-Greek land, or both, and almost all the extant plays refer to barbarian customs or inferiority. In *Inventing the Barbarian*, Edith Hall chronicles the Greek poets' creation of a "discourse of barbarism" composed of "a complex system of signifiers denoting the ethnically, psychologically, and politically 'other'" (Hall 1989: 2). Likewise, Edward Said considers Aeschylus's play *Persians* to be one of the first instance of "orientalism" (Said 2003: 56).

The Romans inherited the idea that the world is ontologically divided into light and dark, into civilization and barbarism. In Cicero's *Somnium Scipionis*, the Roman general Scipio Aemilianus is visited by the shade of his dead grandfather, the general Scipio Africanus. The elder Scipio tells the younger Scipio:

> You see that the earth is inhabited in only a few portions, and those very small, while vast deserts lie between them. [...] You see that the inhabitants are so widely separated that there can be no communication whatever among the different areas; and that some of the inhabitants live in parts of the earth that are oblique, transverse and sometimes directly opposite your own, from such you can expect nothing surely that is glory. (quoted in Pagden 2015: 154)

In the first century CE, Pliny the Elder, in his *Natural History*, described in detail grotesque races from faraway lands. These creatures were understood not as figments of the imagination but as real groups of people.[5]

Once these monstrous races were integrated into Christian thinking, they were associated with the lineage of Cain, whose progeny were creatures whose grotesqueness and suffering were a consequence of his sin (Stannard 1992: 167). For example, Augustine spends chapter 8 in *City of God* debating whether the descendants of Adam or those of the sons of Noah produced the monstrous races of men. By the Middle Ages, these monstrous races were associated with a single, generic type who combined human and animal characteristics: the wild man (*sylvestres homines*) (Bernheimer 1952: 1). The wild man as a passionate infidel was both animalic and antithetical to the light of Christian salvation. As a merely passionate bodily being, he was understood as "little more than ambulatory genitalia," that is, as sexuality incarnate (White 1972: 24). Like the barbarian of the Greek imagination, the wild man was all body and lust without reason and discipline. In the Bible's Old Testament, the wild man was associated with the children of Babel and Sodom and Gomorrah and represented "a state of degeneracy below that of 'nature' itself, a peculiarly horrible state in which the possibility of redemption is all but completely precluded" (13). Like Aristotle's natural slave, the wild man cannot change his essence and so salvation is beyond him. That the wild man represented the forces of the Antichrist can be seen in Saint Jerome's Latin translation of the Bible; there he explains the prophet Isaiah's description of demons through the concept of "wild men" (Bernheimer

1952: 96–97; Williams 2012: 144). During the medieval Christian era, the biblical wild man, because he represented the dark side of the West's imagined dualism, embodied the irreconcilable barbarian (Williams 2012: 159).

In the following section, we will see the development of the barbarian as a hermeneutic concept that shaped European perceptions of non-Europeans during their historical encounters.

The Civilization-Barbarian Dualism in History

Throughout his oeuvre, James Baldwin diagnosed the psychology behind the dualistic thinking underlying Western racism that we have described. Baldwin repeatedly noted that white American racism toward blacks is rooted in a "schizophrenia in the mind" (Baldwin 1998: 313) that is foundational to Western civilization. That is, white racism ultimately stems from white civilization's inability to accept its fundamentally embodied and therefore fallible human condition.[6] Their refusal to accept the totality of their human nature has led white peoples to a fragmentation of the self into a dualism of pure (white) reason and impure (black) corporeality that makes black peoples the scapegoat onto which white peoples project the unwanted side of the dualistic divide.[7] Blacks bear the burden of the white desire to transcend their own corporeality, and because they symbolize this corporeality, blacks are despised for it. "If Americans were not so terrified of their private selves," Baldwin observes, "they would never have needed to invent and could never have become so dependent on what they still call 'the Negro problem,'" which white peoples invented to "safeguard their purity" (Baldwin 1998: 386).

In what follows, I cover a broad range of sources, from the Spanish colonization of the Americas to the later European settlement in North America and the European colonization of Africa. Although casting a lens this wide might seem to threaten chaos, my purpose is to show the uniformity in European views of natives across actors, places, and historical time periods. Doing so reveals a pervasive mode of thought and testifies to Baldwin's insight that at the heart of Western racism is a dualism founded on European civilization's fear of the human condition.

To Western civilization and European colonists, beset by this "schizophrenia in the mind," the non-European native stood for the wilderness itself: the native was, in the words of the American historian Richard Drinnon, the "dark others" whom the "white settlers were not and must not under any circumstances become" (Drinnon 1997: xxvii–xxviii). In his history of the American western frontier, *Facing West: The Metaphysics of Indian-Hating and Empire-Building*, Drinnon notes that "consistently regard[ing] Indians as persons with a psychology of their own would have upended" everything the settlers of the time knew about the world. "It would have meant recognizing that the 'state of nature' really had full-fledged people in it and that both it and the cherished 'civil society' had started out as lethal figments of the European imagination" (Drinnon 1997: 139). In accord with this dualistic view that the inhabitants of the American continent lived in a state of nature that could not possibly become a civil society, the conventional scholarship of the time—whose legacy is still influential today—typically described the "peoples" of the Americas as perverse and barbaric "lurking beasts" who took part in "strange ceremonies" (quoted in Stannard 1992: 12). This paradigm for framing the indigenous peoples followed a well-established precedent. The Spanish, for example, attributed to the indigenous peoples they encountered a primitivism they did not actually exhibit. Europeans unfailingly characterized the native via the negative tropes in a reason-passion dualism, including, among others, irrationality, sodomy, incest, and cannibalism (which European colonists associated with natives just as compulsively as Aristotle attributed it to "barbarians").[8]

Europeans did not question these tropes because their expectations had been structured by sources of the tropes like Aristotle, who defined these negative features and practices as essential characteristics of the barbarian. For instance, we can see how the views passed down from antiquity provided the hermeneutic ground for Spaniards' interpretations of the Amerindians. For Tomás de Mercado (1523/1530–1575), an economist of the school of Salamanca and a Dominican theologian, the Indians were clearly barbarians, as barbarians "are never moved by reason, but only by passion" (quoted in Pagden 1982: 47). For Mercado, the native was a living embodiment of the negative side of the reason-passion dualism. Because this pervasive view required that the native be the antipode to reason, spirit, the good, the mind, and so forth, Europeans of the Middle Ages necessarily saw "the Amerindians and the Africans [...] [as] defective members of their own species" (17). It was this Manichean demonization of the other that justified European crimes against the natives as well as the dispossession of their lands, their murder, and their exploitation.

Such demonization can also be seen in the literature produced by the European settlers in North America. Richard Slotkin, the celebrated scholar of the western frontier in American literature, notes that, in the literature of the Puritan settlers, "the Puritan could stand for reason and religion against utter and passionate infidels" (Slotkin 2000: 58). Since the native represented evil itself, the idea of intermarriage with them was repulsive.[9] For the early Puritan settlers, to engage in "miscegenation" with the barbarian native was to commune with an indescribable horror that would bring ruin to civilization and throw humanity itself into oblivion. These fears of the Amerindians and the wilderness were projections of Puritans' Calvinist views of the postlapsarian and fallen nature of the human soul.[10] For the European settlers on the American continent, the Indian—the "wild man" in the European imagination—"must cease to exist, must either be civilized or sacrificed to civilization—which amounts to the same thing" (Turner 1992: 205).

In *The Wretched of the Earth*, Frantz Fanon also notes the Manichean nature of the relationship between the colonizer and the colonized. The colonial world is a "Manichaean world" divided into the colonist as the light and good, and the colonized as the dark and evil. Being the "negation of values" or the "enemy of values," the native is the "absolute evil" or "the quintessence of evil." "He is the corrosive element, destroying all that comes near him; he is the deforming element, disfiguring all that has to do with beauty or morality; he is the depository of maleficent powers, the unconscious and irretrievable instrument of blind forces" (Fanon 1963: 41). Colonialism is not merely characterized by the material domination of one group of peoples over another. Underlying the material exploitation of the colonized is the Manicheanism of the civilization-barbarism dualism. The ideology underlying colonialism redounds to ancient views about cosmic order.

Robert Williams's point that Europe needed to invent the "barbarian" as part of its own exercise in self-definition can be seen in the othering of Jews within Europe. Absent a racial other of visible physical differences, an other needed to be created out of the European population itself, and so the Jew was designated to serve as the antithetical monster (Hannaford 1996: 127). Writing of the anti-Semite's psychological need for "the Jew," Jean-Paul Sartre makes the point eloquently: "If the Jew did not exist, the anti-Semite would invent him" (Sartre 1995: 13). What the Jew is or does is no of consequence, as "the Jew only serves him as a pretext; elsewhere his counterpart will make use of the Negro or the man of yellow skin" (54). James Baldwin makes the same point in relation to US white-black relations: "What white people have to do is try to find out in their hearts why it was necessary to have a 'nigger' in the first place, because I am not a nigger, I am a man. But if you think I am a nigger, it means you need him" (Baldwin and Darnell 1989: 45).

The culture of racism requires an other for the construction of the personhood of the racist. Without this invented other, the person who operates under a racist culture will have no way to be a self. Within Europe, therefore, the monstrous Jew allowed for the self-definition of the European in the same way that the savage allowed for the self-definition of the Greeks. As the historian of anti-Semitism Paul Lawrence Rose writes:

> For nineteenth-century Germans, so unsure of their own "Germanness," the Jewish Question was ultimately the German Question. It was, in effect, another way of asking "What is German": and receiving the satisfying answer—"whatever is not Jewish." (Rose 1990: 41)

The invented scapegoat—the racial other, such as the Jew—serves this exercise of self-definition by acting as an inverted mirror image of all that the Western imagination wishes to believe about itself. Defining what one is through rejecting what one is not—that is, this negative exercise in self-definition—relies heavily if not essentially on the ontologically bivalent nature of Western metaphysics.[11] We see this in European representations of the Jew, who is uniformly depicted as carnal, associated with unbridled lechery, marked by an odious stench, and commonly associated with excrement (Wistrich 1999: 4). The Jew represented the mortal natural body itself. Relatedly, therefore, the Jew was understood as a Manichean threat to Christianity itself. The Antichrist was often portrayed as the child of a union between the devil and a Jewish harlot and was perceived as an apocalyptic threat coming to annihilate Christendom (5). As we explained at the beginning of this chapter, and as would apply to all racial others of the European imagination, the Jew is perceived simultaneously as matter without form (and so driven by passion and an animalic nature) and yet as having the form of evil, and thus being driven by a perverse telos to overthrow form and order. This view of the racial other as embodying these two (paradoxical) qualities underlies Europeans' historical belief that they must annihilate or dominate the racial other in order to safeguard order.

Colonialism as Holy War

In addition to believing themselves the embodiment of form and, as such, sanctioned by natural law to secure order in the world by dominating the (formless) native, medieval Christians at the time of the "discovery" of the Americas believed that they were on the threshold of the "second coming." While the signs of Christ's second coming were everywhere, it remained the obligation of Christians to prepare the way. Christians were thus required to spread the gospel throughout the entire world and ensure that all the world's people (once they had been located) accepted Christianity. All non-Europeans so encountered were thus faced with "the total conversion or extermination of all non-Christians" (Stannard 1992: 192). This Manichean, eschatological worldview informed European settlers' idea of colonization, as the historian Jorge Cañizares-Esguerra explains: "In the eyes of the European settlers, colonization was an act of forcefully expelling demons from the land." That is, "Europeans saw colonization [. . .] as an ongoing battle against the devil," and "as an ongoing epic struggle against a stubbornly resistant Satan" (Cañizares-Esguerra 2006: 14, 5).

The same view of colonialism was shared by the Protestant settlers in North America: "By the mid seventeenth century, colonists of European descent were absolutely certain of the overwhelming presence of demons in the New World" (Cañizares-Esguerra 2006: 12). Cañizares-Esguerra sees striking commonalities in the discourse of demonology between the Catholics and the Protestants, rooted in their shared Christian culture, which "from its inception had understood the history of the elect to be an ongoing spiritual and physical battle against the hostile demonic enemies, including heretics, pagans, Jews, and Muslims, part of a cosmic confrontation between good and evil" (5). It is this shared history of Manicheanism—whereby the good is preserved (by Christians) insofar as they succeed in destroying evil—that accounts for the militaristic terms in which countless texts in the Old and New Testament speak of religious life.

Although historical tradition has misleadingly reduced the Crusades to five Christian campaigns against Islam between 1095 and 1229, recent scholarship has shown that the Crusades were not an aberrant variety of religious violence, but in fact were "a peculiar form of religious piety, second only to monasticism," and their "violence was regarded as penitence and charity." "War as pilgrimage" was seen as "a form of sacrifice and atonement aimed at sympathetically re-creating Christ's suffering" (Cañizares-Esguerra 2006: 30). It bears remembering that for almost half a millennium prior to Columbus's departure for the "New World," Christians had been launching destructive holy wars and massive enslavement campaigns against enemies they viewed as carnal demons and described as infidels in their efforts to recapture the Holy Land (Stannard 1992: 190). The colonizers of the Americas were habituated to a culture that not only assumed the existence of evil others but also identified violence against and destruction of perceived evil enemies with religious virtue. Under this view, Satan's agents necessarily exist, as otherwise the world would be perfect; the very imperfection of the world testifies to the reality of Satan and his agents. Once this ideological framework is in place, it becomes very easy to parse those perceived as different as being metaphysically evil.

It is against this background of demonology and Crusade violence as religious piety that we should understand why the Puritan John Mason, the deputy governor of the Connecticut Colony, best known for leading the English settlers in an attack on the Pequot, "gleefully" cited Deuteronomy 20:16–17 ("Of the cities [. . .] which the Lord thy God doth give thee for an inheritance, thou shalt save nothing alive nothing that breatheth [. . .] but thou shalt utterly destroy them") as "justification for the extermination of Indians" (quoted in Stannard 1992: 177). The native was identified with cosmic evil that impeded the good. It is also against this background that we can understand why Christopher Columbus, an ex-slave trader, "thought nothing of enslaving or killing such people simply because they were not like him" (200) and launched a campaign of horrific violence against the inhabitants of Hispaniola. Columbus embodied the medieval man, "a religious fanatic obsessed with the conversion, conquest, or liquidation of all non-Christians" (199), and like all later settlers in the Americas, was a product of "more than a thousand years of Christian culture" (200).

The framing of the West's relationship to the non-West in the Manichean terms of civilization vanquishing barbarians persisted into the twentieth century and can be seen in how the United States understood its role in Vietnam. As Frances FitzGerald put it in her book *Fire in the Lake: The Vietnamese and the Americans in Vietnam*, one of the most famous accounts of the Vietnam War:

> The Americans were once again embarked upon a heroic and (for themselves) almost painless conquest of an inferior race. To the American settlers the defeat of the Indians had seemed not just a nationalist victory, but an achievement made in the name of humanity—the triumph of light over darkness, of good over evil, and of civilization over brutish nature. Quite unconsciously, the American officers and officials used a similar language to describe their war against the NLF [National Liberation Front/Vietcong]. (quoted in Drinnon 1997: 450)

FitzGerald's account supports the argument that the modern American empire and its agents see the relationship between themselves and the non-West in the same Manichean terms used by the medieval colonists.

Seeing the world in terms of an irreconcilable dualism between civilization and barbarism is a deep-seated and persistent habit of thought or hermeneutic horizon that structures the Western understanding of the non-West. In his analysis of the modern political myths that flourished in the aftermath of the 9/11 attacks, Sheldon Wolin explains that the narrative of terrorism falls into this age-old Manicheanism: "Typically, one force [the United States] portrays itself as defending the world, and it depicts the other as seeking to dominate it by a perverse strategy that thrives on chaos" (Wolin 2008: 11). Terrorists are seen as "primitive, satanic, invisible denizens of an 'underworld'" (14). Speaking to the US Military Academy in West Point, New York, in 2002, President George W. Bush used language redolent of the Crusaders as he announced that the United States was "in a conflict between good and evil" and that "we must uncover terror cells in 60 or more countries."[12] The same language of irreconcilable dualism still structures the Western understanding of and engagement with the non-West: all contemporary foreign policy enemies of "the West" are invariably depicted through the Manichean tropes of the barbarian.

This discussion of the barbarian has two important implications for our understanding of the Chinese tradition. First, since the Chinese tradition does not have a dualistic ontology comparable to that of the Western tradition, the Chinese historically have had no comparable desire to scapegoat a racial other and to associate that other with the negative side of a perceived ontological dualism. The rampant universalizing in Western Sinology of the Western idea that (Chinese) self-identity was understood through the foil of the other must be corrected, as this is reading Western dualistic notions of subjectivity into Chinese records. Othering the foreigner as an exercise in self-definition is coherent only under a dualistic ontology. Second, even when Chinese texts do use animal imagery in castigating non-Chinese peoples, this does not have the same meaning in their metaphysical context as it does when Aristotle describes non-Greeks as bearing a bestial disposition. In the Chinese tradition, pejoratively castigating someone as a beast does not imply, as it does in the West, that they belong to the bad side of an ontological, bivalent dualism.[13]

We have to remember that in the Greco-biblical tradition there is an ontological difference between man and beast. "A transcendent God, outside his creation, symbolized the separation between spirit and nature," the historian Keith Thomas tells us. "Man stood to animal as did heaven to earth, soul to body, culture to nature" (Thomas 1983: 35). The assumption of such an ontological difference between man and the rest of nature, including animals, caused an "anxiety, latent or explicit, about any form of behavior which threat-ened to transgress the fragile boundaries between man and the animal creation" (38). As we will see in chapters 3 and 6, since the Chinese tradition assumed that all natural beings, including humans, are part of an immanent continuum without discrete boundaries, there was no metaphysical background that pre-disposed people toward the existential anxieties that have long plagued people in the West.

Conclusion

This chapter has described the Western tradition's invention of the barbarian as an exercise in self-definition. By placing the barbarian on the negative side of the dualism between the barbarian and civilization, between unreason and reason, the (Greek) white race is able to escape its own human, embodied nature. Reserving freedom and reason exclusively to the white race is tanta-mount to saying that only the white race has the capacity to transcend the human condition. Hegel, for example, believed that only the Caucasian race experienced the subjective capacity for freedom (Hegel 1978: 57). This chapter has shown the ubiquity of the idea of the barbarian throughout European history, the projection of the barbarian onto non-Western peoples, and the influence of the idea of the barbarian on Western policies toward the racial other. It is important to recognize the deep-seated nature of the often subcon-scious paradigm of the barbarian in the Western tradition, as the assumption of a Manichean foe (barbarian) as the inverse of the good is a key element in the structure of Western racism. The uniform use of the same tropes to char-acterize all non-Europeans testifies to these attributions being more ideologi-cal than empirical.

This background needs to be borne in mind throughout the coming discus-sions. To understand the Chinese relationship to foreigners we must recognize that the metaphysical and ontological dualisms that have long structured Western interpretations of nature are not present in the Chinese cultural con-text. Instead, we find a processual account of nature and human beings. The absence of such an assumption explains why Chinese history is not marked by the same missionary zeal to destroy a racial other who symbolizes all that is perceived as antithetical to humanity. As we will see in the following chapter, the Chinese tradition lacks the Western concept of the barbarian owing to the nondualistic nature of its metaphysics—what I call its "processual holism."

3

Chinese Processual Holism and Its Attitude toward "Barbarians" and Nonhumans

CHINESE METAPHYSICS' CHARACTERISTIC attitude toward nonhumans such as animals and demons is best described as a "processual holism." Under this view that all things are constantly in process and form a continuum, an ontological distinction between "species" becomes impossible to delimit. Distinctions are instead understood as perspectival and provisional. These metaphysical assumptions explain the Chinese tradition's lack of interest in classifying the distinctions between humans and the nonhuman. And since, in this view, the distinction between humans and nonhumans is tenuous, precarious, and subject to change, a key implication is that the Chinese worldview did not assume an ontological distinction between those considered "Chinese" and those considered "non-Chinese."

Without ontological distinctions (as accurate representations of the divisions of reality) to explain differences, phenomena perceived as anomalous, such as demons, ghosts, and spirits, are attributed to the *perspective* of the human agent. Human agents perceive these phenomena as anomalous only because they are unable to see that all things form a continuum. Ultimately, all things are part of the same immanent cycle of change, and so there is nothing truly anomalous in the world.[1]

This chapter argues that the metaphysics underlying the traditional Chinese worldview makes its attitude toward nonhumans markedly different from the attitude of the Western tradition. In the metaphysics of processual holism, because all things are constantly subject to change, it is very difficult to categorically define things and draw discrete boundaries between them. The implication of there being no discrete boundaries between things is that ultimately all things are manifestations of the same underlying continuum, and so there exists a commensurability between all things. This metaphysical background explains why the Chinese canon is pervaded by representations of animals, demons, and spirits (nonhumans) forming a continuum with the human. The differences between humans and nonhumans are not ontological and fixed, but rather dynamic and subject to change.

The metaphysical assumption that there are no ontological distinctions between things and that all things form a continuum places a (moral) premium on the agent's ability to perceive nature as a holistic continuum. Under this model, humans do not see themselves as separate from or transcending nature. Thus, there is no ontological boundary to a person's moral concern with anything in nature, including those perceived as non-Chinese. Anomalous phenomena such as ghosts, spirits, and demons are attributed in classical China to the human agent's lack of virtue clouding their view of the oneness of all phenomena. The premium placed on all things forming a continuous whole has important implications for the Chinese view of foreigners. In the Chinese tradition, non-Chinese-ness is understood as: (1) a provisional state that is subject to change, and (2) not *essentially* different from Chinese-ness.

Before we begin, the use of the term "holism" needs clarification. The "whole" in Chinese thought is a dynamic, *organic* harmony that obtains between all the particulars of the world, and it is best understood as the dynamic, functional whole of an ecosystem, or that of a living organism.[2] Under this organic view of order and the whole, a "thing" is essentially, existentially, and definitionally an *event* that arises only because of a confluence of relationships with other things (understood as relationships). Previous scholars have variously described Chinese cosmology in this "organismic" way. Joseph Needham, for example, writes that "the key-word in Chinese thought is Order and above all Pattern (and, if I may whisper it for the first time, Organism)" (Needham 1956: 281). This conception of organic holism is implicitly expressed by Eric Nelson when he notes that the "holistic naturalism" found in the metaphysics of the *Yijing* "does not proceed by subsuming a particular under a universal or mediating it within a totality" (Nelson 2011: 389; see also Mote 1971: 20; Tu 1989: 69). Under the metaphysics of this holistic naturalism, "the whole is not totalitarian but a harmony among multiple individual singularities that addresses and allows each to respond according to its own natural propensity" (Nelson 2011: 389). This conception of holism is also evident in

Brook Ziporyn's description of wholeness in Daoist philosophy as a structuralist dependence of the part on its environment (Ziporyn 2012: 139–62).

I would argue that Ziporyn's conception of wholeness applies to Chinese metaphysics in general. In the relationship between the part and the whole under the model of organic holism, each part is *sponte sua* but requires for its completion the other parts of the whole, and the whole is understood as the functional law derived from the spontaneous arising of novelty from the interaction of the parts.[3] This whole functions as a whole, but is not a whole in the sense of a single, finite unity. Under organic holism, a thing is not seen as ontologically discrete, but as dependent for its definition on its relationship to that which it is not, that is, its relationship to the whole.

In "A Chinese Philosopher's Theory of Knowledge," Zhang Dongsun (张东荪) contrasts the "correlative" nature of Chinese logic with the Aristotelian logic of identity. Whereas the logic of identity (substance ontology) allows one to describe something only in relation to itself, Chinese (correlative) logic defines a thing in relation to something beyond itself. Zhang takes the example of "wife," which in Chinese would be defined as "a woman who has a husband" (Chang 1952: 213). On the other hand, a definition of "wife" that corresponds with the logic of identity might be "a married woman." This "correlative" logic that Chang describes is the logic of organic holism. The idea that ultimately all things are connected and interdependent leads to the idea that all things ultimately form a oneness, which is understood in terms of the relationality of all things.

Chinese metaphysics sees every living thing in the world as its own spontaneous source of action (*ziran*). Order is not metaphysically predetermined and eternal. Under a system of metaphysical determinism such as the medieval harmony of the spheres and the Great Chain of Being (see chapter 4), nothing in the world is self-willed.[4] Rather, each thing's source of movement is derived from the given (single), eternal, and static ontological order. Under this view, the world is completely rational and has no room for contingency or novelty but is metaphysically determined, and things are different not because of the confluence of various circumstances, but because they are necessarily so for all eternity. If, as under Chinese metaphysics, there is no one stable ontological order, then it is harder to abide by the Aristotelian concept of each thing in nature having just one telos and being definable *in se est et per se concipitur*. There is no concomitant assumption of a single, eternal, static ontological order. A thing is instead defined momentarily and relationally, both in time and space (in relation to past and present) and with other things. Relationality and holism thus become the defining characteristics of Chinese metaphysics.

This chapter will proceed as follows. The first section introduces the concept of "processual holism" as it is currently used in the philosophy of biology and shows that traditional Chinese metaphysics, in its attitude toward the biological realm, follows the key characteristics of processual holism. Then the discussion moves on to a more detailed description of the traditional Chinese attitude toward nonhuman phenomena in terms of the characteristics of processual holism. The next section shows the continuity between the Greek philosophical attitude toward nonhumans (specifically animals and non-Western "barbarians") and the later Western attitude. For the Greco-Western tradition, the human being and the animal are natural kinds that are ontologically distinct. The two sections that follow describe in more detail the Chinese idea of animals forming a continuum with humans. The chapter then moves on to show the implications, with regard to their attitudes toward foreigners, of the Western view of the human being as ontologically distinct from all other natural kinds and the Chinese view of the human being as forming a continuum with the rest of nature. Whereas under the Greek view, the "barbarian" is so in essence and nothing can be done to change the barbarian's status, such a philosophical viewpoint is impossible under Chinese processual holism, which views the human being as a moral category to be achieved, not a natural kind to which some "races" of people but not others congenitally belong. In the Chinese tradition, it is only through the process of acculturation that any of us become human. The last section discusses the main Chinese traditional philosophic schools and the fact that all of them make the same assumption of the fundamental commensurability of the myriad things. The philosophical views surveyed here also find wide resonance in other aspects of Chinese culture, such as popular literature.

Processual Holism: A Perspective from Biology

The processual holism of the Chinese worldview can be described through a process understanding of biology. In his foreword to *Everything Flows: Towards a Processual Philosophy of Biology*, the scientist Johannes Jäger writes of how deeply engrained "the fallacy of misplaced concreteness"[5] is in Western cognitive habits as well as in the practice and theorization of biology. This fixation with substance "consists in the unwarranted reification of objects, which become fundamental and replace the underlying dynamic reality in our thinking"

(Jäger 2018: xi). Furthermore, the ideology of substance (fixity, endurance, boundary) is unempirical. Modern science suggests that boundaries are often ambiguous, that it can be hard to say where one thing ends and another begins. In addition, all things change, emerge, and decay, and it is impossible to say precisely when they are themselves, or when they cease be themselves (Jäger 2018: xii).

There is a consensus in contemporary process philosophy of biology that biological entities can be divided into kinds in multiple overlapping ways: "The assumption that there is some unique natural kind to which a given organism belongs is false" (Dupré and Nicholson 2018: 23). This "classificatory pluralism"—or "promiscuous realism," a term coined by John Dupré—to characterize the views of contemporary process philosophy of biology is coherent with the Chinese philosophic assumptions about the continuity of nature and the related provisional nature of classification. It also, as Dupré and Nicholson write, "finds metaphysical justification in process ontology." The "processual character of biological entities" provides "a deep explanation of why a multiplicity of ways of classifying such entities is precisely what we should expect to find" (23).

The holism of organic life makes defining the boundaries between biological entities very difficult. Given the interdependence of ecological life, it is hard to definitively and unambiguously define where an individual entity begins and ends. Reality is a continuum of overlapping processes that provide no single, real way of dividing up reality into distinct "kinds" or "classes" of entities. The individuation of nature into distinct individual entities proves to be a slippery matter under a view of nature as continuous, processual, and holistic. A "promiscuous individualism" appears when we attempt to define individual entities, just as a "promiscuous realism" appears when we attempt to pinpoint natural kinds (Dupré and Nicholson 2018: 2–4).

We see all the characteristics of a processual understanding of biology—holism and continuity, the "promiscuous" nature of boundaries between species and kinds, and pluralistic, perspectival classifications of animals—in the Chinese attitude toward animals. According to Roel Sterckx's *The Animal and the Daemon in Early China*, the traditional Chinese attitude toward animals has certain features: (a) there is no insistence on stark categorical or ontological boundaries between humans and nonhumans such as animals and ghosts, demons, and spirits; (b) any demarcations made are constantly subject to change; (c) because change and transformation are pivotal to perceptions of animals and conceptions of the human-animal relationship, the fixity of species is neither self-evident nor desirable; (d) the animal world is navigated and ordered through the Chinese naming of animals; (e) the nonhuman world is seen as an organic part of the natural order in which all beings are mutually interdependent; and (f) as such, animals and humans form a continuum and are subject to the same natural and moral forces.[6] In other words, a oneness underlies all phenomena (Sterckx 2002: 6–7). I deal with all of these points in the following sections and will also highlight the characteristics of the Chinese understanding of nonhumans by contrasting it with the Western attitude to nonhumans.

The Moral Agent and the Perception of Oneness

As we will see in the next chapter, the existence of noncontinuous, ontological hierarchies of the things of the world—the "Great Chain of Being"—has been the most potent and persistent idea in the West about the general order of things (Lovejoy 1964: vii). The Chinese tradition, on the other hand, assumes a radically different metaphysical framework. In lieu of a single ontological order, the Chinese worldview is characterized by the assumption that all particulars are *ziran* (*sponte sua*), that order is emergent, and that all things are interrelated. Given that there is no single ontological order, the Chinese understanding of the world is inalienably perspectival. There is no one position that is isomorphic with the (one) structure of the universe as the structures of the universe are infinite.

The assumption that there is no one single ontological order clarifies Sterckx's point (d). When the Chinese *did* order the animal world, it was a hermeneutic exercise in "tracing the occurrence of certain key terms and comparing the semantic fields of similar graphs in different contexts" (Sterckx 2002: 21). For example, lexicography frames the zoological analysis in the *Erya* and *Shuowen Jiezi*, the two earliest Chinese dictionaries. In the classical Chinese tradition, taxonomizing linguistic descriptions of animals was seen as sufficient for epistemologically understanding and navigating the animal world (30). Through associated words, Chinese taxonomy recognized that categories are human, perspectival, and provisional, not ontological facts, and that the human relationship to animals is one of hermeneutic understanding and so merely conventional names suffice. As I have argued in *A Philosophical Defense of Culture: Perspectives from Confucianism and Cassirer*, the Confucian tradition understands language as an invention of the human agent's creative spontaneity that reads the implicit patterns of the world (as we see in *Xici* 2.2; see

Xiang 2018a). In the Chinese tradition, language is not understood within a representationalist framework in which the mind functions like a mirror reflecting preexisting facts and things. The Chinese view of language is neither an idealism nor realism. Language is seen as nondualistic in that the symbol (language) is a creative product of the human interpretation of the patterns and meanings of the world (which is itself a product of the interaction between humans and the world).[7] The Chinese attitude toward animals reflects the same anti-representationalist assumption of the relationship between language and reality. Linguistic descriptions of animals were understood as sufficient for understanding and controlling animals not because they reflect the essence of animals but because language is the only way of coordinating and navigating reality. The linguistic family resemblance between the names of different animals sufficed in understanding the animal world because of the critical awareness that our access to the world is inalienably mediated by the symbolic medium of language.

This same attitude about the role of human agency in constituting reality can be seen in the Chinese attitude toward anomalous phenomena like ghosts, spirits, and demons (鬼神). As we will see in more detail in the next chapter, Mary Douglas, in her classic *Purity and Danger*, follows William James in remarking that dirt signifies disorder, and that dirt qua disorder needs to be understood in terms of a *subjective* classification of "matter out of place" (Douglas 2001: 165; James 1985: 133). What is deemed to be dirt depends on context. Nothing is ontologically dirt; rather, dirt is the antithesis of order such that our elimination of it is a positive and creative act of bringing coherence to our environment and experience (Douglas 2001: 2). Crucially, our reaction of disgust, loathing, or fear in the presence of what we perceive as dirt is akin to "reactions to ambiguity or anomaly" and is rooted in our desire for order, being, and form and our antipathy toward disorder, nonbeing, and formlessness (5).

In Confucian discourse, we find two paradigms in response to the phenomenon of ghosts or the category of the anomalous. One is what I call a "moral rationalism," and the other what I call a "naturalism." Both paradigms are representative of James's and Douglas's critical attitude in that the anomalous is not understood as *ontologically* anomalous. (For something to be defined as ontologically anomalous, its attribute of anomalousness would not depend on context but would be essential to it. Furthermore, its essence would bear no relation to the essences of things that are defined by order.) In the Confucian context, the perception of anomaly is attributed either to the human being's lack of virtue or to her inability to see the dynamic continuity of the myriad things. The category of the anomalous is ultimately understood as a product of human artifice or convention. Whether the anomalous exists or not is fully within the control of human agency. Anomaly, in Chinese metaphysics, is *not* understood as ontological.

We can see the first paradigm of "moral rationalism" in the thought of Dong Zhongshu. Even as one of the most religiously inclined of Confucians, Dong Zhongshu saw freak events as the outcome of a lack of virtue in the human realm, such that the only way to address these events was for humans to correct their conduct. The Confucian way of making order is not to extirpate the anomaly but to view the human agent's action as responsible for that order. A typical example of this view can be found in the *Luxuriant Gems of the Spring and Autumn*. In the chapter "The Necessity of [Being] Wise and Humane" (必仁且知), we read: "Concerning the source of natural disasters and bizarre events [異], ultimately they are caused by the faults of the ruling family of the state" (Queen and Major 2016: 322). As the chapter "Biography of Dong Zhongshu" of the *Book of Han* explains:

> When the state is about to lose the *dao*, then *tian* will send out natural disasters and catastrophes to criticize and censure it, [when the state] does not examine oneself, [*tian*] again sends out catastrophes and freak events [怪異] in order to warn and frighten it. [If the state] still does not know to change, then harm and vanquishing will befall [it]. From this one can see the humaneness and love *tian* has for the sovereign and its desire for the state's chaos to end. (Ban 1962: 2498, my translation)

The existence of the anomalous (異) is ultimately attributable to the human agent's actions. We find similar humanistic ideas about the interactive nature of human action and naturalistic order in *Luxuriant Gems of the Spring and Autumn*:

> When aberrations in the Five Phases occurs, one ought to remedy it with virtue [*de*, 德] and disseminate it throughout the world. Then calamities will be eradicated. If one does not remedy it with virtue [*de*, 德], before three years have passed, *tian* will send thunder and rain down stones. (Queen and Major 2016: 484, my modifications)

Under the Confucian worldview, matter is not out of place because it was metaphysically determined or ontologically so; instead, matter being out of place is a sign of a failing in the human being's own behavior, and anomalies are symptoms of the human's moral failings. The only way to put matter back in its correct place is to demand moral behavior from the self. To merely extirpate the anomaly would be to miss the point, to mistake symptom for cause. The Chinese worldview has no notion of ontological evil to explain why bad things happen. The only reason bad things happen is due to the lack of virtue in the human realm.

We can see naturalism, the second paradigm, in the thought of Zhu Xi for whom ghosts and spirits do not transcend the naturalistic process of qi-transformation itself. Like everything else, they arise from the workings of yin and yang. Ghosts and spirits are as much a part of nature as phenomena that we do not find anomalous. As such, they "are merely the traces of creation. All that exists between heaven and earth is qi. The extending [yang qi] are spirits and the constricting [yin qi] are ghosts" (Zhu 1986: 1547, my translation). Ghosts and spirits are thus nothing but "the innate ability of the two qi" (1686, my translation), that is, merely the manifestations of qi. Zhu Xi goes so far as to say that "ghosts and spirits are merely qi" (34, my translation).[8] For him, once one has thoroughly understood the li (理) of such phenomena, they no longer appear strange. Zhu Xi quotes Xie Liangzuo (谢良佐), a student of the Cheng brothers, to make this point clear: "When I want them to exist, they exist; when I want them not to exist, they do not exist" (3289, my translation). As all things are ultimately merely qi-transformation, nothing should be perceived as beyond their bounds. Some people regard certain phenomena as anomalous because they are unenlightened about the fundamental structures of the world: the immanent transformation of qi. Zhu Xi's views about ghosts and spirits exemplify Confucians' "fundamental point of faith that the universe is ultimately harmonious" (Li 2014: 43). Thus, there is nothing radically anomalous within the universe because there is nothing external to the emergent order of nature itself. Thinking that there is indicates merely a lack of epistemological insight.

Ubiquitous in the Chinese tradition is Zhu Xi's view that exemplary persons understand the immanent processual holism of all phenomena and are able to see that all things are rooted in the ceaselessly generative power of dao. All things are but (different) manifestations of a common oneness. In the "Change as the Ultimate Mandate" (易本命) chapter in the Records of Ritual Matters by Dai the Elder (Da Dai Liji, 大戴礼记), for example, we see what we might anachronistically call the Cheng-Zhu idea that "li is one but its instantiations many" (理一分殊):

It is due to change [yi, 易] that creativity and fecundity is ceaselessly generated. Humans, birds, animals, and all the varieties of creeping things have
their own reason for becoming and being. Some living solitary, some in
pairs, some flying and some running on the ground. And no one knows
their true nature. Only the person who profoundly achieves identity with
Dao and De can fathom their origin. (Wang 1983: 256, my translation)

Although it is easy to see the multiplicity of the world, it is harder to understand its processual holism or "oneness" and to act on this understanding.
Likewise, we read in the *Luxuriant Gems of the Spring and Autumn*, "Only a
sage is able to link the myriad things to the One and to bind them to the Origin" (Queen and Major 2016: 172). The same implicit understanding of oneness can be found in Wang Bi's commentary on chapter 42 of the *Laozi*:

> Therefore, the myriad things are begotten, and I know the master [主] that
> controls this. Although they have myriad forms, the fusion of *qi* makes
> One [一] out of them all. Each of the common folk has his own heart-mind,
> and customs differ from state to state [异国殊风], yet any lord or prince
> who attains to the One becomes master over them all. (Lynn 1999: 135, my
> modifications)

What the person of perfected virtue sees is that underlying the manifold
variety of phenomena is the ceaselessly generative power of *dao* itself. This
power of generation, because it is the source of all things and their flourishing, is understood in moral terms as virtue (*de*, 德). We find many instances
in the Chinese classics of the idea that the source of the world is morality or
virtue itself. For Wang Yangming, moral knowing (良知) "is the spirit of creating and transforming and this spirit creates heaven and earth, realizes ghosts
and gods [成鬼成帝]. They all arise from this. Truly nothing can be equal to
this" (Wang 1963: 216, my modifications). Thus, morality is itself creation and
transformation—that is, the naturalistic process of the world. It is this naturalistic process qua morality that gives rise to the myriad things, including
ghosts and gods.

The inability to see the oneness of all things is understood as a moral and
epistemological failing. As Zhang Junmai (张君劢, 1886–1969) explains, for
the Confucians, "the [D]ao itself is always considered as self-existent like the
sun and the moon but whether it shines or remains hidden depends upon the
human beings who illuminate it" (Chang 1957: 59). In the *Luxuriant Gems of
the Spring and Autumn*, we see that only the person of perfected virtue is able

to see what connects the myriad things, not in terms of categories but in terms of morality (that is, the ceaselessly generative and transformative action of nature):

> Those who can discuss the [various] categories [类] of birds and beasts are not those with whom the sage desires to converse. The sage desires to discuss humaneness [仁] and righteousness [义] and lay out their inherent patterns. He knows their divisions [分] and classes [科], their categories [条] and distinctions [别], and threads those together that fit together. The sage clarifies things that have been investigated by means of righteousness, so that there will be no instances of deceptive resemblance [between things]. This, and only this, is what the sage prizes [贵]. (Queen and Major 2016: 173)

The person of perfected virtue is not focused on understanding the distinctions between things, but rather on seeing how they are manifestations of the same natural continuum and ultimately are all related to one another. The inability to see that the world ultimately forms a continuum is attributed to the agent's lack of virtue. In the *Luxuriant Gems of the Spring and Autumn*, only those of perfected morality can extend to all things (in the Mencian sense of *tui*, 推[9]) the feeling of not bearing to see the suffering of others (不忍人之心):

> The love of the king [王] extends to the tribes of the four directions [四夷], the love of the hegemon [霸] extends to the Lords of the Land; the love of the secure [ruler] [安] extends to those within his territory; the love of the imperiled [ruler] [危] extends to his dependents and aides; and the love of the [ruler] bereft [of his state] [亡] extends only to his person. (Queen and Major 2016: 315, my modifications)

The sovereign of the utmost virtue is able to extend concern even to those beyond his governance. Diminishing virtue in the sovereign is correlated with the ever-decreasing breadth of his concern. The more virtuous the sovereign, the greater the geographic extent of his care for others. Here, being unable to extend love to all under heaven is seen as a privation, a debilitation, or a deprivation of what should be the case in a healthy situation. This interpretation of the inability to sympathize with all things as pathological can also be seen in the philosophy of Cheng Hao, for whom "being one body with things" (与物同体) is the state of humaneness (*ren*, 仁; the cardinal virtue of Confucianism). Cheng Hao used the idea of unobstructed *qi* from Chinese medicine to talk about this state of oneness with the myriad things:

Books on medicine describe paralysis [瘘痹] of the four limbs as absence of humaneness [仁]. This is an excellent description. The man of humaneness regards Heaven and Earth and the myriad things as one body. To him there is nothing that is not himself. Since he has recognized all things as himself, can there be any limit to his humaneness? If things are not parts of the self, naturally they have nothing to do with it. As in the case of paralysis of the four limbs, the *qi* no longer free-flowing, and therefore they are no longer parts of the self. (Cheng and Cheng 1981: 15, my translation)

To take the myriad things as one's body is the state of humaneness. The equivalence drawn with paralysis analogizes the inability to feel all things as a part of oneself to the loss of limbs, and seeing ontological distinctions between things is analogized to being numb and unfeeling. This is understood in terms of a privation, as not humane. Two disciples of the Cheng brothers, Xie Liangzuo (谢良佐) and Yang Shi (杨时), both inherited Cheng Hao's definition of humaneness as "being one body with things." Xie Liangzuo developed Cheng Hao's use of a pathological numbness in one's body as a metaphor for a lack of humaneness and talked about humaneness in terms of "birthing" (生), "feeling," and "awareness" (觉). In *Recorded Sayings of Shangcai* (上蔡语录), he says:

What is the heart-mind? It is humaneness. What is humaneness? Being alive is humaneness, the dead are not humane. Presently, those whose bodies are numb [麻痹] and do not know pain and itchiness are called not humane. The pits of peaches and apricots[10] that can grow and germinate [生] is called humane, it refers to the idea of birthing. Extending this, humaneness can be seen. (Xie 2010: 6, my translation)

Wang Yangming famously taught that the person of perfected moral cultivation sees all in the world as a part of himself to such an extent that when he sees tiles and stones being shattered and crushed, he cannot help but feel sad that a part of himself is being broken. For Wang Yangming, the humaneness of the original heart-mind, when extended externally, forms what is called "the humanity which makes him form one body with heaven, earth and the myriad things" (天地万物一体之仁; Wang 1963: 119). Although we are all congenitally endowed with the same potential for feeling sympathetically connected to all things, in actuality the petty person's heart is numb to the suffering of others. As Wang Yangming puts it in *Inquiry on the Great Learning*:

That the great person can become one body with the myriad things, it is not that they intended it, the humaneness of their heart-mind was originally so, it is one with the myriad things of heaven and earth. Forming one body with Heaven, Earth and the myriad things is not only true of the great person, even the heart-mind of the small person is also no different. Only he thinks too low of himself. [...] This means that even the heart-mind of the small man necessarily has the humane-ness that forms one body with all. This is rooted in the human nature that is mandated by heaven, and is naturally intelligent, clear and not beclouded. Therefore, it is called enlightened virtue [明德]. (Wang 2011: 1066)

For the Confucians, not being able to feel sympathetic connection with others is a pathology, a disability, whereas feeling that all things are a part of one's self is the original nature of the human being (性), and so the source of utmost humaneness (仁). This is why, for Wang Yangming, nothing prevents the petty man from being able to feel one with all things in the same way that the great person does. *All* human beings have this original nature or potential, since this is the very definition of being human. Expanded to the political realm, this assumption that the correct human behavior is to feel at one with all things means that nobody is outside the bounds of moral concern. In the *Gongyang Zhuan* (公羊传), a commentary on the *Spring and Autumn Annals*, we read that,

in the winter, during the twelfth month, the Earl of Zhai arrived. Who was the Earl of Zhai? *He was a grand officer of the Son of Heaven.* Why is it not said that he was "dispatched" to Lu? *Because he had fled to Lu.* If he had fled to Lu, why does the record not say "fled"? *Because the Zhou kingdom was believed to be all-encompassing, and the word "fled" would imply something beyond it.* (Miller 2015: 10)

As can be seen, the moral ideal for the ruler is to cultivate a state in which he sees no boundaries to his concern. A commentary from the Han Confucian He Xiu (何休) makes the meaning of this passage explicit: "The king treats all under heaven as his family [天下为家]" (Ruan 2009: 4773, my translation). The idea that the true sovereign has sympathetic concern for all under heaven is ubiquitous in the Chinese classics. For example, in the *Annals of the Former Han* (前汉纪), Xun Yue writes, "Today all under heaven is united as one, this is the fundamental spirit of the *Spring and Autumn Annals* [春秋之义], there is nothing external to the King [王者无外]" (Xun 2002: 223, my translation).

The "Conveyance of the Rites" (*liyun*, 礼运) chapter of the *Classic of Rites* echoes this idea that the sovereign should not see anything as beyond the pale of his concern, the ruler being "a sage [who] can look on all under heaven as one family, and on all in the central states as one man" (Wang 2016: 268, my translation).

Prevalent in traditional Chinese political thought is the ideal of the holistic oneness of the myriad things of the world that we have described here in Chinese moral metaphysics. The ideal of processual holism that we see in Chinese metaphysics contrasts with the metaphysical view of nature in the Western tradition. Just as the Chinese metaphysical view of the relationship of the self with the myriad things has repercussions for Chinese political ideals, the Western metaphysical view that the human is ontologically distinct from the rest of nature has repercussions for Western political ideals. Among these repercussions is the idea that those who are properly human—which historically amounted to the Western European man—can dominate all that is not "human." To understand how this idea came to prevail we need to begin with the Greeks' view of humans as ontologically distinct from the rest of the natural continuum, as this was the view that, having been adopted in the later history of Western thought, would contribute to the racialized violence that characterized the colonial period.

The Western View of Nonhumans: Ontological Boundaries

In the history of Western philosophy, there is a striking obsession with defining and delimiting the property that makes humans distinct from the rest of the natural world. As early as the sixth century BCE, the Pythagoreans singled out animals as a category of discussion. In *Republic* 430 B, Plato talks about the precarious form of true belief that can be found in the nature of animals and slaves (Plato 1997: 1062; Sorabji 1993: 11). Aristotle's gradualism in biology is interrupted by introducing a sharp distinction between animal and man (Sorabji 1993: 13–14). For Aristotle, animals are without reason (*logos*), reasoning (*logismos*), thought (*dianoia*), intellect (*nous*), and belief (*doxa*) (14). Much of his treatise *On the Soul* is concerned with distinguishing between plant, animal, and human souls (15). For the classicist and philosopher Richard Sorabji, Aristotle's denial of rationality to animals was inherited by the Stoics, the Epicureans, and both the Jewish and Christian traditions (7–8). The assumption that there are ontological boundaries between things or that things are discontinuous has the practical moral implication that those marked as beyond the boundaries of one's kind are not subject to the same moral concern. In *Animal Liberation*, Peter Singer coins the neologism "speciesism" to describe the indifference of humans to the suffering of animals they consider nonhuman and thus as located beyond the sphere of their moral concern. What Singer has in mind is reflected in Kant's *Lectures on Ethics*: "So far as animals are concerned, we have no direct duties. Animals are not self-conscious, and are there merely as a means to an end. That end is man" (Kant 1963: 239–40). Race-consciousness operates in a similar way: "other" races are seen as lacking "intrinsic value" and are marked as beyond the sphere of moral consideration. If the human being is a fixed, natural kind, then the human's categorical delimitation also sets the boundaries of the human's moral concern.

A clear and consequential example of morality's dependence on ontology can be seen in the European attitude toward the newly "discovered" Amerindians. In his work *The Invasion of America*, for example, the historian Francis Jennings writes that, in the view of the European colonizers, "to invade and dispossess the people of an unoffending civilized country would violate and transgress the principles of international law, but savages were exceptional. Being uncivilized by definition, they were outside the sanctions of both morality and law" (Jennings 1975: 60). As the ontological status of the Amerindian was determined to be the natural slave (barbarian) of which Aristotle spoke, the Amerindian was deemed to be beyond the pale of moral concern. How to treat the Amerindians depended first on determining what ontological *kind* they were.

The relationship between Spaniards' moral behavior toward the Amerindians and their perceived place in the Great Chain of Being is not controversial. In one of the pioneering works in this regard, *Aristotle and the American Indian*, the celebrated historian of colonial America, Lewis Hanke, writes that the Europeans had to become clear about Amerindians' ontological status— whether they were the (subhuman, barbarian) natural slave that Aristotle talked of or were actually human beings—before they could know how to associate with them: "And it is certain that the question of the *true nature* of the Indians agitated and baffled many Spaniards throughout the sixteenth century, and that it became a prime issue of the Spanish conquest" (Hanke 1959: 24, emphasis added).

We can also see how the bounds of one's moral concern followed the bounds of one's species in the thought of Arthur de Gobineau, one of the most infamous racial theorists. For Gobineau, an individual's potential as a human being was determined by his position in the racial hierarchy. That Gobineau's views were no inexplicable deviation from the norm but part of a prevailing orthodoxy is detailed by Charles Mills in *The Racial Contract*. In this work, Mills uses the idea of a non-ideal or naturalized racial contract as a theoretical concept for recognizing, describing, and understanding how racism actually structures the polities of the West and elsewhere. The racial contract is better able to explain the nature of our world than the color-blind or "raceless" theories that dominate mainstream political theory, as race has always been central in shaping Western ideals, not an afterthought (Mills 1997: 14). Under the racial contract, which has governed the world since Western colonialism, Western populations have been living under a two-tiered moral code, with one set for whites and another for nonwhites (23). As in Gobineau's view, under the racial contract, morality depended on ontology and so only "whites" were the subject of moral concern or had moral status. Nonwhites, being nonsubjects, were not subjects with the moral concerns and rights afforded to "persons" (understood historically as European males).

As we will see in the next section, the Confucian tradition does not so strictly distinguish between objects that are of moral or nonmoral concern; as we have already seen, even roof tiles, for example, can stir the emotions of moral sympathy.

The Continuity between Humans, Animals, and Demons in Chinese Thought

In the processual holism of Chinese metaphysics that characterizes the Chinese tradition, humans are not seen as radically distinct from the rest of the natural continuum. In contrast to the great preoccupation with distinguishing between humans, animals, and plants in the early Greek tradition, early Chinese writing did not single out animals as a category of discussion (Sterckx 2002: 24). This processual holistic character of Chinese metaphysics explains why the Chinese tradition has no classificatory tendency similar to that of the Greek tradition. In early Chinese writing, there is no one single denotative definition summarizing the essential ontological properties of an animal, such as the Greek *zoon* (ζῷον), which approximates the Greek or Western notion of an "animal."[11]

The same metaphysical background explains why the term "barbarian," common in a number of European languages, does not have a single analogue in the Chinese language. When the myriad things are assumed to be in process and continuous with each other, it makes less sense to erect rigid classificatory boundaries such as the Greek boundary between the human and the nonhuman (be that animals or "barbarians"). Consistent with its other bivalent dualisms, Greek philosophy assumes an ontological gap between civilization and barbarism; the law of the excluded middle ordains that all that is different will be parsed as non-Greek and thus barbarian. The inapplicability of the term "barbarian" to the Chinese context is discussed in more detail later in this chapter.

If we recall Sterckx's points (a), (b), and (c) about the Chinese attitude toward animals (there being no insistence on ontological boundaries between humans and nonhumans, any demarcations made are constantly subject to change, and the fixity of species is neither self-evident nor desirable), we can say that there was no fixity of species in the classical Chinese worldview because it did not assume the existence of a single (static) ontological order. The Chinese attitude that there are no ontological boundaries between humans and animals evidences the Chinese metaphysical assumption that the universe is an-archic, *ziran*, or, in Brian Bruya's phrase, is "spontaneous[ly] self-causing."[12] Under this view that each thing is *sponte sua*, no-thing has a *telos* or a strictly delimited way in which it can develop; every particular can develop in ways that are not predictable (as each particular is related to all that is not itself). As such, it becomes impossible to define a thing absolutely, and so order is understood as emergent and perspectival. A typical expression of this view that order is emergent as things change in unpredictable ways can be found in the "Reaching Utmost Happiness" (*zhile*, 至乐) chapter of the *Zhuangzi*, which declares the impossibility of defining and delimiting the constant transformation of things:

The seeds of things have subtle workings [几]. In the water they become Break Vine, on the edges of the water they become Frog's Robe. If they sprout on the slopes, they become Hill Slippers. If Hill Slippers get rich soil, they turn into Crow's Feet. The roots of Crow's Feet turn into maggots and their leaves turn into butterflies. Before long the butterflies are transformed and turn into insects that live under the stove; they look like snakes and their name is Qu-Duo. After a thousand days, the Qu Duo insects become birds called Dried Leftover Bones. The saliva of the Dried Leftover Bones becomes Si-Mi bugs and the Si-Mi bugs become Vinegar Eaters. I-lo bugs are born from the Vinegar Eaters, and Huang-Kuang bugs from Jiu-You bugs. Jiu-You bugs are born from Mao-Rui bugs and Mou-jui bugs are born from Rot Grubs and Rot Grubs are born from Sheep's Groom. Sheep's Groom couples with bamboo that has not sprouted for a long while and produces

Green Peace plants. Green Peace plants produce leopards and leopards produce horses and horses produce men. Men in time return again to natural spontaneity[机]. So, all creatures come out of natural spontaneity [机] and go back into it again. (Chen 2016: 533–34, my translation based on Zhuangzi and Watson 1964: 117)

Under this worldview, there is little motivation to categorize the things of the world as species and genera as things do not exist within ontologically discrete boundaries. Relatedly, this worldview would agree with John Dewey in arguing that the Aristotelian species-genera model falls afoul of the "philosophical fallacy," that is, "the abstracting of some one element from the organism which gives it meaning, and setting it up as absolute," then revering this one element "as the cause and ground of all reality and knowledge" (Dewey 1969: 162). When we select "similar" properties from a manifold, we are arbitrarily—and from our own perspective—taking a part to characterize and represent the whole. It is this Chinese metaphysical assumption that explains the absence of interest in categorizing animals in the same way that the Aristotelian mode of genus and species does, as well as why the Chinese tradition lacks the Western tradition's obsession with defining the essential (cognitive) element separating humans from animals.

The Continuity between the Human and the Animal in Confucianism

As Chinese metaphysics does not explain difference via ontological boundaries, the Confucian tradition understands human and animals instead as different points on a continuum and sees individuals' humanity as achievable through increasing embodiment of culture and virtue. Under this Confucian view, "human" is a moral category that is achieved, not a natural category to which a person congenitally belongs. The implication here is that even the biological human being, when not shaped by the right cultural forms, is not yet fully human. As Mencius famously puts it in *Mencius* 4B19, "That wherein human beings differ from the birds and beasts is but slight. The majority of people relinquish this, while the morally exemplary person retains it" (Mencius 2009: 89, my modifications). In *Mencius* 3B9, we see the statement that the difference between humans and animals is not ontological: "Yang holds for egoism, which involves denial of one's sovereign; Mo holds for impartial care, which entails denial of one's parents. To deny one's parents or to deny one's sovereign is to be an animal [禽兽]" (Mencius 2009: 70). Humanness is not an element or essence that one either has or does not have. For Mencius, those who abandon the morality of filial piety have already abandoned their own humanity.

In the Chinese classics, animal imagery is commonly used to stigmatize behavior that breaks the commonly accepted rules of the period. This is why the Chinese themselves can become like animals and are often described as such. In the *Records on the Warring States Period* (战国策), composed during the Western Han, the state of Qin—a Chinese state that embraced legalism and unified China—is described in terms of animal imagery:[13]

> Qin shares the same custom with the Rong and the Di peoples. Like savage tigers and wolves, Qin is covetous, tyrannical and dishonest. It doesn't adhere to any rules of proprieties or righteousness, and has no virtue at all. Whenever there is a chance to gain some profit, the rulers of Qin don't mind hurting their relatives or even their own brothers. They are nothing but beasts. Qin knows no deeds or admirable virtues. (Zhai 2008: 1071, "Third Volume on Wei," my translation)

"Human" is not a natural kind to which a person essentially belongs, but a moral category that a person achieves by embodying certain practices; as such, a person's human status is not fixed, but dynamic and subject to change (see Sterckx 2002: 123). Although this passage speaks derogatorily about the Qin, Rong, and Di by comparing them to animals, it also elucidates how the early Chinese defined animality. It is significant that all the qualities attributed to the Qin, Rong, Di, and animals are behaviors that a person could change or correct, not an ontological essence. When the Qin, Rong, and Di renounce aggression, leave off coveting gain, and stop putting advantage before virtuous action, they will no longer be analogized to aggressive predatory animals.

The key point here is that, in the Chinese worldview, human beings, such as the Qin, Rong and Di, can regress to a predatory animal-like state if they do not preserve that which distinguishes humans from animals: behaviors that accord with normative cultural-moral standards. Under this process metaphysics, the human *being* is a human *becoming*, and the human being is not defined ontologically as a natural kind, but as a moral category that is achieved. The view that humanness lies in the demonstration of certain behaviors and can thus be cultivated, not that it is an essence that one may or may not congenitally possess, distinguishes the Chinese attitude toward non-Chinese from the Greco-Western attitude toward non-Greeks.

Chinese Processual Holism and
the Absence of the "Barbarian"

The Chinese tradition's assumptions, under a metaphysics of processual holism, that there are no ontological boundaries between what is immanent to nature, that nothing transcends this processual whole, and that a person *becomes* human through acculturation have important implications for traditional Chinese attitudes toward the non-Chinese. As I have argued elsewhere (Xiang 2019b, 2019c), otherness became problematic in the Western context only because the (racial) other was understood, under a substance ontology, as *essentially* other—that is, ontologically distinct from what is properly human. Under the traditional and processual Confucian Chinese metaphysical view of the self as a human becoming, however, humanness is not a congenital and eternal essence, but a quality acquired through acculturation and the practice of culturally appropriate actions. Under this view, those who are (initially) perceived to be other can always *become* acculturated according to Chinese norms and so become Chinese. This cultural-processual identity as opposed to a racial-ontological identity is reflected in the central tenet of Confucianism: the perfectibility through education of all humans. In the dualistic Greek-Western view, by contrast, the barbarian is a Manichean other who is ontologically distinct from proper humans and so is incapable of becoming "properly human."

In the Confucian view (and coherent with process metaphysics), one is not born human but becomes human through the ceaseless process of acculturation and practice. Thus, there are no ontologically superior groups of people and no *natural* hierarchies, as in the Aristotelian, Platonic (with the different grades of soul), and later Christian (Great Chain of Being) conceptions. The implication of Aristotle's theory of natural slavery is that because of barbarians' ontological inferiority, their domination by Greek men is justified. The barbarian (natural slave) improves through subjugation by the rational agents (Greek and later Western males). The master and slave have the same interest because the slave can partake of reason only by imitating his master; in his natural state he is incapable of fulfilling his proper *telos*. Similarly, it was through assuming that the Amerindians were the natural slaves of whom Aristotle spoke that the Spanish legitimized their colonial takeover of the Americas (Pagden 1982: 27–56). In the eyes of the Spanish, the Amerindian's "barbarism"—his ontological nature—and his, to the Spanish gaze, unreflective, passion-dominated, half-reasoning man-child nature gave them a legitimate right to political dominion over him. By contrast, the Chinese metaphysics of processual holism lacks any one stable ontological order and so cannot sustain a conception of each thing as having one *telos*, as in the Aristotelian view. Instead, a thing is defined only momentarily and relationally (both in time and in space, that is, in relation to past and present, and to other things). Under the Chinese metaphysics of processual holism, it is impossible to justify the ontological domination of foreigners ("barbarians") by Chinese men.

Thus, the common practice of translating Chinese terms that designate non-Chinese peoples (such as *yidi*, 夷狄) as "barbarian," is mistaken, for the following reasons. To equate the Chinese view toward non-Chinese peoples with the Greek and later Western view toward barbarians makes three insinuations: (1) that dichotomies between civilization and barbarism, human and animal, freedom and determinism, and reason and nature exist under Chinese processual holism; (2) that Western colonial and genocidal history has a comparable parallel in the Chinese tradition; and (3) that it is possible to justify domination of the barbarian on the basis of his ontological inferiority under Chinese processual holistic philosophy. The Chinese understanding of non-Chinese, though often derogatory, simply cannot be equated with the Greek-Western conception of the "barbarian" once we acknowledge the falsity of these insinuations.[14]

The history of how the term *yi* (夷) became commonly translated as "barbarian" helps clarify why equating Chinese designations for non-Chinese with "barbarian" is problematic. As the historian of China and Vietnam Kathlene Baldanza notes, the wide use during the Qing period of *yi* as a generic term for Europeans demonstrates that it was "used more as a neutral marker of foreignness than as a specific ethnic designation." Baldanza cites a contemporary observer, Samuel Wells Williams, who in his 1848 history of China, *The Middle Kingdom*, considers the term benign and deems "savage" and "barbarian" to be overtranslations (Baldanza 2016: 32–33n57). In a telling episode in the history of the term, Lydia Liu traces the identification between *yi* and "barbarian" to agents of the British state in mid-nineteenth-century China who took offense at being designated as *yi* because they identified it with "barbarian." Despite Chinese protestations that the term was innocuous, in article 51 of the Anglo-Chinese Treaty of Tianjin of 1858 (an unequal treaty that ended the first phase of the Second Opium War), the British stipulated that Britain and British subjects were never to be referred to as *yi* (Liu 2004: 31–69). From this historical episode we can see that the British read their Western understanding of the "barbarian" as the irredeemably ontological, Manichean other into the Chinese designation for the non-Chinese. That the British understood *yi* as "barbarian" shows only that they assumed Western racism to be universal, not that it in fact was.

The Commensurability between All Things

There is no greater example of the Chinese worldview that all the myriad things belong to an immanent whole than its assumption of the commensurability between humans and demons. Summarizing his observations about the genre of the accounts of the anomalous (志怪),[15] Robert Ford Campany concludes that, "if one surveys the entire body of anomaly account narratives depicting interactions between living and dead persons, one's deepest impression will be a sense of sympathy, community, and fellow-feeling across the boundary between the 'light' and 'dark' realms" (Ford Campany 1996: 383), as these "tales emphasize the commonality of moral principles across social as well as ontological boundaries" (378–79). What is commensurable across humans and spirits, and what ties the light and dark realms together, is the same moral code that "govern[s] our interactions with them as with each other" (376).[16]

The extent of this Chinese optimism about the commensurability of all things can be seen in one of the most famous stories from Pu Songling's *Strange Stories from a Chinese Studio* (聊斋志异), "Nie Xiaoqian" (聂小倩). In this story, a beautiful female ghost who has been coerced into murdering unsuspecting human males is moved by the moral uprightness of one of her potential victims, a scholar, and falls in love with him. Following him back to his home, she slowly becomes a member of the household as she gains acceptance by fulfilling the obligations of filial piety. Her gradual acculturation through reading the Buddhist sutras and eating human food ultimately results in her becoming human again: that status is restored when she marries the scholar, bears three children for him, and becomes skilled in producing elegant paintings. This story demonstrates processual holism in action: humanity is a continuum that one embodies through increasing competence in culture, not a substance that one either possesses or does not possess.[17] It bears stressing that this story also gives us an account of the relationship between humans and nonhumans very different from the standard Western account.

Since it made no incommensurable (ontological) divisions between humans, animals, and ghosts and demons, the Chinese tradition had little reason to insist on incommensurable divisions or exclusive distinctions between those considered Chinese and those considered foreign. Indeed, the textual tradition often intones that although different peoples around the world have different customs, those differences are not incommensurable. Difference is merely a local manifestation of the same immanent process that underlies all phenomena. For example, in the chapter "Question of Tang" of the Daoist text *Liezi*, we are told that far beyond the realms of the Middle Kingdom the peoples are the same as they are in the Middle Kingdom:

> "What is there outside the four seas?"
> "Countries like the Middle Kingdom."
> "What is your evidence for that?"
> —"I have traveled east as far as Ying; the people were the same as here. When I asked what lay east of Ying, it proved to be the same as Ying. I have traveled as far as Bin; the people [人民] were the same as here. When I asked what lay west of Bin, it proved to be the same as Bin. This is how I know that the four seas, the four borderlands, the four limits, are no different from here. (Graham 1990: 96, my modifications)

What is demonstrated here is an optimism about the fundamental commensurability between all peoples. Although differences do exist, incommensurable differences do not. As such, peoples from regions with different habits from those of the central states can still become acculturated in the norms of the central states and so achieve great social esteem there. This assumption of fundamental commensurability explains why the Chinese had no equivalent of the concept of the "barbarian" and no ethnographic interest in the other, as there was in the West. For example, Pliny the Elder's *Natural History* (first century CE) describes in great detail "grotesque races" from faraway lands, *not* as figments of the imagination but as actually existing (Stannard 1992: 167). Throughout Chinese history, Richard Smith notes, "China's foreign relations did not occupy a special place in the dynastic histories. [. . .] For the most part, foreigners were viewed by the Chinese in terms of military security and/or trade—not as objects of independent ethnographic interest" (Smith 2015: 216).

Since the Chinese tradition has no view of the universe as static and sees all things as existing within the continuum that is nature, it has no epistemological predisposition to drawing sharp ontological distinctions and thus does not assume the Manicheanism between good and evil that endowed the

Western tradition with such fear and revulsion toward the (barbarian) racial other. The Chinese poetic genre of the "frontier fortress" (边塞诗) can be productively contrasted with the genre of American frontier literature. The juxtaposition of Chinese representations of northwestern peoples (*hu*, 胡) with the European settler's representation of the (savage) native American eloquently shows the divergent relationship to difference that governed the two cultural consciousnesses. It is beyond the scope of this project to provide an exhaustive survey of the depiction of foreigners in the "frontier fortress" genre of poetry, but a few literary examples representative of the genre can be provided, drawn from the Chinese encounter with foreigners on its northwestern borders. From these representative examples, we can see that the Chinese gaze knew nothing of parsing difference in terms of Manichean otherness.

In Yan Ren's (严仁; *fl.* ca. 1200) "Frontier Fortress" (塞下曲), we read:

The still and solitary city in the setting sun,
The yellow elms and white reeds fill the *Guan* mountains entire.
Thousands upon thousands of *Qiang* [羌] pipes arise from the
    horizon,
[I] know it is the *Hu* [胡] returning from herding horses
    (my translation).[18]

Gao Shi's (高适) (704–765) "The Song of Yingzhou" (营州歌) is a eulogy on the masculinity of the nomads:

The youths of Yingzhou are well versed in the ways of the grasslands,
Wearing robes made with fox fur they hunt outside the city.
They do not become inebriated even after drinking thousands of cups
    of wine,
The sons of Hu can ride horses from the age of ten (quoted in Yan
    2014: 282, my translation).[19]

In Zhou Pu's (周朴) (?–878) "Frontier Fortress" (塞下曲), we see again a harmonious depiction of nomads and a celebration of the natural landscape:

The Hu from Chach [modern-day Tashkent] go east of the desert,
[He] likes to play the horizontal flute to lead the autumn wind.
In the coming of night, the clouds and rain are all flown away
The moon shines on the rippleless sand stretching leagues and leagues
    into emptiness (quoted in Yan 2014: 283, my translation).[20]

Another vivid example of the difference between the Western and Chinese attitudes toward diversity is found in comparing the European encounter with the American opossum with the Chinese encounter with the giraffe. Both animals were previously unknown in their respective locales. Susan Scott Parrish has shown that the female opossum represented for Europeans in the "New World" "an alien mixture of familiar forms" and was thus a demonic animal to them, owing to the prodigious generative capacity of its two uteruses and nursing-pouch for its young (as a marsupial) (Parrish 1997: 485). As Parrish writes:

> Such female generativity represented [...] the earthly degeneracy from God's pure creation: at one pole was God's disembodied singularity and at the other was a polymorphous female spawning and redigesting still more sundry shapes. In this netherworld of mixed forms, all generation was, by definition, degeneration, and the more generative the creature, the more perilously she was marked by the divergence from that unity that came with material incarnation. (Parrish 1997: 480)

In its prodigious capacity for reproduction, the opossum symbolized birth, decay, death, change, and becoming; it pointed to the impossibility of "being," of form remaining eternal. To the medieval mind encountering the female opossum, she would have embodied the formless nature that is the enemy form. Making the "composite creature" even more monstrous to the medieval European mind would have been her "borrowed parts from familiar animals [from Europe] and even from the human body" (Parrish 1997: 485). In Aristotle's classification of animals, biologically perfect animals reproduce themselves by passing on their form and "imperfect" animals, such as insects and some reptiles, are spontaneously generated from the earth or from the fusion of rotting matter (*Generation of Animals* 762a10–763b16; Aristotle 2007: 1179–81; *Meteorology* 381b10; Aristotle 2007: 612).[21] By not possessing the form of a single animal recognizable to the European, the opossum would have been associated with the odious idea of biological imperfection, formlessness, and creation from decay—that is, as the most complete antithesis of God as "being," form, perfection, and nonchange.

In contrast to the Western gaze, which saw so much of nature as the enemy of form and perfection, the Yongle emperor (1360–1424), when presented with a giraffe by the king of Bengal, interpreted the gift as the auspicious *qilin* (麒麟), whose appearance augured the arrival of an illustrious ruler. That the Chinese did not parse difference as demonic speaks to their

FIGURE 3.1. The female opossum and her two whelps, in John Ogilby, *America* (London, 1671). William L. Clements Library, Ann Arbor, Michigan.

worldview that all things are a part of nature, and that nature is never formless or meaningless. Nothing is feared because nothing is external to the continuum of nature itself.

Conclusion

This chapter has argued that the processual holism of the Chinese metaphysical worldview has important implications for the Chinese attitude toward nonhumans, especially juxtaposed against the Western attitude toward nonhumans. Seeing all things as forming a continuous whole, the Chinese worldview did not see ontological differences between humans and nonhumans. All boundaries were seen as dynamic and all things as capable of transformation into each other given the right circumstances. In other words, there was understood to be a fundamental commensurability or oneness underlying all things, whether animals, demons, or non-Chinese. This assumption of the dynamism of all things makes the human naming of things inherently perspec-

FIGURE 3.2. Tribute Giraffe with Attendant, sixteenth century.
Formerly attributed to Shen Du, Chinese, 1357–1434. Philadelphia
Museum of Art: Gift of John T. Dorrance, 1977, 1977-42-1.

tival and provisional. The recognition that human understanding is perspectival and provisional is reflected in the Chinese attitude toward the anomalous. What is *perceived* as anomalous is not understood as ontologically anomalous. Instead there is a tendency to rationalize anomaly as caused by the human agent's lack of virtue or lack of acuity in understanding that all phenomena are manifestations of a fundamental (dynamic) oneness. The inability to understand that there are no ontological boundaries is understood as an epistemological and moral failing. The epistemological assumption about the oneness of all things is thus related to a moral prescription. The moral agent is one who can see all things as one (that is, as a processual, dynamic continuum), whereas the person of lesser morality trades in ontological distinctions and does not see the oneness of phenomena. Whereas the Chinese understood the world as a processual whole, the Western tradition assumed the fact of ontological boundaries between all immanent things ranked in an ascending hierarchy of worth, as we will see in the next chapter.

4

Race, Metaphysical Determinism, and the Great Chain of Being

THIS CHAPTER PROVIDES a philosophical background to the Greco-Roman ideas about ontological hierarchy, later inherited by Europeans, that we briefly discussed in chapters 2 and 3. It shows that the racism that governed European colonialism (defined as the era succeeding Columbus's "discovery" of the "New World") shares many similarities with the Great Chain of Being (hereafter referred to as "GCB") that A. O. Lovejoy discussed in his classic *The Great Chain of Being*. Under this racial worldview, difference is not understood as emerging from dynamic processes but as ontological; it is parsed hierarchically, and the only relationship among the different ranks of difference is one of domination of the lower by the higher. In this chapter, I use representative examples from European racism and colonialism, most notably the European colonization of the Americas, to substantiate these parallels.

The GCB is characterized by several key features: (1) that there is a single ontological order in which all finite beings are fixed in an eternal order; (2) that the world is completely rational because it is metaphysically determined, with no room for contingency or novelty; (3) that things are different not because of the confluence of various circumstances, but because they have been necessarily so for all eternity; (4) that difference is ontological, not emerging constantly from dynamic processes; (5) that these ontological differences are also hierarchical; (6) that the only relationship between the different stations of the hierarchy is domination of the lower by the higher; and (7) that violent domination within the hierarchy is ontologically justified.

The paradigmatic example of difference being parsed in terms of an ontological hierarchy is Aristotle's theory of natural slavery. As a corollary of these GCB axioms, a final characteristic is that (8) diversity is tantamount to conflict.

The idea of the "just war" arises from this claim, which ontologically legitimates violent domination. Plotinus—one of the formative figures in the theorization of the GCB—wrote that conflict in general is only a special case and a necessary implicate of diversity; "difference carried to its maximum," he argued, "*is* opposition" (quoted in Lovejoy 1964: 65–66). The GCB view of the world as a single ontological order cannot accommodate novelty and is thus incredibly inflexible and brittle. What novelty it encounters has to be forced into its hierarchical framework if the whole system is to be safeguarded from chaos. In practical terms, this meant historically that newly encountered peoples who were different from the Europeans in physical appearance and customs were *necessarily* inferior to the Europeans. Given the static nature of this ontological hierarchy, an individual's classification in this hierarchy could not be changed. One of the collaterals of Western philosophy's assumption of hierarchical order is the diminished status of those considered nonhuman—or only liminally human, such as the racial other. "Nonhumans" are seen as ontologically inferior and thus justifiably subject to domination.

The GCB resolved two issues: it explained why there is diversity[1] in the world, and it proved that the world is intrinsically rational. The implication of the world being intrinsically rational is that the universe is absolutely determined, that all things or events of the immanent world could not have been other than precisely what they are. This tenseless "block universe" (in William James's words) in which all space-time is determined through necessary truths admits of no additions, omissions, or alterations. There is therefore no possibility of change, contingency, or potentiality in the universe. A consequence of the intellectual security provided by a fully rational, fully determined universe is a strictly delimited way in which the things of the world can develop that leaves no room for freedom and novelty. This view of the universe is psychologically comforting, but it is also incredibly precarious, because the empirical fact is that there is in fact change and novelty in the world. To secure the truth of this rational and determined system is necessarily to deny or obliterate the existence or possibility of change and novelty. The totalitarian and absolutist nature of this view of the world became manifest, with the most devastating consequences, in the colonial period, when Europe encountered previously unimagined diversity.

Relying on the works of James Baldwin, William James, and Mary Douglas, I close this chapter with a critique of the epistemological errors implicit in the ontologization and hierarchization of difference and the moral failures attendant upon these epistemological errors. By way of the observation of the philosopher

William James and the anthropologist Mary Douglas that dirt is "matter out of place," I show that the epistemological error of an ontological hierarchy is its failure to recognize that value is subjectively ascribed, and so when we rank things in terms of value, we inevitably encode our perspectival and socially biased preferences. I also argue that both the epistemological and moral failures of the GCB are rooted in an aversion to the contingency of existence that psychologically motivates the obsession with metaphysical determinism and a "fully rational" world. The inability to embrace the constancy of change, and so the emergent and contingent nature of order, results in a fanatical devotion to perceiving the structure of the world (the GCB) as having an inviolable sanctity. Simultaneous with a system of metaphysical determinism (the GCB) is an abnegation of human agency and an inability to accept the human condition (our own contingency and agency in constituting order).

A Brief History of the Great Chain of Being

Since antiquity, the GCB has been the most potent and persistent Western idea about the general order of things (Lovejoy 1964: vii). Until the nineteenth century, the GCB was one of the most famous vocabularies and concepts in Western thought; it dominated Western conceptions of the general order of things and underlay some of the most potent and persistent presuppositions of Western thought, even up to modern times (vii).

There are two sources of the GCB: Plato and Aristotle. Plato equated the source of ideas with perfect goodness, making it a dialectical *necessity* that the world be exactly as it is. The Platonic equation of the Good with fecundity and necessity, combined with an Aristotelian ontological scale,[2] required that all existing things be placed in a unilinear *scala naturae* according to their degree of perfection (Lovejoy 1964: 58).

One of the most representative accounts of the GCB is from Sir John Fortescue, a fifteenth-century jurist, who claimed that there are no two identical things in the world. The uniqueness of each thing is its difference from all other things, and this difference is tantamount to a thing's superiority or inferiority to any other thing:

In this order angel is set over angel, rank upon rank in the kingdom of heaven; man is set over man, beast over beast, bird over bird, and fish over fish, on the earth in the air and in the sea: so that there is no worm that crawls upon the ground, no bird that flies on high, no fish that swims in the depths, which the chain of this order does not bind in most harmonious concord. [...] God created as many different kinds of things as he did creatures, so that there is no creature which does not differ in some respect from all other creatures and by which it is in some respect superior or inferior to all the rest. So that from the highest angel down to the lowest of his kind there is absolutely not found an angel that has not a superior and inferior; nor from man down to the meanest worm is there any creature which is not in some respect superior to one creature and inferior to another. (quoted in Tillyard 1943: 24–25)

Fortescue assures us that, as there are no two identical things in the world, difference is tantamount to hierarchy. Another representative work based on the GCB was Alexander Pope's *An Essay on Man*, a popular poem of the eighteenth century:

> Vast chain of being! which from God began,
> Natures ethereal, human, angel, man,
> Beast, bird, fish, insect, what no eye can see,
> No glass can reach; from infinite to thee,
> From thee to nothing.—On superior powers
> Were we to press, inferior might on ours;
> Or in the full creation leave a void,
> Where, one step broken, the great scale's destroyed:
> From Nature's chain whatever link you strike,
> Tenth or ten-thousandth, breaks the chain alike.
> [...]
> Order is Heaven's first law: and, this confest,
> Some are and must be greater than the rest.[3]

As we see from Pope, order is tantamount to a hierarchy stretching from the most perfect (God) to the most imperfect. As order is tantamount to hierarchy, the consequence of breaking even one step of this chain would be the general dissolution of the cosmic order. Necessary to the order of the world is the impossibility of novelty and change.

Another expression of this view can be seen in the observation in *An Essay on the Origin of Evil* by William King (1650–1729), archbishop of Dublin, that "an equality of perfections in the creatures is impossible." In the natural hierarchy of perfection, those of "the inferior orders could not aspire to a higher station without detriment to the superior which possesses that station; for he must quit his place before another can ascend to it" (King 1732: xxiv). The ontological order of the world is such that no two things can have the same worth. We will see repeatedly the eight characteristics of the GCB listed earlier reflected in Western engagement with difference.

Diversity and Hierarchy

Since the GCB was the operative European assumption for millennia, it is no surprise that the European encounter with difference historically led to both the hierarchization of difference and the violent domination of difference. The first time the European world picture was challenged by an unforeseen difference was the Spanish encounter with the Amerindians late in the fifteenth century. The Spanish were confronted with a continent and a people whose existence they had not anticipated. We can catalog in that encounter the ways in which the Spanish parsed the different customs of the Amerindians as signs of their subhuman nature. Seeing difference in hierarchical terms, the Spanish saw only inferiority and transgression in the differences between themselves and the Amerindians.[4] Under this metaphysical determinism, they took cultural difference as a sign of ontological inferiority.

It is important to note that since the "Age of Discovery," the GCB has often been temporalized, as can be seen in the discipline of ethnology, a product of European colonialism. Confronted with a previously unconscionable diversity, the European colonizers sought to explain diversity without divesting Europe of its preeminence among the multitude of world cultures (Pagden 1982: 146–98). Ethnology grew out of the need to reconcile the recently discovered cultural diversity of "the Rest" with the European claim of universalism. Seeing that there were real differences among peoples, the Europeans treated these differences hierarchically by deciding that some cultures were just lower down on the evolutionary path. Difference was not understood horizontally, but hierarchically. Plotting cultural diversity on an ascending graph of progress, the European view was that the closer one was *spatially* to the heart of empire, the closer one was to modernity—that is, to the *temporal* present. Following this ethnological conception of a temporalized teleological hierarchy, conventional scholarship has depicted the near-extinction of the Amerindians as an inevitable and "unintended consequence" (Stannard 1992: 286) of the march of history, progress, and civilization.

Diversity and Domination: Natural Slavery and Just War

One of the most representative examples of the GCB is Aristotle's theory of natural slavery, which equates all non-Greeks with barbarians and barbarians with natural slaves. Under the GCB, as the world is rationally determined, the *social* category of slave is parsed as an *ontological* category. To the question, then, of whether some humans are slaves by nature, Aristotle's answer is yes, as "from the hour of their birth, some are marked out for subjection, others for rule" (*Pol.* 1254a22–23; Aristotle 2007: 1990). Under Aristotle's theory of natural slavery, difference equals inferiority, and inferiority legitimizes domination:

> For that which can foresee by the exercise of mind is by nature lord and master, and that which can with its body give effect to such foresight is a subject, and by nature a slave; hence master and slave have the same interest. Now nature has distinguished between the female and the slave. For she is not niggardly, like the smith who fashions the Delphian knife for many uses; she makes each thing for a single use, and every instrument is best made when intended for one and not for many uses. But among barbarians no distinction is made between women and slaves, because there is no natural ruler among them: they are a community of slaves, male and female. That is why the poets say,—
>
> It is meet that Hellenes should rule over barbarians; as if they thought that the barbarian and the slave were by nature one. (*Pol.* 1252a31–b9; Aristotle 2007: 1986–87)

Under this view, the only and proper telos of the slave is to be a slave. Even his physical nature is commensurable with his end: the natural slave is built for hard labor, whereas the free man is built for political life. As Aquinas later explained, the slave is "almost an animated instrument of service" (quoted in Pagden 2015: 47). Moreover, the master and slave have the same interest because the slave, who in his natural state is incapable of fulfilling his proper telos, can partake of reason by imitating his master. Like the animal, the slave is all body and no mind, and as such he should be ruled by those who embody mind—free men. Each thing has one telos, and the slave's telos is to be ruled by (Greek) men. That the slave should be dominated is part of the natural hierarchy, because the more rational dominates the less rational.

What Aristotle's theory of natural slavery ultimately naturalizes and legitimizes is the violent domination of difference. Since difference is seen as either superiority or inferiority, superiority can claim the right to dominate while inferiority is tantamount to an invitation to be dominated. In fact, the domination of the slave is *just*:

> And so, from one point of view, the art of war is a natural art of acquisition, for the art of acquisition includes hunting, an art which we ought to practice against wild beasts, and against men who, though intended by nature to be governed, will not submit; for war of such kind is naturally just. (*Pol.* 1256b22–25; Aristotle 2007: 1994)

Metaphysical determinism and ontological hierarchy thus sanction the violent domination of those in the category of slaves and animals by free men because such domination is in the nature of the universe.[5]

The relationship of domination between the master and the slave, when expanded, becomes the relationship between the colonizer and the colonized. In the Athenian pronouncements of Thucydides' Melian dialogue, for example, both the relationship between the imperial state and its subjects and that of the relationship between master and slave are of the same type of relationship which is also considered to be natural and inevitable. For Aristotle, as Benjamin Isaac explains, it was clear that war is a legitimate process whose purpose is to reduce inferior foreigners to the state of slavery that is their intrinsic nature and purpose anyway (179). Similarly, in *City of God* Augustine quotes Cicero's *De Republica* in declaring that the ruling of the provinces is just, because "servitude may be advantageous to the provincials" considering that "they became worse and worse so long as they were free." Once enslaved, "they will improve by subjection" (quoted in Isaac 2004: 183). Subjection of the provincials was seen as operating in the same way as the soul's rule over the body and reason's rule over the passions and other vicious parts of the soul. Similarly, Thomas Aquinas's *De regimine principum* makes explicit the link between the social hierarchy of master and slave and the chain of movement stretching all the way back to the unmoved mover (Pagden 1982: 48). In all of these examples, violence is justified through the framework of the ontological order of the universe. Aimé Césaire would later call this ontological justification the "dependency complex" between the colonizer and the colonized.

What Césaire calls the "dependency complex" is most conspicuously present in the Spanish justification, relying on Aristotle's theory of natural slavery, of their right to enslave the Amerindians.[6] As Aristotle's theory of natural slavery ultimately equates all non-Greeks with natural slaves, it was embraced with great alacrity in the European colonization project. As Anthony Pagden writes,

Aristotle conveniently and simultaneously explained not only "why it was just for the Europeans to deprive the Amerindians of what would otherwise be considered their natural rights" but also the "startling differences between their behavior and all that was held to be in accordance with natural law in Europe" (Pagden 2015: 109). In the infamous Valladolid dispute of 1550 over the legitimacy of Spanish conquest, the philosopher Juan Ginés de Sepúlveda defended colonization and the enslavement of the Amerindians on the basis of this very idea that ontologically the Amerindian were barbarians. As he wrote in *On the Just Causes of the War against the Indians*, "the perfect should dominate the imperfect, the excellent its contrary" (Dussel 1995: 169n13). Similarly, the Spanish jurist Juan de Matienzo (1520–1579), in his *Gobierno del Perú*, characterized the native Americans as Aristotle's natural slaves, that is, as incapable of possessing reason for themselves. Instead, they are "participants in reason so as to sense it, but not to possess or follow it. In this they are no different from the animals (although animals do not even sense reason) for they are ruled by their passions" (quoted in Pagden 1982: 42).

In more recent history, as Richard Slotkin (2000) has shown, the governing motif of European settler-colonial literature in north America is "regeneration through violence." The governing theme of American frontier literature again manifests the GCB. Here, virtue, in this case a regeneration or rebirth of the self, is achieved through violent conflict.

To the European colonizer, the ontological nature of the non-European as a natural slave—that is, his ontological position below the European—simply required that he be dominated. The European *knew* that the Amerindian was a natural slave because he was different (that is, not European in either appearance or custom). In real terms, difference is tantamount to hierarchy, and the relationship between differences (between Greek and non-Greek, between European and non-European) is either dominating or being dominated. The ontology of the GCB is perfectly suited, if not designed for, dominating difference.

The Tragedy of Metaphysical Determinism

Racialized violence and genocide under European colonialism and its inability to grant dignity to difference are attributable to the metaphysics of the GCB. This section explores what psychologically motivates the ideology of the GCB.

The metaphysical concept of "Being" is characterized by absolutism. It allows no room for "Being" of a different type, as this would lead it to the crisis between being and nonbeing that we find in Parmenides. Metaphysical determinism cannot tolerate novelty, for the possibility of novelty would *ipso facto* invalidate metaphysical determinism. As fifteenth-century Europeans subscribed to a static and ontologically determined map of the world, the introduction of any new element to this ontology threatened the entire structure. We see the empirical consequences of metaphysical determinism's inability to intellectually give place to novelty in Europeans' encounter with difference during their discovery of the inhabitants of the "New World." Pagden writes that, for the Spanish scholastics who had to interpret this newfound reality, "any judgment on the *nature* of the Indians" had to be rooted "in a scheme which offered an explanation for the structure of the whole world of nature and the behaviour of everything, animate or inanimate, within it. Any attempt to introduce a new element into that scheme could, if ill-conceived, threaten the whole" (Pagden 1982: 28).

Pagden's assessment that the Western system of reality required that the Amerindian, as an ontological threat, be kept in a particular place in the established hierarchy has been echoed by James Baldwin's assessment of the intransigence of American antiblack racism. In *The Fire Next Time*, Baldwin observes that white Americans' fear of blacks ultimately stems from their fear that cosmic chaos would ensue from any change in the fixed place occupied by blacks in the white's sense of reality. It is worth quoting Baldwin in full:

> Try to imagine how you would feel if you woke up one morning to find the sun shining and all the stars aflame. You would be frightened because it is out of the order of nature. Any upheaval in the universe is terrifying because it so profoundly attacks one's sense of one's own reality. Well, the black man has functioned in the white man's world as a fixed star, as an immovable pillar: and as he moves out of his place, heaven and earth are shaken to their foundations. [...] I said that it was intended that you should perish in the ghetto, perish by never being allowed to go behind the white man's definitions, by never being allowed to spell your proper name. You have, and many of us have, defeated this intention; and, by a terrible law, a terrible paradox, those innocents who believed that your imprisonment made them safe are losing their grasp of reality. (Baldwin 1998: 294)

American racism is so chronic because it is rooted in a worldview that will not countenance any changes ("to its definitions"). The black population has long symbolized an unchangeable aspect of the white man's system of reality, with a fixed definition within that system. Because any changes to the status of the black population threatens that system of reality itself, the system's stability has depended on the imprisonment of black people. Baldwin's insights into the perniciousness of American racism uncannily echoes the following passage from Plotinus, which is also worth quoting in full:

> How, if there is to be a multiplicity of forms, can one thing be worse unless another is better, or one be better unless another is worse? [...] Those who would eliminate the worse from the universe would eliminate Providence itself. [...]
>
> It is the [cosmic] Reason that in accordance with rationality produces the things that are called evils, since it did not wish all things to be [equally] good. [...] Thus the Reason did not make gods only, but first gods, then spirits, the second nature, and then men, and then animals, in a continuous series—not through envy, but because its rational nature contains an intellectual variety. But we are like men who, knowing little of painting, blame the artist because the colors in his picture are not all beautiful—not seeing that he has given to each part what was appropriate to it. And the cities which have the best governments are not those in which all citizens are equal. Or we are like one who should complain of a tragedy because it includes among its characters, not heroes only, but also slaves and peasants who speak incorrectly. But to eliminate these low characters would be to spoil the beauty of the whole; and it is by means of them that it becomes complete [literally "full"]. (quoted in Lovejoy 1964: 64–65)

As it is within the rational structure of the universe for things to be of different grades of "good"—that is, for there to be a hierarchy of value—things considered to be of lower value must necessarily and eternally stay in their appointed value grade.

The "tragedy" of metaphysical determinism is that, as William James wrote in *The Varieties of Religious Experience*, a monistic view, with its foundations in God, the Absolute, or the Good, runs into paradox when it has to explain why evil exists. The worst parts must be *essential* parts of the whole unit, for otherwise the whole would vanish or it would not be what it was meant to be (James 1985: 132). Since the world is completely rational and metaphysically determined, the perceived imperfections within it *necessarily* exist. Those who would change these imperfections would be bringing chaos to the world and thus challenging the perfect design of providence. Thus did European colonialism, imbued with the medieval presumption that the Aristotelian natural slave (barbarian) existed, parse the non-European as this very natural slave, and thus rightfully to be subordinated by Europe.

The solution to the tragedy of metaphysical determinism, whereby the empirical world is forced with great violence to conform to an unempirical ideal, is to do away with this system. "The only *obvious* escape from [the] paradox" of the necessary existence of evil in a beneficent world, William James notes, "is to cut loose from the monistic assumption altogether, and to allow the world to have existed from its origin in pluralistic form" (James 1985: 132). James's sentiment about the inhumanity of metaphysical absolutism was powerfully echoed by James Baldwin in a speech entitled "The American Dream and the American Negro," which he delivered at the Cambridge Union in 1965. There is scarcely any hope for the American dream, Baldwin argued, unless the American identity reconciles itself to its multiracial background and society. "What one begs the American people to do, for all our sakes, is simply to accept our history." If they do not, he warned, "the people that are denied participation in it [the American dream], by their very presence, will wreck it" (Baldwin 1998: 718–19).

If one's ideology is radically out of sync with empirical reality, then the very existence of empirical reality is a threat to that ideology. Conversely, clinging to an ideology that is radically out of sync with empirical reality amounts to oppression of that reality. In the case of the GCB, the empirical reality is that the world is not rationally determined. The world is characterized by emergent novelty, change, contingency, and diversity. Unless we are able to accept this fact, the very presence of unforeseen novelty is a threat to our sense of reality. The inability to accept the differences, change, and novelty of the world would thus predispose people in detrimental ways. It would involve an epistemic violence (the predisposition towards seeing the world as a threat). Since our perception of the world would reflexively be shaped by these attitudes, it would be natural, then, to reflexively engage in physical violence towards that perceived differ-ence. Our inability to accept the differences, change, and novelty of the world will simultaneously entail that we impose an ideology that does violence, both epistemic and physical, to the empirical particulars of the world in order to perpetuate the validity of its metaphysically deterministic worldview. But metaphysical determinism is epistemologically mistaken and morally per-ilous in its parsing of difference as transgressional. Difference should instead be understood as enriching.

A Threat to Order: The Racial Other as Matter Out of Place

In a sentiment similar to Baldwin's about the irrationality of unempirical ide-ologies, Lovejoy writes in the conclusion to *The Great Chain of Being* that the GCB was doomed to fail, since it tried to fit the empirical fact of our changing world into a system of eternal and necessary truths, which required a static and constant world. The concept of race as the biological manifestation of the GCB likewise tried to find an eternal fact about different human beings that would conclusively determine what the different races were and would become. To wish for this kind of intellectual security is understandable, but it is also cowardice in the face of the human condition. What Lovejoy is saying in philosophical terms is echoed by James Baldwin when he observes that Americans' fear of their private selves is what "makes them so baffling, so moving, so exasperating, and so untrustworthy" (Baldwin 1998: 385). It is the fear of mortality—"a terror of human life" (386)—that drove Americans to invent a racial other to symbolize and scapegoat what they did not wish to face about their human condition: the fact that it is *not* eternal and unchanging.

In *Melville and the Idea of Blackness: Race and Imperialism in Nineteenth-Century America*, the literary scholar Christopher Freeburg shares Baldwin's insight that the ferocity of American racism is due to the white subject's own sense of existential frailty. In Herman Melville's novels, Freeburg contends, the white characters see in blackness their own "failed attempts to control themselves, others, nature, and the course of history" (Freeburg 2012: xi). Blackness signifies the inevitability of human mortality, the "unpredictable violence of nature," and "one's unavoidable susceptibility to the whims of other," and is thus correlated with the human desire to seize one's destiny by amassing scientific or spiritual knowledge and so becoming master of one's fate (4). Similarly, for the historian Richard Drinnon, American "Indian-hating" is rooted in the ascetic, Puritan "white metaphysics" of repression, which makes binary oppositions—"subjective/objective, imagination/understanding, reason/passion, spirit/flesh, and not least, civilization/savagery"—out of what is in fact the "relatedness of everything." For Drinnon, this repression is rooted in the fear of "our own inescapable mortality" (Drinnon 1997: xviii). Out of this repressive complex "arose the generic *native*, that despised, earthy, animalic, suppressed, 'shadow self' projected by the Western mind" (xxvii). Drinnon sees the European's virulent loathing of natives as a projection of their self-loathing over being subject to the human condition, to the fact that we are ultimately corporeal beings (xxiii). "In short, Native Americans were to Puritans and their descendants unwelcome mementos of their own mortality" (463).

Summarizing Lovejoy, Baldwin, Freeburg, and Drinnon, we can say that the psychological motivation underlying an obsession with a thoroughly rational, metaphysically determined universe is a fear of the contingent nature of the human condition itself, that is, the fact of our embodied nature and the attendant inevitability of change and mortality. What makes white Americans, in Baldwin's words, so "untrustworthy" is the irrationality of people who wish for a rationality that excludes all change and contingency at all costs. As Love-joy writes, to wish for the kind of rationality that is "conceived as complete, as excluding all arbitrariness, becomes itself a kind of irrationality" (Lovejoy 1964: 331). The GCB's obsession with eliminating all irrationality is compara-ble to an obsession with eliminating any speck of dirt. Which is to say, the GCB's obsession with rationality is akin to an obsession with purity. Thus, Mary Douglas's anthropological work on the perception of dirt can help us better understand the psychology that motivates the GCB.

In her classic *Purity and Danger*, Douglas, following William James, speaks of dirt as signifying disorder and points out that dirt is a subjective classifica-tion of "matter out of place" (Douglas 2001: 165; James 1985: 133). Our elimi-nation of this antithesis of order is thus a positive act that creates coherence in our environment and experience (2). Our perception of dirt and our anx-ious need to eliminate it are rooted in the desire to dominate our environ-ment and make it conform to our ideals. Our reaction of disgust, loathing, or fear of what we perceive as dirt is akin to "reactions to ambiguity or anomaly" and arises from our desire for order, being, and form, as well as from our desire to avoid disorder, nonbeing, and formlessness (5). Applying both Douglas's diagnosis of our fear of dirt and Baldwin's account of why racial hatred is so chronic in the United States, we can say that the racial other is (psychologically perceived as) the dirt and pollution that signify disorder, nonbeing, formlessness, and death.

It is thus no coincidence that etymologically "race" has affinities with the term *ratio*, in the sense of referring to "the order of things" (Pagden 2015: 98). The social categories of race provide a means of ordering the world. The racial other, perceived as dirt, disrupts the ideal vision of order that white metaphys-ics wishes to impose on the world and represents that "ambiguity or anomaly" that disrupts the illusion of an eternal and unchanging order. Douglas observes that the "recognition of anomaly leads to anxiety and then suppression or avoidance" (Douglas 2001: 5). As dirt, the racial other threatens the possibility of order and therefore needs to be controlled by being restricted to a particular place, subordinated, or eliminated.

As Douglas observes, the desire to safeguard purity, the association of dirt with disorder, and the habit of reordering the environment through the elimi-nation of dirt are perhaps universal traits. What is *not* universal, however, is the association of the racial other with dirt, for what constitutes dirt is a matter of subjective judgment. It is a "guilty and constricted white imagination"

(Baldwin 1998: 386) that associates the racial other with dirt, which must be eliminated or subordinated in order to safeguard purity and order. Although Douglas was writing about "primitive" cultures, what she says in the following about a culture's avoidance of contagion aptly describes Western societies' obsessive perception of the racial other as dirt:

> It may seem that in a culture which is richly organised by ideas of contagion and purification the individual is in the grip of iron-hard categories of thought which are heavily safeguarded by rules of avoidance and by punishments. It may seem impossible for such a person to shake his own thought free of the protected habit-grooves of his culture. (Douglas 2001: 5)

The "habit-grooves" of Western culture's "iron-hard categories of thought" dictate that the "racial other" as dirt be avoided. The tragedy of what Baldwin calls the "constricted white imagination" is that, once formed, it seems "impossible for such a person to shake his own thought" of the identification of the racial other with dirt, and so he remains obligated to ritually sacrifice (either through elimination or subordination) the racial other so as to preserve the purity of his own conception of order.

One of the outcomes of this identification of the racial other as dirt, in the words of the legal scholar Robert Williams, is that the Amerindian is "pushed to the brink of extinction by the premises inherent in the West's vision of the world and the Indian's lack of place in that world" (Williams 1990: 328). Western metaphysics' system of reality could not make room for the Amerindian. Likewise, in her account of Theodor de Bry's voyages to the "New World," Bernadette Bucher references Mary Douglas's *Purity and Danger* in noting that

> beings and things that participate in two or more categories as fixed by a given culture appear ambiguous and monstrous for that reason, and become instantly burdened with interdictions, horror and disgust. [...] At first, the Amerindian, by his very existence on a previously unknown continent and the mystery surrounding his origins, introduced chaos into the order of things such as the European imagined it in their own cosmogony, moral code, and ideas on the origin of man. (Bucher 1981: 142–44)

It is a particular configuration of a person's habit of thought, or system of reality, or ideology that identifies the racial other as a threat to order. The extreme form of racism found in the Western tradition ultimately is attributable to the "iron-hard categories of thought" of a "constricted white imagination" that perceives the racial other as the dirt that destabilizes order.

Although the psychological human desire for ordering the world and distaste for disorder are innate and universal, their manifestation in the ideology of the GCB, with its related need to dominate or eliminate the racial other, which it identified with dirt, was a culturally contingent phenomenon. That ideology, though based on universal human affects, contributed to the egregiousness of Western racism.

Conclusion

In this chapter, we have seen that Western philosophy traditionally dealt with difference and diversity by appealing to a metaphysically determined, ontological hierarchy with a predetermined position for each thing. Under Aristotle's theory of natural slavery, for example, the slave was ontologically determined to fulfill a role as a slave. This paradigm for hierarchizing difference was temporalized during the era of European colonialism, so that the different peoples and practices encountered were understood by the Europeans as lower in the evolutionary chain of civilization. This metaphysical determinism and ontological hierarchy had two important outcomes. First, Europeans were able to ontologically justify the domination of difference, since they believed that natural law required that those higher in the hierarchy dominate those lower in the hierarchy. This view gave way to the idea that there are just wars. Second, metaphysical determinism justifies violently forcing novelty to fit a preconceived picture of the world.

Mary Douglas's observations on humans' psychological responses to dirt elucidate the psychology that motivates the GCB: the racial other, being perceived as dirt, is a threat to the fully rational order represented by the GCB. Her observations also helps to explain the visceral aversion toward the racial other manifested by the singularly egregious phenomenon of Western racism.

As we will see in the next two chapters, inherent in the Western ordering of the universe is a violent domination that is ontologically parsed. Because of this framework, the Western tradition is predisposed towards seeing violent domination in efficacious, virtuous terms. The Chinese tradition, not being based on such a metaphysics, has a very different understanding of efficacy and virtue. In the next chapter, we will explore the differing accounts of efficacy of these two traditions.

5

The Metaphysics of Harmony and the Metaphysics of Colonialism

IN CONTRAST to the metaphysical determinism of the Western tradition, a key characteristic of Chinese metaphysics is the assumption that all things are *ziran* (*sponte sua*): all things are self-causing and so already have form. Chinese metaphysics does not assume the dualism of form and matter.

Since all things are *sponte sua* and the myriad things of the world form an interdependent continuum, it is senseless to talk about a hierarchy of perfection. The philosophical assumption that all things are *ziran* precludes any idea of a "great chain of being." This absence of a metaphysics of dualism and hierarchy, as will be seen in this chapter, explains why China, despite consistently being one of the most powerful states throughout human history, with more than ample resources to have been a great maritime empire builder, never demonstrated the colonizing tendencies of the West. Put positively, Chinese history includes no colonizing missions because of a foundational characteristic of Chinese philosophy, namely, a metaphysics of "harmony."

Colonialism, as Edward Said reminds us in *Orientalism*, is not simply the political and physical domination of one group of peoples by another. "To say simply that Orientalism was a rationalization of colonial rule," he wrote, "is to ignore the extent to which colonial rule was justified in advance by orientalism, rather than after the fact" (Said 2003: 39). Colonialism was an ideology before it was a practice. The material practice of colonial conquest was shaped, if not motivated, by colonial ideology. Likewise, Said writes in *Culture and Imperialism*, "neither imperialism nor colonialism is a simple act of accumulation and acquisition. Both are supported and perhaps even impelled by impressive ideological formations." The intellectual underpinnings of colonialism preceded its material practice, as "the enterprise of empire depends upon the *idea of having an empire*." It is this idea of empire that allows otherwise "decent people" to "think of the *imperium* as a protracted, almost metaphysical obligation" (Said 1994: 8, 10). European colonialism cannot be understood as an epiphenomenon of a stable and universal human nature; the activities that define European colonialism were shaped by a particular culture and its philosophical assumptions.

That European colonialism is ideological in nature can be seen from the fact that before the Portuguese or Spanish knew anything about the newly discovered continent, they were already thinking about how to dominate it. In his study *The Ottoman Age of Exploration*, Giancarlo Casale reminds us that when the Europeans embarked on their voyages of discovery in the first half of the fifteenth century, Muslim merchants were already traveling unobstructed from Morocco to Southeast Asia. The western Europe of this era existed, both physically and intellectually, in "relative isolation" (Casale 2010: 5). Despite its isolation, and even before any European power controlled "one square inch of territory (or even a single ship) anywhere in Asia or the New World," Europeans were already laying claim to the entire extra-European world. For example, under the famous Treaty of Tordesilla (1494), Portugal and Spain "agreed to nothing less than a partition of the entire extra-European world, with each side claiming the right to conquer and rule all lands within its own hemisphere and to maintain exclusive control over its navigation and maritime trade" (5). This treaty exemplifies the strength of the European ideology of world domination. From the very start of the "Age of Discovery," Portugal or Spain assumed that control or domination would characterize the operative relationship between Europe and the yet-to-be-encountered other peoples and their lands.

This chapter takes up Edward Said's point that colonialism is impelled by ideology. Because any understanding of colonialism is incomplete without an analysis of the ideology of colonialism, this chapter attempts to formulate the nature of this ideology by describing the "metaphysics of colonialism" and its conception of efficacy, which follows the Platonic paradigm of the genesis of the images of forms (*Timaeus* 49a1–4, 52a8, d2–4). Here the material substrate (*chora*) is without character, and so causal efficacy for the generation of things lies with the forms. This conception of efficacy can be seen in its enactment in the European conquest of the "New World," which, both in practice and in later recountings was perceived as a vacant *terra nullius* onto which was printed the form of Western civilization. The same ideal of efficacy as imposing an ideal form onto passive matter can be seen in Carl Phillip Gottfried von Clausewitz's *On War*.

Two Accounts of Efficacy: Colonialism and Harmony

This chapter will bring into relief the metaphysics of colonialism through its juxtaposition with the Chinese historical experience and argue that the Chinese tradition had no conception of colonialism because of how its metaphysics shaped the Chinese understanding of efficacy, agency, and power. That is, its metaphysics, which we shall designate as a metaphysics of "harmony," had no place for a Western-style colonizing tendency.

Under a metaphysics of harmony, causal efficacy involves the capacity to recognize the particularity of things, from which follows the capacity to create insightful relationships that allow the participants to mutually enhance and complement each other, thus realizing "harmony." The Chinese conception of harmony is of a universal enriched and deepened by all of the coexisting particulars. This conception of harmony can be understood through the idea of equilibrium (中) or the maintenance of equilibrium in a timely fashion (时中) of the *Doctrine of the Mean*. Under this conception, the sage is the one who has the capacity to bring coherence to all particulars. They can achieve this because they have cultivated a sensitivity to the incipient order of things. They can thus creatively transform situations because they bring the different aspects into relationships that are mutually responsive. Like the conductor who can maximize the individual musical effects of the different sections of an orchestra, the sage is one who can maximize the individual effects of all particulars.

This chapter focuses on the divergent Chinese and Western understandings of efficacy through their respective understandings of war. The violent imposition of one agent's will onto another, war is the most oppressive form of interaction between different social and political groups, and the last resort when all other forms of engagement have fallen short. The best-known Western contribution to the theory of warfare is Carl Philipp Gottfried von Clausewitz's (1780–1831) treatise *On War*. In the Chinese case, we have Sunzi's *The Art of War*.

The first two sections establish that historically the Chinese had the material, technological, and economic wherewithal to wage colonizing campaigns in a manner comparable to the West's "Age of Discovery." Further, throughout history the Chinese tradition had developed a great deal of knowledge about other peoples and cultures. No lack of resources, competence, or knowledge explained Chinese disinterest in colonizing other peoples and places, nor did the absence of a colonizing tendency stem from any ignorant belief that China was the full extent of "all under heaven." Instead, the Chinese diverged from the West in this cultural behavior because of the divergence in their philosophical outlook.

A Maritime Power

A (racist) fallacy habitually made by Western audiences is the assumption that the Chinese failed to colonize the earth in the Western mode because it lacked the wherewithal. As Frederick Mote writes, "An enduring misconception of Chinese history must be scuttled: China has a very long and successful history as a maritime power" (Mote 2003: 717). Sea voyages were commissioned from the time of the Qin and the Three Kingdoms to the Song and Ming dynasties, and the records of these expeditions are still considered epic today (Zheng 2012: 2). As the historian Zheng Yangwen points out, one compelling indication of the extent of China's maritime activities in Southeast Asia is that for generations Southeast Asian historians have conducted research on maritime China (Zheng 2012: 10–11). Indeed, these historians have shown that Chinese diaspora entrepreneurship shaped the modern economies of the region (Sakurai 2004: 35–52). This section provides a brief chronology of the maritime activity of historical China.

From as early as the *Book of Han* we see records of Chinese maritime trade routes to modern-day Vietnam, Malaysia, southeast India, and Sri Lanka, among others. The *Book of Han* mentions a region called Yue, which stretches from modern-day Guangdong and Guangxi provinces to central Vietnam. The region is recorded as "close to the sea and it has buffalos, elephants, tortoiseshells, pearl, silver, copper, fruits, cloth. Many of those who go there to trade became rich and Fanyu [番禺] is one of its big cities" ("Treatise on Geography II" [地理志下], *Book of Han*; Ban 1962: 1670). In what historians take to be the earliest official account of the Han's maritime trade (Zheng 2012: 21; Gernet 1982: 127), the "Treatise on Geography II" of the *Book of Han*, we read:

> From the barriers of Rinan [日南, central Vietnam], Xuwen [徐聞, Guangdong], Hepu [合浦, Guangxi], you can sail and reach the country of Duyuan [都元] in five months, the country of Yilumei [邑盧没] after another four months, the country of Shenli [諶离] after twenty or so days, and the country of Fugandulu [夫甘都卢, Myanmar] after more than ten days of walking.

From here, you can sail for another two months to reach the country of Huangzhi [黄支, Kanchipuram, southeast India].

The customs in this country bear resemblance to these in Zhuya [珠矼, Hainan Island]. This is a big country with many people and many exotic things. They have paid tribute since Wudi's time (141–87 BCE).

There are translators, they belong to the imperial household, and together with those who were recruited they went to the seas to trade pearls, glass wares, precious stones and exotic things with gold and silks. . . .

The big pearls can be as wide as two inches in circumference. At the time of Pingdi when Wang Mang (AD 9–23) was running the court, he asked the King of Huangzhi for live rhino as tribute. From here, you can sail for eight months to reach the country of Pizong [皮宗, Pulau Pisang], the place of Rinan, Xianglinjie [象林界云] after another two months. To the south of Huangzhi lies the country of Yichengbu [已程不, Sri Lanka] from where the Han's translator envoy returned. (Ban 1962: 1671; quoted in Zheng 2012: 20–21, modified)

Yü Ying-Shi believes that this passage is "maybe the earliest reference in Chinese literature to Malaysia" (Yü 1986: 453).

During the Three Kingdoms period (220–280 CE), the kingdom of Wu sent missions to modern-day Taiwan, Hainan Islands, Funan (today's Cambodia and the Mekong Delta), and the Hindu kingdom of Champa (today's central and southern Vietnam) (Zheng 2012: 23–24). The Indian historian R. C. Majumdar writes that Chinese interest in these regions was defensive, as "the dismemberment of the Chinese empire into three parts (220–265) emboldened them [the Champa] to cross the frontier and carry their raids far into the Chinese territory" (Majumdar 1985: 22). According to the *Records of the Three Kingdoms* (*San Guo Zhi*, 三国志), the Wu kingdom traded with Japan, Korea, and many small principalities in and around the Malay Peninsula (Zheng 2012: 25). After the return of the first Chinese monk to travel to India, Fa Xian (法显) (ca. 337 CE–ca. 422 CE), he described in great detail the countries and places he visited, which included Khotan, Gandhara, Gaya, and Ceylon. Fa Xian's records of his journey tell us that there were ships with the capacity to carry two hundred or so merchant passengers between Ceylon, Java, and Canton, and that such journeys were frequently undertaken. The distances traveled by these ships also suggest the availability of technology that made these frequent trips possible (27–29).

During the Northern and Southern dynasties (420–588 CE), the Song, Qi, Liang, and Chen courts encouraged maritime trade with the region spanning the Philippines, the Straits of Malacca, Sri Lanka, India and West Asia, Japan, and Korea (Zheng 2012: 29). With the increase in trade, as many as fifty thousand foreigners lived in Luoyang at this time (Zheng 2012: 30). The Tang regime so welcomed foreigners to do business in China that Emperor Xuanzong (ruled 712–756 CE) even established a "maritime trade bureau" (市舶司) (32). By the middle of the ninth century, peoples from the Middle East regularly sailed to China (Hourani 1995: 66). The historian Oliver Impey gives an impression of the extent and reach of Tang maritime trade:

> By the year 800, huge quantities of Tang pottery, mostly bowls with painted decoration in brown or green, and green or black glazed jars were being imported into the Persian Gulf for distribution throughout the Near East, attesting to the large volume of the sea-borne traffic (Impey 1977: 21).

The Song continued to reach out to the maritime world, cultivating good relationships with dominant maritime powers in Southeast Asia, such as the kingdom of Shrivijaya in modern-day Indonesia. Technological advances brought about by the use of the compass and the stern-post rudder made it possible for Chinese vessels in this period to carry exports as far as the coast of Africa (Xu 2003: 10). *The History of the Various Foreign Countries* (*Zhu Fan Zhi*, 诸番志)[1] records that the Song established trade relations with more than fifty countries. Like many previous dynasties, the Song solicited foreign trade, and even rewarded foreign traders when they came to China (Zheng 2012: 38). The extent of Song trading activity can be seen in the Song's institutionalization of foreign trade management and publication of the legislation "Guangzhou Maritime Trade Regulation" (广州市舶条列) in 1080, which outlined rules for foreign trade, custom control, and punishment. So lucrative was the taxation on foreign trade that 20 percent of the Song's revenue, it has been suggested, came from this source (39). Testifying to the pervasiveness of contact with neighboring states[2] is the publication of two scholarly works on southern China and Southeast Asia during this time: *Impressions from South of the Five Ridges* (*Ling Wai Dai Da*, 岭外代答) and *History of Foreign Places* (*Yi Yu Zhi*, 异域志) (42).

For around four and a half centuries, from the consolidation of the Song dynasty until the seafaring expeditions (1405–1433) of Zheng He (1371–1433, an assimilated Muslim), China had the greatest navy in the world (Gernet

1982: 326–29; Fairbank and Goldman 2006: 93). Zheng He's fleet set sail at the behest of the Chinese emperor to Southeast Asia, South Asia, West Asia, and East Africa, reaching Java, India, the Strait of Hormuz and the Horn of Africa.[3] His fleet was vastly bigger and technologically more advanced than Columbus's armada, the *Niña*, *Pinta*, and *Santa Maria*. At the time of Zheng's voyages, the European "Age of Discovery" had not yet even begun. In 1418, eighty years before Vasco de Gama rounded the Cape of Good Hope, Zheng He had already reached Malindi near present-day Mombasa (Kenya). No less a personage than Henry Kissinger has written, "China's fleet possessed what would have seemed an unbridgeable technological advantage: in the size, sophistication, and number of its vessels, it dwarfed the Spanish Armada (which was still 150 years away)" (Kissinger 2011: 9). The Chinese fleet had some one hundred ships, the largest of which measured 120 meters, with crews totaling up to twenty-eight thousand sailors and soldiers. It was an armada that was not to be surpassed until the invasion fleets of World War I. When Vasco da Gama landed in East Africa in 1498, he and his crew encountered natives who wore embroidered green silk caps with fine fringes. The Africans scoffed at the trinkets the Portuguese offered and were underwhelmed by their small ships. Village elders told tales of white ghosts who wore silk and had visited long ago in large ships (Levathes 1994: 19–21).

A dominant folk assumption, inherited from the Greeks, is that the capacity for *techne* displays one's humanity, and that Europe, unlike other more primitive nations, had this technological capacity (Pagden 1982: 72–75). Contrary to this widely held opinion in the West, however, colonialism does not necessarily follow from technological know-how. Zheng He's voyages show that the China of the fifteenth century had not only the technology but also the organizational capacity and wealth to become "a great maritime empire builder." Had they so wished, the Chinese could have tried "to expand by force the territories ruled by the Chinese state." One hundred and fifty years before the beginning of the "Age of Discovery," they "could have pre-empted the Europeans in that regard had they wished to do so" (Mote 2003: 616). As Louise Levathes writes,

> Half the world was in China's grasp, and with such a formidable navy the other half was easily within reach, had China wanted it. China could have become the great colonial power, a hundred years before the great age of European exploration and expansion. But China did not. (Levathes 1994: 20)

Although the Chinese at certain points had the material means to embark on a colonial campaign of world domination, this potential never became actuality because they "had no conception of a Chinese maritime empire created by the powerful instrument of their naval strength" (Mote 2003: 616). As Chinese maritime history shows, technological superiority does not necessitate domination of those who are technologically inferior. The historian Felipe Fernández-Armesto voices a representative opinion on China's important divergence in this regard from the path taken by the West: "China's 'manifest destiny' never happened and the world predominance, which, for a time, seemed hers for the taking, was abandoned. [. . .] [China's] forbearance remains one of the most remarkable instances of collective reticence in [world] history" (Fernández-Armesto 1996: 129, 134).

The remainder of this chapter proposes that one reason for this forbearance was the lack of certain metaphysical assumptions in the Chinese tradition that would have predisposed the Chinese to see the project of overwhelming the earth as efficacious or virtuous. It would have been neither relevant nor possible within their imaginative horizon. A particular metaphysics is needed if one is to think that dominating the earth is a relevant pursuit. Before we get to the philosophical argument, we need to address and dispel another common and mistaken reason given for the absence of a colonizing campaign in China's history: that China did not know of the existence of other lands and peoples.

Knowledge of Non-Chinese Peoples

An awareness of peoples who did not belong to the "Chinese" sphere can be seen from the earliest examples of Chinese writing. "Barbarians" figure prominently in Shang 1600 BCE–1046 BCE oracle inscriptions, the earliest known form of Chinese writing (Creel 1970: 194). The term *wai guo* (外国; foreign countries) has a long history that goes back to the Han (Yang 1968: 21). The idea that the Chinese, in some primitivist delusion, thought that "all under heaven" literally referred to the geographic space of their central states does not stand scrutiny.[4]

Sima Qian's *Shiji*,[5] the *Book of Han*,[6] and the *Book of the Later Han*[7] all contained detailed accounts of many of China's neighbors during the Han dynasty. The "Biographies of the City-States of the Western Territories" (西域传) of the *Book of Later Han* even mentions Tiao Zhi (条支), which probably refers to Babylonia and is in present-day Iraq (Sima 2010: 7275n2).[8] Many interesting historical encounters between the Han and its neighbors can be seen in these records. In the "Biography of Dayuan" (大宛列传) of the *Shiji*, we read that Zhang Qian, a Chinese official and diplomat who served as an imperial envoy to the regions west of China (died ca. 114 BCE), is said to have described

for the Han court and emperor the following: Dayuan (大宛),which designates the descendants of Alexander the Great's army who lived in the Fergana
Valley, Uzbekistan (see Christopoulos 2012: 35); Kangju (康居), an area covering
contemporary Pakistan, Azerbaijan, Uzbekistan, and southern Kazakhstan;
Dayueshi (大月氏), in contemporary Afghanistan; and Daxia (大夏), near
contemporary Kashmir. He also related what he had heard about Wusun (乌孙),
in contemporary Kyrgyzstan (Sima 2010: 7278n5), and Anxi (安息), or "Parthia," in contemporary Iran (7282n3), Tiaozhi in contemporary Iraq (7284n5),
and Yuandu (身毒), in contemporary India or Pakistan (7286n5). In the *Book
of the Later Han*, we read that in 97 CE the king of the country of Shan (掸
国, in contemporary Myanmar), who was named Yong Youdiao (雍由调),
sent treasures to the Chinese emperor and was given seals and money by the
Chinese emperor in return. Yong Youdiao was later invested as a tributary
prince (大都尉) of the Chinese empire (Fan 1965: 2851). In sum, from at least
the Han dynasty the Chinese had an understanding of the geography and
peoples of Asia.

Also from at least the Han dynasty, the Chinese knew about the existence of
Eurasia. Both the *Book of Han* (Ban 1962: 3890) and the *Shiji* (Sima 2010: 7309)
record the Chinese emissaries to Parthia being greeted by twenty thousand on
horseback at the behest of the Parthian king. The *Shiji* further records that after
the Chinese emissaries had returned home, a Parthian emissary was sent to the
Han to see the extent and greatness of its empire. The *Shiji* also contains the famous story of Emperor Wu's desire to acquire the "heavenly horses" (天马) of
the Dayuan people (Sima 2010: 7301, 7314). In the archive of a Han dynasty
garrison at Xuanquan discovered in 1987 is a record of a Sogdian diplomatic
mission to China in 52 BCE comprising two envoys, ten aristocrats and their
entourage, and nine horses, thirty-one donkeys, twenty-five camels, and a cow
(Graf 2018: 466). As Valerie Hansen writes, the Xuanquan documents show that
the rulers of these places participated in "systematized exchange of diplomatic
envoys with the Chinese emperor of the Han dynasty" (Hansen 2012: 17–18).
In the *Book of Han*, it is recorded that the Han had communications with the
state of Jibin (罽宾) in northwest India (Ban 1962: 3885–86; Hulsewé and
Loewe 1979: 107–8).[9] David Graf provides a helpful summary of Chinese relations with the peoples of the Northwest who came along the Silk Road:

> During the reign of Emperor Wudi (140–87 BC), diplomatic missions to
> the Western Regions exposed the Chinese to the wealth of the Central Asia
> states. Substantial gifts to the Sogdians, Scythians, Bactrians, Indians, and
> Parthians precipitated commercial exchanges. (Graf 2018: 506)

As Valerie Hansen writes, China's major trading partner from the Silk Road was Samarkand, on the edge of the Iranian world (Hansen 2012: 3).[10]

The most interesting part of Han dynasty encounters with the places beyond its borders is Han China's knowledge of the existence of the Roman empire. According to the *Book of Later Han*, the Roman empire (Daqin) was called the "Great Qin" because its people and civilization were comparable to China's (Fan 1965: 2919; Yu 2013: 69). Similarly, the *Records of the Three Kingdoms* (三国志) explains that the term *Daqin* was used because the people of this state were tall and honest, their manner comparable to that of the Chinese, although they wore *hu* (Western) clothing. It even says that the peoples of the Daqin say that they themselves were originally from China (Chen 1982: 860–61; Yu 2013: 92). In the *Book of Later Han*, it is mentioned that in 166 CE, Andun (安敦)—who may have been Marcus Aurelius Antoninus (r. 161–180 CE)—sent emissaries with gifts to the Han court (Fan 1965: 2920; Yü 1986: 461; Graf 2018: 478; Hirth 1885: 175). The *Book of Later Han* also provides a geographic account of Daqin, say that they themselves its cities, foliage, cultural customs, political institutions, natural produce, and foreign relations with other countries (Fan 1965: 2919–20; Yu 2013: 67–73).[11] The *Records of the Three Kingdoms* describes the feudatory (vassal) petty kingdoms of Daqin.[12] The *Book of Former Tang* (written in the mid-tenth century CE about the period 618–906 CE) describes Byzantium (Fulin, 拂菻) in great detail.[13] One passage describes the Sui empire's relationship with Byzantium:

The emperor Yang of the Sui dynasty [604–618 CE] always wished to open intercourse with Fulin [拂菻], but did not succeed. In the 17th year of the period Zhen Guan [贞观, 643 CE], the king of Fulin, Bo Duo Li [波多力, Constans II Pogonatus, emperor 641–668 CE], sent an embassy offering red glass, *lü Jinjing* [绿金精, green gold gems], and other articles. Taizong [太宗, then the ruling emperor] favored them with a message under his imperial seal and graciously granted presents of silk. Since the Dasi [大食, the Arabs] had conquered these countries, they sent their commander-in-chief, Moyi [摩栧, Mo'awiya], to besiege their capital city; by means of an agreement they obtained friendly relations and asked to be allowed to pay every year tribute of gold and silk; in the sequel they became subject to Dasi [大食]. In the second year of the period Qian Feng [乾封, 667 CE] they sent an embassy offering *Di Ye Jia* [底也伽]. In the first year of the period Da Zu [大足, 701 CE] they again sent an embassy to our court. In the first month of the seventh year of the period Kai Yuan [开元, 719 CE] their lord sent the *Da Shou Ling* [大首领, an officer of high rank] of Tu Hu Luo [吐火罗, Tokharestan] to offer lions and *ling-yang* [羚羊, antelopes], two of each. A few months after, he further sent *Da De Seng* [大德僧, priests of great virtue] to our court with tribute. (Liu 1975: 5314–15; Hirth 1885: 55–56, my modifications)[14]

The *History of the Song* (宋史, written in the late thirteenth century CE about the period 960–1279 CE) describes a tribute in 1081 CE to China by the Caesar of Byzantium (presumably Michael VII Doukas), as well as the customs of Byzantium and its penal codes (Tuo 1985: 14125; Hirth 1885:).[15] China remained knowledgeable about the non-Chinese world throughout the imperial era such that, by the Song dynasty, "accounts of foreign countries" (外国列传) emerged as a standard category in historical writings (Yang 1968: 21).[16]

Relative to the medieval European tradition of the time (when Columbus "discovered" the American continent), the Chinese tradition of the same period had a more empirical understanding of human difference. The image of the world from which Columbus and his navigators were operating was not that different from the prevailing image of Herodotus's day of the world as a single landmass divided into three continents: Europe, Africa, and Asia (Pagden 2015: 153–54). As we see through his writings, Columbus's frame of reference for what to expect beyond the shores of Europe included Pliny's (23–79 CE) *Natural History*; *The Travels of Sir John Mandeville*, the most popular prose work of the Middle Ages (Stannard 1992: 197); and one of the most important geographical works of the late Middle Ages, Pierre d'Ailly's *Imago Mundi* (*Image of the World*), which was written in 1410 (197).[17] All these works gave fantastical accounts of grotesque races in faraway lands. Pierre d'Ailly's *Imago Mundi* talked of "savage men who eat human flesh and have depraved and frightening faces" and are so "dreadful in aspect, that one can tell only with difficulty whether they are men or beasts" (quoted in Lauren 2018: 10). *The Travels of Sir John Mandeville* details the monstrous races of the East and describes the dog-headed human Cynocephaly and men with one eye.[18]

Given this world-picture, it is unsurprising that Columbus wrote in his journal on April 11, 1492, as he was sailing to the Indies, that he expected to find "men with one eye, and others with dogs' heads" (quoted in Todorov 1984: 15). In a letter of February–March 1493, he wrote, "There remain to the westward two provinces where I have not been, one of which they call Avan, and there the people are born with tails" (quoted in Todorov 1984: 16). Nevertheless, in his letter to the Spanish king and queen while returning from his first voyage, Columbus had to admit that "in these islands I have so far found no human monstrosities, as many expected" (quoted in Stannard 1992: 197).

Europeans had an "obsession" with cannibalism, though modern scholarship has failed to find any real evidence of it.[19] Not surprisingly then, as soon as Columbus entered unknown water in 1492 he started inquiring about the existence of cannibals (Pagden 1982: 81). It bears stressing that Columbus's views were by no means unusual for his time (Stannard 1992: 199; Todorov 1984: 15).

Since its earliest records and throughout its imperial history, China knew that peoples radically different from itself existed, and that they populated radically different regions. It also had the material wherewithal to dominate these known peoples and places. In what follows, I argue that China did not manifest the behaviors seen in European colonialism because it lacked an ideology of colonialism, which is described in the next section.

The Ideology of Colonialism

Colonial discourse describes the relationship between the (European) colonizer, the (non-European) colonized, and the colonized land as follows: Prior to European colonization, the colonized land was a vacant *terra nullius* that was stagnating in the "eternal return" of Mircea Eliade's primitive man. The entry of the European man into this yet-to-be colonized land pushed these lands into the league of civilization. The American continent, for example, in the mind of its "discoverers" and in later academic accounts, was "merely recognize[d] as a material or potency upon which Europe could invent its own *image and likeness*," in the words of the Latin American philosopher Enrique Dussel (Dussel 1995: 34, emphasis added). The Americas were merely docile matter that awaited the imprint of the European form of civilization.

Relatedly, as the historian of South Africa Leonard Thompson tells us, a "myth" that is deeply embedded in the historical consciousness of white South Africans is that Afrikaners came upon a vacant land (Thompson 1985: 70). An expression of this view can be found in the *South African Digest* of 1982:

> When the whites came to Africa in the 16th century, there were no native blacks in South Africa—only some nomadic tribes, including the Hottentots, who were of Arabic origin. So whose country is it by virtue of original settlers? (quoted in Thompson 1985: 70)

The stories of the founding of the United States often repeat, in mythic fashion, this trope about the vacancy of the land prior to European arrival. In *Of Plymouth Plantation*, William Bradford, leader of Plymouth Colony, which was established by the first Puritans in present-day Massachusetts, talked of the Americas as "unpeopled": "There were only savage and brutish men which range up and down, little otherwise than the wild beasts of the same" (quoted in Drinnon 1997: 49). The same trope of the Americas as an unpeopled waste-land is repeated by Theodore Roosevelt in *The Strenuous Life*:

> Of course our whole national history has been one of expansion. [. . .] That the barbarians recede or are conquered, with the attendant fact that peace follows their retrogression or conquest, is due solely to the power of the mighty civilized races [. . .], and which by their expansion are gradually bringing peace into the red *wastes* where the barbarian peoples of the world hold sway. (Roosevelt 2009: 15, emphasis added)

The truth, of course, is that North America, like South Africa, was peopled before the arrival of the Europeans. The existence of the native American peoples and the taking of their land are well documented. Indeed, the myth of North American vacancy is belied by the historical and legal records of the protracted process of Indian removal and land dispossession.[20] Nevertheless, current scholarship perpetuates this myth of the vacancy of the Americas prior to European arrival. The orthodox narrative today goes something like this: "Prior to the arrival of Europeans," North, South, and Central America, with the exception of the Aztec and Incan civilizations, "generally is seen as a bar-baric wasteland" (Stannard 1992: 12). In contrast to this myth, the historian Francis Jennings provides an eloquent account in which, contrary to the myth, the European settlers "did not settle on a virgin land." Rather,

> they invaded and displaced a resident population. This is so simple a fact that it seems self-evident. All historians of the European colonies in Amer-ica begin by describing the natives' reception of the newcomers. Yet, para-doxically, most of the same historians also repeat identical mythical phrases purporting that the land-starved people of Europe had found magnificent opportunity to pioneer in a savage wilderness and to bring civilization to it. [. . .] The basic conquest myth postulates that America was virgin land, or wilderness, inhabited by nonpeople called savages; [. . .] that their mode of existence and cast of mind were such as to make them incapable of civilization [. . .] that civilization was required by divine sanction [. . .] that civilization and its bearers were refined and ennobled in the contest with the dark powers of the wilderness; and that it was all inevitable. (Jennings 1975: 15)

In a colonizer's description of pre-settlement Australia, we see again this trope of an empty wasteland: "At the time of first settlement in the Australian colonies all lands were deemed to be waste lands and the property of the Crown" (quoted in Mills 1997: 50). As an Australian historian, Russel Ward, wrote in 1961: "Before the Gold Rush there were, after all, few foreigners of any one race in Australia—except for the Aborigines, if we may, sheepishly I hope, call them foreigners after a manner of speaking" (quoted in Mills 1997: 50). For Ward, the "Aborigines" were not quite human; consequently, preconquest Australia was empty of inhabitants. Ubiquitous in all the European settler-colonial accounts of the preconquest land is the myth of the vacant *terra nullius*.

In colonizing discourse, the idea of the vacancy of the yet-to-be colonized land is related to the idea that those few peoples who populate the land are part of nature themselves and so, having no civilization, have no claim to the land. For example, James Bryce (1838–1922), who served variously over his career as an Oxford don, historian, politician, and later ambassador to the United States, speaks of the native races of South Africa in his *Impressions of South Africa* as comparable to wild beasts that merely roam the land:

> Here in South Africa the native races seem to have made no progress for centuries, if, indeed, they have not actually gone backward. [. . .] The elephant and the buffalo are as much masters of the soil as the Kafir [Kaffir], and man has no more right to claim that the land was made for him than have the wild beasts of the forest who roar after their prey and seek their meat from God. (Bryce 2020: 66)

A few more examples will make this point even clearer. George McCall Theal (1837–1919) was the most prolific and influential South African historian of the late nineteenth and early twentieth centuries. For Theal, given the manifest inferiority of Africans (whose minds, he believed, stopped developing around puberty), the only way to explain the existence of the impressive stone buildings in Great Zimbabwe was to attribute them to the hand of "invaders" at some remote point in history whose disappearance was "an unsolved mystery" (quoted in Thompson 1985: 92). Like Theal, Bryce thought that the stone ruins in Zimbabwe were the product of "a more advanced race." "Whoever these people were," he asserted, "they have long since vanished" (Bryce 2020: 82). Arthur de Gobineau's *Essay on the Inequality of Races* epitomizes the assumption that precolonized non-Europeans were incapable of culture. Gobineau resorted to the same logic to explain how a race such as the

Chinese—who, according to his racial logic, were a priori incapable of culture—seemed to exhibit such a rich culture. Given the strength of his a priori principle, Gobineau came to the conclusion that Chinese culture was not the work of the Chinese people: Chinese civilization had in fact been created by a group of Aryan conquerors from India (Gobineau 1915: 212). Under this racial ideology, civilization springs only from contact with the white races (210). Thus, wherever there is evidence of history or culture, we must be on the lookout for the white man.

Charles Mills's outline of the colonizing ideology eloquently describes all of these examples:

> So the basic sequence ran something like this: there are no people there in the first place; in the second place, they're not improving the land; and in the third place—oops!—they're already all dead anyway (and, honestly, there really weren't that many to begin with), so there are no people there, as we said in the first place. (Mills 1997: 50)

Also speaking of the colonizing ideology, Anthony Pagden notes that

> the English accounts of the acquisition of territory in America generally maintained that title had been acquired [. . .] either through purchase or [. . .] by means of the occupation and "improvement" of "vacant lands" or *terra nullius*. [. . .] [The idea of the *terra nullius*] drew heavily on a far earlier assumption that all nature was, in Aristotle's terms, potential and waiting for human agency—human artifice (*techne*)—to make it actual. (Pagden 2015: 16)

In what follows, we will analyze in more detail the metaphysics, originating with the Greeks, that underlies the ideology of colonization.

Colonialism as the Imposition of Form upon Matter

Plato's model of genesis is paralleled by the engendering of new life. The platonic *chora* is designated as a receptacle (*hypodoche*) and a wet-nurse of becoming (*Timaeus* 48e–49a; Plato 1997: 1251). The platonic *chora* is a *passive*[21] receptacle or space (*Timaeus* 52b; Plato 1997: 1255), without character,[22] and it receives all without becoming anything.[23] As such, the *chora* is identified with the mother (*Timaeus* 51a; Plato 1997: 1254). "It is in fact appropriate to compare the receiving thing to a mother, the source to a father" (*Timaeus* 50d;

Plato 1997: 1253). The source of new life is thus the male *form*, and the female *matter* is merely a passive receptacle that contributes no character to the thing's becoming. *Chora* is the space that is neither being (forms) nor becoming (copies), but a kind of interval—a "third type" (*Timaeus* 52a; Plato 1997: 1255)—between them in which things gain their imprints. It exists neither eternally (like forms) nor in time (like the copies). *Chora* is a space between being and becoming. The only characteristic one can attribute to *chora* is the fact of its existence.

Francis MacDonald Cornford described this receptacle as a neutral medium that provides a place for the images or holds them, but that is independent of them, such as a reflecting surface or mirror (Cornford 1997: 177). Peters's *Greek Philosophical Terms* defines *chora* (χώρα) as "land, area, space" and as related to *hyle*, *hypodoche*, and *topos* (Peters 1967: 30). *Hyle* is defined as "material, matter" (88). *Hypodoche* is defined as "receptacle," and according to Plato, it is in this receptacle that *genesis* takes place (*Timaeus* 50b–51b). Aristotle identifies Plato's "receptacle" with matter (*hyle*) (Peters 1967: 91). *Topos* is defined as "place" (197). Plato's interest in *topos*, Peters tells us, is "in the area (*chora*) in which genesis takes place (*Tim.* 52a–c), a role analogous to that played by *hyle* (matter) in Aristotle, hence Aristotle's charge that Plato identified *chora* and *hyle* (*Phys.* IB, 209b)" (197). That *chora* is identified with space (a characterless place), an interim between being and becoming, the female, and matter will be crucial to our analysis of the parallels between the paradigm of Western colonialism and the Platonic conception of genesis.

It is precisely this dualistic paradigm of an ideal form imposed upon matter that we see in the European conquest of the Americas and in later narratives about the "founding" of America in the literature: the Americas were mere characterless, empty matter ready for the imposition of ideal form by the European conquerors. In this conception, the European imagination saw the Americas as a (Cartesian) *space* (as opposed to a *place*) onto which the form of European civilization was to be imprinted. Prior to the arrival of the Europeans, the Americas, like the platonic *chora*, was a pure, featureless expanse. The land found by the Europeans is overwhelmingly described in conventional scholarship as a "virgin land," "a vast emptiness," or even a "void," and of course it is also called a vacant *terra nullius* (Pagden 2015: 16). The Indians are described as "static and passive" features of the landscape, beings with "no towns or villages" who simply "roamed" across the land (Stannard 1992: 12). Histories of the Americas treat the native peoples the same way they treat flora and fauna: "Consigned to the category of miscellaneous information [. . .] they inhabit the realm of 'etc.'" (quoted in Stannard 1992: 14).

Like the "static" *chora*, the Americas, both the land and the peoples, required the imprint of the form of the Europeans before it was possible to be propelled into the realm of becoming—that is, partake in historical time. The Americas, as mere matter was neither being nor becoming, and thus occupied a liminal state before history. There is no conception that the Americas was a *place* constituted of all the particulars of that terrain. It is because the European view of the Americas imbued it with the characteristics of the *chora* that, in the conventional scholarship recounting the European domination of the Americas, the imprinting of European civilization is narrated as having been a peaceful and frictionless process. Since the land is conventionally depicted as empty, the process of its inhabitation would not have met any obstructions. Colonization was thus understood as the frictionless process of imposing form onto matter. In my view, this process is an aspect of what Edward Said has called "the moral epistemology of imperialism," which required that the indigenous peoples be "blott[ed] out from knowledge" (Said 1980: 18, 23). As we saw from Charles Mills's summary, the indigenous peoples are blotted out in two ways: first, by the absence of any acknowledgment that they exist, and second, by the realization, through their extermination, of the very nonexistence always attributed to them. The Western model of order is perfectly suited to this moral epistemology of imperialism, as it dualistically separates order and form from matter and assumes the docility of matter.

The conception of a colonized land as a *chora* can also be seen in the pervasive Western conception of China as a homogeneous entity, landlocked and stagnant before being "discovered" by the West and dragged into "modernity" (historical time). The idea that Chinese civilization is static and therefore prehistorical finds paradigmatic expression in Hegel's *Philosophy of History*: "China and India remain stationary, and perpetuate a natural vegetative existence even to the present time" (Hegel 1956: 173). Teshale Tibebu's characterization of Hegel's India applies equally to Hegel's China: "In Hegel's India, time froze in the cold of permanent hibernation" (Tibebu 2011: 272).

Contrary to this orientalizing stereotype, China was never static, but rather a highly dynamic entity. Like other lands perceived by the West as begging for colonization, China is viewed as a *chora*, and so it exists liminally in an ontological state of not yet becoming, and thus prior to historical time. Only after being imprinted with the form of European civilization can it be brought into historical time. Hegel expresses this paradigmatic view underlying European colonialism in *Philosophy of Subjective Spirit*:

It is in the *Caucasian* race that spirit first reaches absolute unity with itself. It is here that it first enters into complete opposition to naturality, apprehends itself in its absolute independence, disengages from the dispersive vacillation between one extreme and the other, achieves self-determination, self-development, and so brings forth world history. (Hegel 1978: 57, emphasis in original)

Here the Caucasian race, because it is in "complete opposition to naturality" (matter), is the form ("self-determined"). Repeating the same motifs as Hegel's account of the static nature of a non-Caucasian people, Hugh Trevor-Roper, the Regius Professor of Modern History at Oxford University, writes in *The Rise of Christian Europe* of "the unrewarding gyrations of barbarous tribes in picturesque but irrelevant corners of the globe," who are without history:

> Perhaps, in the future, there will be some African history to teach. But at present there is none, or very little: there is only the history of Europeans in Africa. The rest is largely darkness, like the history of Pre-European, pre-Columbian America. And darkness is not a subject for history. (Trevor-Roper 1965: 9)

For Trevor-Roper, as for Hegel, only the Caucasians can be said to belong to history proper. Under Hegel's and Trevor-Roper's view, history begins when the white man imprints his form of civilization on the mere matter of the other races and the environs they inhabit.

The metaphysics of European colonialism is thus premised on a *dualistic* metaphysics whereby nonwhite peoples (and their associated places) are without form. Following this dualistic paradigm, the Greek worldview presents law as one of the key institutions separating the Greek from the savage. Without the law, humans would regress to their animal selves. From the perspective of the Greeks' dualistic imagination, the animal self is antithetical to all that makes humans special (that is, our capacity to be ruled by reason). Without reason and being guided by law, the regression to animality amounts to insanity: bestiality, excessive emotions, and lasciviousness. Driven only by desire, animals are led solely by sensation. As Demosthenes (384–322 BCE) pronounced, "If laws were abolished and each individual were given power to do what he liked, not only does our communal organisation vanish but our very life would be in no way different from that of the animals" (quoted in Isaac 2004: 196). Law is the *form* of civilization that is imposed upon the mere *matter* of a brute, uncultivated nature.

From its beginnings in ancient Greece, the idea that there is an ontological and irremediable divide between civilization and barbarism (savagery) has shaped and directed the West's actions toward the non-Western world. For the Greeks, savage creatures like the centaurs were irrational and so could not understand *xenia*, the universally binding law that made civilized existence possible (Williams 2012: 18–19). The irrational, lawless, hypersexualized centaurs were driven by bestial passions to violate the laws of civilization. The defeat of the centaurs by the earliest Greek heroes thus represented for the Greeks the victory of law and civilization over the lawless, irrational, animalistic savages. As Williams explains:

> Nestor's reference [in the *Iliad*] to the Centauromachy introduces the Western world to its first mythic stereotype of a fierce, lawless savage. A subhuman beast, irreconcilably opposed to the higher law of a superior form of civilization. [. . .] From this point forward, Homer's defining categories of lawlessness, remoteness, habitual intemperance, primitive bestiality, and sexual licentiousness will become foundational elements of the idea of the savage, applied to non-Westernized peoples by Western civilization for the next three thousand years. (Williams 2012: 20)

The Romans took on the Greek idea of the restraining role of law against barbarians. For the Greeks as it was for the Romans, law became the *form* of civilization imprinted on the bestial, barbarian other. Augustine here quotes Cicero's *De Republica*:

> It was replied in behalf of justice, that this ruling of the provinces is just, because servitude may be advantageous to the provincials, and is so when rightly administered,—that is to say, when *lawless* men are prevented from doing harm. And further, as they became worse and worse so long as they were free, they will *improve by subjection*. (quoted in Isaac 2004: 183, emphasis added)

Before being brought under the rule of law, the "provincials" do harm, but they improve when they are subjected to (Roman) law. The imperial project as conceived by the Roman and later Western tradition thus assumes that, because the bestial, nonrational side of the dualism prevails in the land of the barbarian other, by ontological law, the rational side of the dualism must be imposed upon it.

Under this model, there is a one-way relationship between the unchanging center and the periphery. Colonization is premised upon a dualistic paradigm whereby the *only* relationship between colonizer and colonized is the one-way relationship of the colonizer imprinting form onto receptive matter (the colony). This colonial relationship between the colonizer and the colonized against the background of an "empty" land parallels Plato's conception of the genesis of copies. It is therefore fitting that in nonphilosophical usage, *chora* can also indicate the hinterland of the ancient Greek *polis*, which is opposed to the *polis* (Hansen 1997: 17). The assumed metaphysical framework behind the obligation of European imperium can be seen in the association of the hinterlands (*chora*) with the docile matter that is given form by the *polis*.

The Western model of efficacy as the imposition of an ideal form onto a receptive matter is, of course, nothing but an ideal. In practice, the world is never completely receptive to the order that we wish it to have. In the warfare that brings the colonies under the colonizer's rule, there is what the famous military strategist Carl Philipp Gottfried von Clausewitz called "friction" (Clausewitz 2007: 65). As François Jullien explains,

> So just as for Aristotle, matter, an indeterminate power of contraries, always remains more or less recalcitrant to the determination that "form" seeks to impose upon it, similarly the world is never altogether receptive to the order that we wish it to have: inevitably there is always a discrepancy between the planned model for our action and what we, *with our eyes fixed* on that model, manage to achieve. (Jullien 2004: 4–5, emphasis in original)

The amount of violence needed to impose what the Europeans had in mind ("that model") onto the recalcitrant reality of the Americas testifies to this very "friction." Observe what Richard Drinnon has to say about the myth of American settler-colonialism: "Americans in some manner will cling to the traditional idea that they suddenly came upon a vacant land on which they created the world's most affluent society" (Drinnon 1997: xxiii). The land, of course, was not "vacant." Preserving this ideal model of action whereby an ideal form is imprinted onto a receptive matter required: (1) viewing the native populations and species as mere matter and so as non-entities identified with nothingness, thus preserving the idea of the "vacancy" of the land; and (2) having parsed these local populations of peoples and species as non-entities and voids, exterminating them, both in practice and in later recountings of the process of colonization.

Witness how Dee Brown describes the actions of those who succeeded Columbus in San Salvador: they "destroyed its vegetation and its inhabitants— human, animal, bird, and fish—and after turning it into a wasteland, they abandoned it" (Brown 1991: 6–7). In so doing, the colonizers who followed Columbus actualized the ideal of a frictionless imposition of an ideal model on a receptive (empty) matter. Western colonialism puts into practice a medieval metaphysics that assumes the world is matter that needs to be disciplined with form.

Realizing the Existing Tendencies of Things: The Chinese Model of Efficacy

In contrast to the dualistic model of efficacy that we see in Western metaphysics, Chinese metaphysics assumes that all things have a spontaneous source of initiative within themselves. Chinese metaphysics does not assume that anything is without form. The world is instead conceived as a heterogeneous manifold (*wan wu*, 万物) of fully individualistic (*ziran*, 自然), *sponte sua* potencies. There is no dualism between spontaneous free action and merely passive nature or matter.

Under this nondualistic metaphysics that sees all things as already having form, imposing a form onto something is not viewed as efficacious or virtuous, but rather as impeding the original form of the thing and so being a coercive act. It is for this reason that in the *Doctrine of the Mean*, for example, the sage's ability to consummate all things of the world is spoken of in noncoercive (*wuwei*, 无为). The sage's consummation of things is an uncoerced, effortless, and non-instrumental action because it is in accord with and respects the implicit natures and propensities (forms) of things:

> Creativity (*cheng*, 诚) is the way of *tian* (天之道); creating is the proper way of becoming human (人之道). Creativity is achieving equilibrium and focus (*zhong*, 中) without coercion; it is succeeding without reflection [不思]. (chapter 20; Ames and Hall 2001: 104)

The consummation of things that the sage enacts is not an imposition of external forms but the realization of the potential form that already exists within things.

The sage in the *Doctrine of the Mean* embodies the virtue of *cheng* (诚). They are able to consummate things and aid their genesis precisely because of their non-imposing, formless disposition; their sagely conduct can be compared to Plato's *chora*. In the Platonic case, the characteristics associated with the *chora*—characterless, unassertive, compliant, and yielding—are understood as negative, passive qualities. By contrast, the *Doctrine of the Mean* describes them as the qualities of the ecumenical ability to engender and nurture the myriad things (the female metaphor of generation) and understands them in positive, creative terms. That is, in Chinese metaphysics the generative capacity of nature is associated with the order of the world and with feminine attributes.[24] The very non-imposing nature of the female womb, like that of the sage, is in fact the source of its agency and power, its ability to engender all things.

The Western and Chinese traditions thus understand the moment of efficacy differently: the Western tradition attributes causal efficacy to that which makes the impression, whereas the Chinese tradition attributes causal efficacy to the ability to nourish these impressions. The Western tradition speaks in negative terms about the female metaphor of generation, which is seen in positive terms in the Chinese tradition. In the latter case, something like the *chora*, with its attributes of non-assertiveness, characterlessness, tolerance, and ability to yield and be receptive, is venerated and given the commanding role. Whereas Plato sees the function of the female womb in passive terms, Chinese philosophy speaks in active terms of its function of animating and vitalizing in a noncoercive way.

What must be stressed is that these different accounts of the moment of efficacy in the same process of generation arise from the assumption of bivalent dualisms in the Western tradition, on the one hand, and the absence of any such assumption in Chinese philosophy, on the other. Without an assumption of bivalent dualisms, the Chinese tradition assumes that all things already have form, and so form need not be imposed. Efficacy is then understood as aiding the growth of preexisting forms, not as imposing forms onto existing forms. Whereas the Western tradition understands characterlessness as a passive condition, the Chinese understand it in active terms as an infinite potential for carrying the myriad things. The universalism of such potential, which has the power to support everything that exists without partiality, is compared with the powers that generated the world itself: nature or the way of heaven (*tian*) or *dao*. We see the sage described in terms of this characterless, impartial, but universal potency in chapters 30 and 27 of the *Doctrine of the Mean*:

> He [Confucius] modeled himself above on the rhythm of the turning seasons, and below he was attuned to the patterns of water and earth. He is comparable to the heavens and the earth, sheltering and supporting everything

that is. [. . .] All things are nourished together without their injuring one another. The various ways [*dao*, 道] travel together without them causing injury to one another [*xiangbei*, 相悖]. (Ames and Hall 2001: 111–12, my modifications)

Great indeed is the sage's proper path. So vast and expansive, it propagates and nurtures all things; so towering, it reaches up to the skies! So great indeed! (Ames and Hall 2001: 108)

Thus deified, the ability to support all things in an all-inclusive way is tantamount to the power of heaven and earth itself.[25]

In the *Doctrine of the Mean*, the virtue associated with bringing to consummation and with the engendering of things is *cheng* (诚). It is believed that the capacity to help the innate tendencies of things come to fruition is an *active* rather than passive activity. It is for this reason that against the traditional rendering of *cheng* as "sincerity" or "integrity," Roger Ames and David Hall have translated it as "creativity." They note that the graph for *cheng* (诚) is composed of the speech classifier *yan* (言) and the phonetic component *cheng* (成), which means "to consummate, complete, finish, bring to fruition" (Ames and Hall 2001: 62). The "creativity" at work here is a virtue that is "sincere" with respect to the existing "integrity" of things. In the Chinese context, the emptiness and non-imposing (*chora*-like) activity of the sage does not inhibit a thing's becoming but instead helps it grow. It is not understood as a passive process. Thus, being "sincere" with respect to the existing form of things and aiding their growth is itself a co-creative process that requires a kind of attention that allows nature to "enter into" the emptiness of the sage. This attention and perception is not a state of being inactive or static. The non-imposing attention of the sage helps to realize the potentials of things precisely because of their ability to allow nature to enter into their own *chora*-like activities. This does not mean that the sage is then a passive cipher; as a co-creative process, the emptiness of the sage is accommodating to the world that the sage is playing a role in engendering. It is a co-creative process in that it extends both ways.

In the *Doctrine of the Mean*, being sincere (*cheng*, 诚) in respecting the innate tendencies of things allows one to tap into *dao*. Tapping into this natural ordering process elevates the human being to a status on par with the powers of *dao*, or nature, or *tian*. In this way, the human's efficacy becomes like the powers of nature itself.[26] Toward the end of the *Doctrine of the Mean*, an ebullient passage summarizes these ideas about nature's ability to nurture all things being the source of limitless efficacy and exhorts sages to follow this paradigm.[27] This passage (26) is worth citing in whole:

> Thus, the utmost creativity [至诚] is ceaseless. Unceasing, it is enduring; enduring, it is effective; effective, it reaches far into the distance; reaching far into the distance, it is broad and thick; being broad and thick, it is high and brilliant. Its breadth and thickness enable it to bear up everything; its height and brilliance enable it to envelope everything; reaching far into the distance enables it to realize all events. Broad and thick, it is companion to the earth; high and brilliant, it is companion to the heavens; far-reaching and enduring, it is without limit.
>
> This process of utmost creativity [至诚] is in full display without manifesting itself, changes without moving, and realizes without doing anything. [. . .]
>
> Now the firmament [. . .] given its boundlessness, the sun, moon, stars, and constellations are woven through it, and all things are covered by it.
>
> As for the earth, [. . .] it bears up the mountains of Hua and Yue without feeling their weight, circulates the waters of the rivers and seas without any leakage, and bears up all things.
>
> As for the mountains, [. . .] given their expanse and size, grasses and trees grow on them, birds and beasts find refuge in them, and deposits of precious resources are replete within them.
>
> As for the waters, [. . .] given their bottomlessness, giant tortoises, alligators, a variety of dragons, fishes, and turtles live in them, and precious goods and commodities are reproduced within them.
>
> The *Book of Songs* says:
>
> > Ah! What *tian* promotes—
> > So profound and unceasing.
>
> This may describe what makes *tian tian*. (Ames and Hall 2001: 107–8, my modifications)

It is precisely *because* nature (the firmament, earth, mountains, and waters) is all-accommodating that nature can be so broad, thick, far-reaching, enduring, and limitless. Furthermore, the process of sustaining all things is self-effacing: it does not impose itself. Nature's noncoercive actions and ability to act without compromising the innate tendencies of things—nature's *wuwei* actions—are the sources of its power.

This logic—which sees the consummation of things as a *creative* act owing to how the sage abides by and is attentive to the particularity of things—is ubiquitous in the Chinese classics. In *Xici* 1.4, for example, we read:

> *Yi* is a paradigm of Heaven and Earth, and so it shows how one can fill in and pull together the Dao of Heaven and Earth. Looking up, we use it [*Yi*] to observe the configurations of Heaven, and, looking down, we use it to examine the patterns of Earth. [...] As *Yi* [the sage/*Changes*] resembles Heaven and Earth, he/it does not go against them. As his/its knowledge is complete in respect to the myriad things and as his/its *Dao* brings help to all under Heaven, he/it commits no transgression. Such a one extends himself/itself in all directions yet does not allow himself/itself to be swept away. [...] He/it perfectly emulates the transformations of Heaven and Earth and so does not transgress them. He/it follows every twist and turn of the myriad things and so deals with them without omission. [...] Thus the numinous is not restricted to place, and *Yi* is without substance. (Lynn 1994: 51–53, my modifications)

Yi (易), which can be parsed as either the hermeneutic system of the *Yijing* or the sage, follows every twist and turn of the myriad things and so does not transgress them. The issue here is one of attention and proper understanding of the situation. The sage makes no transgression precisely because their conduct is not the passive absorption of information but is instead the capacity to co-creatively interact with the propensity of nature's constant flux.

The idea in the *Doctrine of the Mean* that human virtue and efficacy reside in emulating the all-accommodating nature of heaven and earth (nature) also pervades the Chinese classics. The "Commentary on the Images" for the *Kun* hexagram, for example, states: "Here is the basic disposition of Earth: this constitutes the image of *Kun*. In the same manner, the *junzi* [person of virtue] with his generous virtue carries everything" (Lynn 1994: 144, my modifications). This idea of the *junzi* as one who is yielding and capaciously supports all kinds of life can also be seen in the chapter "Utmost Appropriateness" (至当) of Zhang Zai's (1020–1077 CE) *Correcting Youthful Ignorance*:

> The sage embraces [容] the myriad things and leaves nothing out. He can love the myriad things without partiality for any one of them. This is the way of *tian*. *Tian* nourishes the myriad things with rectitude. The person who governs [理] things on the part of *tian*, follows every twist and turn of

the myriad things without omission without harming *tian*'s rectitude. This is to reach the realm of Dao. (Zhang 1978: 35, my translation)

For Zhang, the utmost virtue embodied by the sage is the key virtue of *tian*, that is, the universal cultivation of the myriad things. The utmost human virtue is to personify the capacious capacity for letting all things be in their becomings. We find the same sentiment in Wang Bi's commentary on the *Daodejing*:

The sage thoroughly understands what people's nature is by nature and allows the innate tendencies [*qing*, 情] of all the myriad things full expression. Therefore, he follows and does not act, complies and does not interfere. (Lynn 1999: 105)

Both Confucian and Daoist metaphysics thus overlap in understanding human virtue and efficacy in terms of respecting and bringing to fruition the innate tendencies of things. This picture of efficacy is modeled on the ability of nature to support all life forms. Chinese metaphysics can thus be said to understand efficacy in terms of *wuwei* (noncoercive) actions that do not impose themselves but instead accommodate all things and help bring them to fruition. The differences between the Western and Chinese conceptions of causal efficacy can be seen in their understandings of how a new life is engendered. The Western conception sees the moment of causal efficacy in the male sperm (the form-giver) fertilizing the egg. The Chinese conception sees the moment of causal efficacy in the female womb nurturing the new life.

We can most effectively get a conceptual grasp on the paradoxical idea (to a Western audience) of the creative realization of the innate form of things by looking at the history of the word *li* (理), which is often translated as "principle" or "order" but is best translated in this context as "coherence" or "pattern." In *Explaining Graphs and Analyzing Characters* (an early second-century dictionary), Xu Shen (许慎) (ca. 58–ca. 148 CE) explains *li* as "working on jade." Working on the jade according to its natural veins is *li*; the inference is that *li* means "administering" and "ordering." As Duan Yucai (段玉裁) (1735–1815) explains in a commentary to *Explaining Graphs and Analyzing Characters*, the ancient Chinese believed that uncarved jade possesses a great quality or potency, but that to bring out that quality craftsmen had to work on it according to its natural veins. The best lapidaries were those who conformed their craftsmanship to the possibilities inherent in the natural striations of the stone itself, thereby maximizing the stone's natural potentialities (Duan 2015: 25). Like the sage of the *Doctrine of the Mean*, these lapidaries did not impose an external form on the existing patterns of a piece of jade, nor were they mere ciphers. Lapidaries' agency lay in creatively bringing to consummation the existing tendencies of the jade.

The Chinese conception of order—what we could call "harmony"—is always already implicit in the world. Those of perfected ability know how to read these existing patterns and how to flesh out and strengthen them. The perception at work in seeing the patterns inherent in all things (*li*, 理)—whether in a piece of jade, the natural world, or social phenomena—is an active, creative perception that consummates those patterns.

This concept of the creative human realization of the innate tendencies of things can be seen in the Chinese account of the origins of civilization. *Xici* 2.2 is a canonical statement of the classical Chinese view of the origins of cultural institutions, language, and civilization. The logic of this passage redounds to the syncretic relationship between the creative interpretative ability of the human subject and the preexisting "symbolic pregnance" of the patterns of the world. *Xici* 2.2 tells of the sage's creation of the institutions that define civilization—among which was writing:

> When in ancient times Lord Baoxi ruled the world as sovereign, he looked upward and observed the images [*xiang*, 象] in heaven and looked downward and observed the models [*fa*, 法] that the earth provided. He observed the patterns [*wen*, 文] on birds and beasts and what things were suitable for the land. Nearby, adopting them from his own person, and afar, adopting them from other things, he thereupon made the eight trigrams in order to become thoroughly conversant with the virtues inherent in the numinous and the bright and to classify the myriad things in terms of their true, innate natures [*qing*, 情]. (Lynn 1994: 77)

The eight trigrams then inspired the creation of key institutions of civilization, such as writing. From this account, it can be seen that the human being is able to phenomenologically understand the meanings (patterns, *wen*, 文) of the (expressive) world that result from his interactions with that world, and that human creativity enables the consolidation and heightening of those meanings. The (symbolic) forms that result—such as language (*wen*, 文)—are the specific forms of patterning that distinguish the activities of human beings.

Several assumptions are implicit in the Chinese (anti-representationalist) theory of the origins of language and civilization: that human patterning forms a continuum with all other kinds of patterns in the world; that human patterning is a result of human-world interaction; and that human patterning heightens preexisting meanings through that human-world interaction. The Chinese tradition views human civilization as a continuum of natural patterning (which is itself already pregnant with meaning). For example, the pattern (*wen*, 文) of rings in a tree stump tell us the age of the tree and the history of the world's impacts on it as it grew. Simultaneously, *wen* designates literature, language, or civilization and refinement in the human realm. That *wen*, the Chinese term for writing and civilization, is the same as the term for (natural) patterning testifies to the continuum (Xiang 2021a).

The Chinese tradition saw the origins of civilization through the sage's ability to comprehensively take into account the particulars of the world creatively synthesized into a symbol.[28] As with the sage of the *Doctrine of the Mean*, order is the result of the ability to creatively harmonize preexisting particulars. For the Chinese tradition, order or culture is not what happens when a preexisting form of being is impressed onto docile matter, as per a representationalist paradigm. Instead, order and culture result from the dynamic and creative systematization (harmonization) of our phenomenological experience of and engagement with the world.

Just as consummate virtue and efficacy are understood as the ability to creatively realize the existing form of things, the Chinese view understands order or "harmony" as already implicit in a situation. The capacity to see how a situation can become harmonized requires both an intimate knowledge of the nature of the particulars and an imagination creative enough to reconcile all these particulars into a coherent and resonant network of relationships. Again, consummate virtue and efficacy strengthen the implicit order of a situation, as in the example of the lapidary, as opposed to imposing a form onto the situation.

We can get a conceptual grasp on what the creative realization of harmony in a situation means by looking at *Analects* 13.23, in which Confucius says: "The morally exemplary harmonizes [和] and does not make himself identical [同]. The petty man makes himself identical [同], but he does not harmonize [和]." Harmonious order is not realized through negating the existing form of any individual, as the petty man does by conforming to the form of others. Harmony requires instead the creativity to imagine the appropriate configurations in which all the elements in a situation can be most optimally ordered. Under this harmony model, the world is constituted by an infinite number of particulars and their relationships. Moral virtue, being particularly sensitive to these relationships, is able to optimize them. There is no harmony within either identity (imposing the same form onto things) or mere heterogeneity. To harmonize is to find an order or coherence that does justice to particularity. It is this harmony model that underlies the famous expression in the *Doctrine of the Mean*: "All things are nourished together without their injuring one another. The various ways [*dao*, 道] travel together without them causing injury to one another [*xiangbei*, 相悖]." This harmony model is inherently cosmopolitan and pluralistic.

As I have argued elsewhere (Xiang 2021a: chap. 6), the paradigm that underlies the Chinese ideal of harmony is the organic world, which exemplifies order amid diversity. We can clearly see the difference between the harmony conception of efficacy and the Western dualistic one in their respective discourses on war, the most representative of which in the Chinese tradition is Sunzi's *The Art of War*, and in the Western tradition Clausewitz's *On War*.

Efficacy in Chinese and Western Accounts of War

We can get a better idea of the importance of harmony in Chinese metaphysics on the practical level by looking at an example of applied harmony in the Chinese attitude to war. As Roger Ames judiciously notes in his introduction to Sunzi's *The Art of War*, what unites the cultivation of the self with the cultivation of victory on the battlefield is the "peculiarly Chinese model of 'harmony'" that is pursued by both the well-cultivated moral agent and the able military commander (Ames 1993: 33). As Sarah Mattice puts it, whereas in Western theory and practice the annihilation of the enemy is the norm, in Chinese theory,

> at the point when one is committed to war, committed to victory, one is precisely committed not to the destruction of the enemy, but rather to doing one's best to make sure that the enemy's state, infrastructure, lands, citizens, and soldiers remain as whole as possible. This is a very different picture of combat than the one drawn by Clausewitz. (Mattice 2014: 28)

Like Ames, François Jullien also suggests that another way to talk about the Chinese strategy of war is harmony.[29] Instead of the Greek idea of action as *creatio ex nihilo* in a frictionless vacuum—the dualistic imposition of form onto formless matter that motivated the Western attitude toward colonization—the Chinese sought to "*harmonize* the development of a situation with the evolution of things in general. [. . .] in China efficacy is effective through adaptation" (Jullien 2004: 51, emphasis in original). The Chinese understanding of efficacy in war is acutely observing all the factors at play and subtly using the nascent forms (existing propensities) of things to transform the overall situation in one's favor. For the Chinese, the best generals were not even seen on the battlefield but instead were engaged in the real battle: the hermeneutic discernment of a situation. The sagely action described in the *Doctrine of the Mean* summarizes well what the military strategist is doing:

> Confucius said, "Exemplary persons (*junzi*, 君子) focus (*zhong*, 中) the familiar affairs of the day; petty persons distort them. Exemplary persons are able to focus the affairs of the day because, being exemplary, they themselves maintain the equilibrium [*zhong*, 中] in a timely way [*shi*, 时]. Petty persons are a source of distortion in the affairs of the day because, being petty persons, they lack the requisite caution and concern. (Ames and Hall 2001: 90, my modifications)

In other words, since the midpoint between any two opposing points is constantly changing in accordance with changes in circumstances and the passage of time, one achieves equilibrium by changing oneself according to the changing circumstances.

We can trace this idea of a timely maintenance of equilibrium to *Analects* 6.29 and 13.21, in which Confucius talks about "applying the mean" (中庸) and "balanced conduct" (中行). This idea of knowing when and how to adapt so as to keep to the mean—like knowing how to find one's center of gravity when walking a tightrope—is harmony in practice. Exemplary persons continuously adapt their conception of order in keeping with the changing circumstances. The Chinese way of thinking about efficacy is well summarized by *Mencius* 2A1: "Though you are intelligent, it is better to take advantage of the force of situations [势]. Though you have a hoe, it is better to wait for the proper season [待时]" (Mencius 2009: 28). The exemplary person does not simply think of imposing an action to promote an outcome; instead, this person takes stock of all the factors of a situation—its *li* (理)—and then, after predicting the evolution of the confluence of these factors, fits his actions within the existing form of the situation so as to maximize its potential.

In the Chinese conception of harmony, the universal is enriched by the coexistence of all particulars, and this can be understood through the idea of equilibrium (中), or what the *Doctrine of the Mean* calls maintenance of the equilibrium in a timely fashion (时中). As the one who is able to bring coherence to all particulars, the sage must be consummately skilled in seeing the incipient dispositions of things and judging how the parts can be mutually responsive to each other to maximum effect. This harmony and applied harmony can also be seen in Sunzi's *Art of War*.

We can clearly see the difference between the harmony conception of efficacy and the Western dualistic conception in their respective discourses on war. Clausewitz discerned that previous Western theorists of war had considered only material, *unilateral* factors that could be mathematically calculated (Clausewitz 2007: 82); they did not consider the *reciprocal* nature of action and so the unpredictable nature of interaction (88). The Western model of war followed the Platonic paradigm of genesis whereby a form was imposed upon compliant matter. For Clausewitz, victory meant defeating the enemy: "What do we mean by the defeat of the enemy? Simply the destruction of his forces, whether by death, injury, or any other means—either completely or enough to make him stop fighting" (xxvi). The dualistic model of ideal form being imposed on docile matter underlies the West's conception of action as *creatio ex nihilo* in a vacuum; further, this contextless action is understood to be determinative of the outcome of a situation. As we saw in the example of the European colonization of the "New World," the Americas were conceived as the docile matter onto which the energizing form of European civilization was to be imprinted. For François Jullien, as befits "a metaphysics of essence," the actual circumstances (*circum-stare*) of an action were seen merely as "accessories or details" that accompanied "that which is essential in the situation or happening" (Jullien 2004: 22). If we analogize what Jullien is saying to the Platonic paradigm of genesis, we can say that in the Western model of war only the action taken by the army is taken into account, as only that action is assumed to have any efficacy. All other circumstances are understood as formless matter that lacks initiative and onto which is imposed the unilinear action. That unilinear action is not considered an interaction, as the formless matter onto which the army imposes its unilinear action, being without form, is not assumed to react in any way. The Western attitude toward war operates like the Platonic paradigm of genesis whereby form is assumed to be frictionlessly imprinted onto a formless matter.

As the Chinese strategist does not operate from a dualistic model of efficacy, his attitude toward the dynamics of war and view of how to be efficacious under this dynamic are radically different. The Chinese strategist, operating under the paradigm of harmony, "consider[s] the potential of a situation to be variable; it cannot be determined in advance since it proceeds from continuous adaptation"; moreover, "the dimension of reciprocity lies at the very heart of what constitutes the potential of a situation." Operating under the assumption that nothing in the world is without form and initiative and that the world is instead a heterogeneous manifold of potencies with their own sources of initiative, the Chinese strategist does not conceive of his action in war as a unilateral action in a contextless vacuum. Warfare, in China, is instead "quite naturally thought of in terms of interaction and polarity, just as any other process is" (Jullien 2004: 23).

It is this idea that an individual's action is merely one insertion in a complex web of existing relations that leads to two key concepts at the heart of Chinese strategy: situation, or configuration (*xing*, 形); and the contours of a situation, which suggest its momentum, direction, and thus potentiality and opportunity (*shi*, 勢). "It is a matter of strategic positioning [*xing*, 形] that the army that has this weight of victory on its side, in launching its men into battle, can be likened to the cascading of pent-up waters thundering through a steep gorge" (Ames 1993: 116). Just like the lapidary, the Chinese model of action inductively starts from the empirical particulars and then, after judging the overall coherence of the situation, proposes a course of action (form) on that basis. As Jullien writes, the Chinese saw that "instead of imposing our plan upon the world, we could rely on the potential inherent in the situation." (Jullien 2004: 16) In so doing one does not have to cope with "friction," since friction is something that comes about when one tries to realize a pre-conceived model in actuality. If one's "model" is a result of the emergence of the situation itself, then friction will not result.

As Chinese metaphysics does not assume the bivalent dualisms of Western metaphysics, its conception of efficacy does not involve the imposition of an ideal form onto a compliant matter, but hermeneutically reading the existing tendencies of things and taking action in relation to them in a way that optimizes (harmonizes) the existing implicit order.

Conclusion

This chapter has argued that both Western colonialism and Chinese non-interventionism are attributable to the characteristics of their respective metaphysics. Western metaphysics is represented by Plato's account of genesis, which ascribes to the forms causal efficacy for the generation of the copies and was the model, it has been argued here, for European colonialism. In Chinese metaphysics, all things already have form, and so causal efficacy is attributed to that which can nurture the (existing forms of the) myriad things. The view that all things are *ziran* or *sponte sua* leads to the Chinese view of efficacy and virtue as the non-coercive respect for the inherent potencies of all nature. The Western conception of an antecedent form imposed upon nature parallels the representational account of human culture and civilization, whereas the Chinese account of culture and civilization is antirepresentationalist. For Chinese metaphysics, if we did not take account of the existing disposition of things, we would be committing ourselves to the Sisyphean labor of placing a rock in a place that geography undermines. For Chinese metaphysics, sustaining the growth of the diversity of things in a way that leads to overall harmony is not a passive act; to create coherence or harmony among diverse things requires creativity, skill, and great effort. The sage, as the one who is able to maximize these relationships, brings coherence to all particulars through creative acts of judging how the parts potentially relate to each other and thus realizing harmony.

These two different accounts of efficacy are epitomized in the two traditions' understandings of efficacy in war. Informed by its metaphysics and conception of efficacy as achieving harmony, the Chinese worldview never had the dualistic conception of other peoples and never saw their lands as formless, passive matter. Nor did they have the conception that Chinese civilization (the "form" in the dualistic view) had a "metaphysical obligation" to impose its civilizational form on the other (as mere matter) so that the other could be propelled into historical time. The Chinese tradition was more empirical than the Western tradition with regard to its understanding of human difference in that it did not assume that some groups of human beings are "barbarians" (mere matter without form). Unlike the Greco-Christian tradition, the Chinese tradition did not default to an unempirical, facile dualism to account for human difference.

6

The Metaphysics of Harmony
in Practice

WE CAN SEE THE CHINESE understanding of efficacy in the Chinese ideal of
how to conduct oneself in a relationship with someone of a different persuasion. The Chinese tradition recognizes that others already have form—in this
instance, a particular moral worldview. Given this reality, to remove this preexisting form and replace it with one's own would only court the other's resentment. Such resentment—which can be likened to the "friction" discussed
in the previous chapter—greatly impedes the other's acceptance of the form
one wishes to impose, be it moral, political, social, or cultural. Instead of imposing form onto others, the Chinese tradition assumes that the minds of
others will be changed as one wishes only if they choose to do so of their own
accord. And the best way to motivate others to change their behavior and
beliefs is by example—that is, by acting as a moral exemplar with whom others
spontaneously resonate.

The idea of seeking constant self-improvement to increase the attractiveness of one's virtue and so become a moral exemplar is ubiquitous in the
Chinese canon, as are the many explicit injunctions against censuring the
perceived moral flaws in others. The predominant thought is that, if we
are truly correct in our own bearing, others will be drawn to our virtue and
seek to follow our example. Relatedly, because China did not see its neighbors as matter without form (that is, they were not seen as "barbarians"), it
did not conceive of its relationship with its neighbors in terms of the imposition of form onto its neighbors. Instead of the Platonic *chora* or the (Platonic
and Aristotelian) craftsman metaphor of the mechanical imposition of form,
China envisioned its relationship to its neighbors as organic interactions of
exchange.

The Chinese term for organisms responding to and interacting with their environments is *ganying* (感应), or "mutual responsiveness." This chapter details how we can conceptualize Chinese identity as a product of *ganying*.

The Ideal of Efficacy in the Chinese Account of Virtue

The Chinese notion of efficacy as harmony can be seen in the Chinese understanding of efficacy in personal relations and, by extension, foreign policy. Given that the Chinese tradition does not assume the existence of "barbarians" who are (dualistically) mere matter without form, the concept of one agent imposing its will onto others with different dispositions from itself is not understood in the virtuous or efficacious terms of giving form to something that was previously formless. Since the other already has her own form, to violently disenfranchise her from her preexisting form and replace it with the agent's own form would result in resentment toward the agent. This is an inefficacious way for the agent to conduct her affairs with others. As Eric Nelson puts it, "Confucian ethics requires one to consider the negative emotions that one's own behavior can cause in others." Such consideration can only arise from "the asymmetrical acknowledgement of the other person as non-identical with oneself" (Nelson 2013: 288).

In its appreciation of the other's legitimate difference—her preexisting form—the Chinese tradition realized how inefficacious it is to force one's own form onto others. We could think of the resulting resentment as a moral-psychological equivalent to the non-ideal "friction" of the Clausewitzian ideal of war. The reality of battle always resists being completely subsumed under the ideal model we might like to impose on it. Inevitably, the world and matter will never be completely docile or receptive to the form we wish to impose.

Whilst the Platonic, Clausewitzian and, Western moral ideal is that of a frictionless imposition of form onto a formless, passive matter, the non-ideal reality is that of friction when we try to realize our ideal designs. Unfortunately for Western moralists, as for Clausewitz, racial others with divergent moral practices are not quite their ideal, matter-without-form barbarians crying out for form to be imposed on them. Far from being the barbarian of Western metaphysics, all peoples already have form, and the imposition of (Western) forms on the cultural other creates resentment. This is why Western "universalism" and the project of its dissemination so often require violence. The reality of the imposition of Western moral forms on the recalcitrant other is a process that rarely accords with the ideal frictionless imprinting of form onto matter. As Frantz Fanon famously wrote:

> But it so happens that when the native hears a speech about Western culture he pulls out his knife—or at least he makes sure it is within reach. The violence with which the supremacy of white values is affirmed and the aggressiveness which has permeated the victory of these values over the ways of life and of thought of the native mean that, in revenge, the native laughs in mockery when Western values are mentioned in front of him. (Fanon 1963: 34)

The Western myth or ideal has always been that the West brought civilization (form) to barbarians (matter) in a frictionless manner, but the "barbarians" in question remember the violence of that event and the great friction that resulted.

Given their assumption of the appreciable differences of others and their understanding that resentment necessarily results from imposing one's own form onto (the form of) others, the Chinese tradition saw efficacy as drawing other people spontaneously to one's position. Under the Chinese view, because all agents are assumed to already have form and to be *sponte sua*, what demonstrates true virtue and efficaciousness is having others come to you and willingly fall under your influence through no coercion or effortful action on your part (*wuwei*). It is this notion of efficacy that is on display in *Analects* 2.1: "One who exercises government by means of his virtue [德] is analogous to the North Star: which keeps its place and all the stars turn towards it." It should be noted that the Chinese term for "morality" and "virtue," *de* (德), is homonymous with "power" and "efficacy" (*de*, 德). Further, both are understood as the "ability to influence charismatically but without overt effort the behavior of others in the same direction; esp. associated with sages, ideal rulers, exemplary figures who live in harmony with all elements of existence" (Kroll 2015: 80). *De* is the "innate power," "potency," "efficacy," "projection of the *dao*, the Way and its Power (Force, Working, Process)" as well as "moral power" (80). Traditionally, *de* is compounded with *dao* to suggest that *de* is a potency that is vouchsafed by cosmic processes itself. Those who can tap into the very nature of the world can be potent and act with efficacy or virtue in the world. (Moral) virtue and efficacy both refer to the same phenomenon of having potency in one's dealings in the world and with others. For example, the *Dao*

De Jing (道德经), which also has the term *de* in it, is often rendered as *The Classic of the Way and Its Power or Virtue. De* also encompasses the sense of "kindness, favor, gracious treatment" (80) and the related sense of being grateful or thankful.[1]

The Confucian account of efficacy embodies these four senses of *de*—virtue, power, gracious treatment, and gratitude: the agent gaining the power to influence others not by coercing them but by enabling their mutual growth. The agent's capacity to affect the dispositions of others comes from both their gratitude to her and their understanding that collaboration with her or her point of view will benefit them. The agent who is able to benefit the greatest number of people is the one with the most power and as such draws other agents to her, as captured by Confucius's metaphor of the North Star. An ability to promote the flourishing of others makes an agent effective as a social actor, bringing her the esteem, respect, and high regard of social others. It is this social currency that animates the Confucian understanding of efficacy or virtue.

The Confucian account recognizes that the virtuous agent is not the one who submits to a transcendent moral law and thereby acts in accordance with a preestablished moral order. Rather, efficacy stems from the co-creative actions of the agent bringing benefit to others by promoting their flourishing and having a positive impact on their experience of the world. This capacity to co-creatively transform each other by promoting mutual growth of character is the basis of the Confucian understanding of "virtue." The term most often translated as virtue, *de* (德), combines these conceptions of efficacy and virtue, as captured in *Daodejing* 7: "The reason the world is able to be lasting and enduring is because it does not live for itself. Thus it is able to be long-lived. Therefore the sage puts his own person last, and yet it is found in the foremost place" (Ames and Hall 2003: 86, my modifications). An example of the *Daodejing*'s meaning can be seen in how the most popular teachers have been the ones who had the most to offer their students. Similarly, the most beloved leaders have been the ones who unselfishly and competently promoted the well-being of their citizens.

We can see this idea about virtue in the images of composite animals that were commonly carved into the walls of tombs and shrines during the Eastern Han dynasty (25–220 CE). These animals were either a two-headed beast, a two-headed bird, or a two-bodied fish. As Martin Powers explains, in these animals one head represents the government and the other represents the people (Powers 1991: 247). An inscription on one such image reads: "The two-headed beast appears when the king's [virtuous] policies benefit the poor and vulnerable [比肩兽: 王者德及孤孀则至]". Powers explains that the underlying assumption in these images was "that the effects of harmonious government would resonate in the natural world, resulting in the appearance of auspicious omens in the form of composite creatures" (4). Virtue, understood as the ability to benefit the people, is a sign of political power and authority and is captured in the image of auspicious mythological creatures.

What is understood as efficacious in each cultural tradition is ultimately indebted to each culture's metaphysics. As we saw in chapter 4, domination in Western metaphysics is seen as an efficacious, virtuous act. Those higher in the ontological Great Chain of Being (those with form) have a natural mandate to dominate those inferior to themselves (those with no form). That which is virtuous is what is efficacious. Confucianism did not espouse a model of virtue and efficacy that is comparable to the Western model indebted to the GCB. Rectifying deviant behavior is only possible through spontaneous attraction to a moral agent's exemplary conduct demonstrating the efficacy of virtuous behavior and not by imposing an external form onto others.[2] All that moral agents can do to attract others is to increase the appeal of their virtue.

The ideal of self-cultivation or moral self-improvement as the panacea for rectifying the non-optimal behavior in others is ubiquitous in the Chinese canon. As Edward Slingerland comments in reference to the *Analects*, "This idea of 'ruling by not ruling'—concentrating on self-cultivation and inner Virtue and allowing external things to come naturally and noncoercively—has been a constant theme throughout the *Analects*" (Slingerland 2003: 176). *Mencius* 4A4 advises, "Whenever one acts to no avail, one should turn within and examine oneself. When one has made one's own person correct, the rest of the world will follow" (Mencius 2009: 76). Similarly, as Mencius puts it in 4B28, when the morally virtuous person finds himself in a less than ideal situation, he first examines himself:

Here is a man who treats me with malice. [Receiving such treatment,] the noble person must turn within [*zifan*, 自反] : "I must not have been humane; I must have been lacking in courtesy, or how could such a thing have happened to me?" If, on turning within [*zifan*, 自反], one finds oneself to be humane, if on turning within [*zifan*, 自反], one finds oneself to be courteous and yet the maliciousness continues, the noble person must *again* turn within: "I must not have shown good faith." If, on turning within [*zifan*, 自反], one finds good faith in oneself and still the maliciousness continues, the noble person will say, "This is a wild man. Since he is like this, how then can one choose between him and the animals? Why should I contend with an animal?" (Mencius 2009: 92–93)

Upon finding no blame in his own conduct for the non-optimal situation, the moral exemplar's source of anxiety is then removed. His concern does not lie in the prospective misdemeanors of others in the world, but in his own moral imperfection.

Relatedly, in *Analects* 14.29 we read, "Zigong was given to criticizing and judging others. The Master remarked, 'Zigong must have reached an acme of virtue! This affords him a leisure that I do not possess.'" Concomitant with the Confucian stress on cultivating the self is the realization that frequently critiquing other persons is actually a sign of moral failure. In other words, part of cultivating the self is not to focus on the failures of other persons, as this is a sign of a lack of virtue and is exactly the kind of behavior that is not efficacious for bringing about moral change. Forgoing any self-congratulatory assumption that one is in a position to voice judgment of others is understood as a sign of virtue and cultivation. Having examined himself and satisfied himself that he has done nothing to provoke the harshness of the other, the moral exemplar simply moves on, making no demand on the offender to rectify his offense. This is because virtue has an affective dimension. To teach virtue, one must be noncoercive. We see this idea in the *Mencius* 4B28:

> Therefore the noble person has anxiety [*you*, 忧] that lasts a lifetime rather than troubles [*huan*, 患] that occupy a morning. And indeed the anxiety has a cause: "Shun was a human being; I, too, am a human being. Shun was a model for the world, one that could be transmitted to later generations. If I am nothing more than a villager, this is something to be anxious about." And what kind of anxiety is it? Simply to be like Shun; that is all. There is nothing that troubles the noble person. Taking no action that is not humane and engaging in no practice that is not courteous, the noble person, in case of a morning's troubles, would not be troubled. (Mencius 2009: 93)

The moral exemplar should only ever rectify himself. His only concern is with not being morally perfected himself. We see the same sentiment in *Mencius* 4A4: no demands need be made to rectify the behavior of others, as merely making sure of the correctness of one's own conduct will be infectious enough to rectify the behavior of others:

> Mencius said, "If one loves others and yet they show no affection in return, he should turn within and examine [*fan*, 反] his own humaneness; if one rules others and yet they are not well governed, he should examine [*fan*, 反] his own wisdom; if one behaves with propriety toward others yet they do not respond appropriately, he should examine his own reverence. Whenever one acts to no avail, one should turn within and examine oneself. When one has made one's own person correct, the rest of the world will follow [*gui*, 归]. (Mencius 2009: 76)

For Mencius, the one who acts in this self-directed way "will have no enemies in the world, and one who has no enemies in the world is the agent of Heaven" (*Mencius* 2A5; Mencius 2009: 35). One indication that Mencius's sentiment ("Whenever one acts to no avail, one should turn within and examine oneself [行有不得者, 皆反求诸己]") was foundational to the Chinese tradition is the fact that it became one of the rules of Zhu Xi's (1130–1200 CE) White Deer Grotto Academy (白鹿洞书院). The same ideal is expressed by Zhang Zai (1020–1077 CE) when he writes, "In holding oneself to account [责] with the same desire to hold others to account [责] is the utmost Dao" (Zhang 1978: 32). The Chinese tradition understood that imposing one's own moral standards and customs on others who are set in their ways only impedes whatever influence on their behavior one hopes to have by evoking their resentment. The most efficacious route to influencing the behavior of others is to shape oneself into such an exemplar that others seek to emulate you.

Of course, this Chinese way of thinking about moral influence is premised on the assumption that there exist no antithetical barbarian others in the world who are insensible to the attractiveness of moral behavior (that is, behavior that promotes the flourishing of others). The Chinese way of thinking about moral influence is coherent with its own assumptions that all peoples in the world are born with moral-knowing (*liangzhi*, 良知). Indeed, the essence of the human being is moral-knowing—that is, to be human is to potentially have an intuitive understanding of moral behavior. Moral behavior, in the Chinese worldview, is understood to be universal in that all peoples intuitively understand it. No one is born without the faculties to understand this behavior. Even those whose moral faculties have been blighted by an upbringing in a hostile environment will become sensitized to moral actions after sustained influence or moral therapy. A person's moral muscles may have atrophied, but they never disappear, and moral rehabilitation will restore this innate moral capacity and its functional strength. The Chinese view assumes that there is no unredeemable moral sociopath who cannot be rehabilitated after sustained reintroduction to moral behavior. This assumption underlies the particular Chinese understanding of efficacy and virtue where the moral agent influences others to spontaneously come to them for moral instruction.

Conversely, under the Western assumption that the world is divided into the forces of morality and the forces of immorality, and that the different races embody these respective forces, the Chinese understanding of efficacy is nonsensical. Barbarians (in Western metaphysics) are preternaturally determined to remain blind to morality. How could they possibly be drawn to moral behavior if they can neither see nor understand it? Their resistance to this imposition of form is parsed as the inevitable "friction" that develops because matter is never fully compliant to form in an ideal Platonic paradigm of the genesis of the images of forms.

This is not to say that the Confucian does not judge; in fact, it is imperative for the moral agent to always be judging. One judges, however, not to exert power over others, but for the sake of one's own moral improvement. Confucius criticizes Zigong in *Analects* 14.29 precisely because Zigong's criticism of others merely asserts his superiority over others and does nothing to improve himself. Similarly, in *Analects* 4.17 we read: "When you see someone who is worthy, concentrate upon becoming their equal; when you see someone who is unworthy, use this as an opportunity to look within yourself" (Slingerland 2003: 35). The failings of others do *not* present an opportunity to feel an egoistic self-affirmation, but rather an opportunity to reflect on one's own conduct. Likewise, in the *Luxuriant Gems of the Spring and Autumn* we read an explicit criticism of the hypocrisy of judging others while simultaneously evading self-critique:

> The standard of righteousness lies in correcting [正] the self, not in correcting others. If we do not correct ourselves, even if we are capable of correcting others, [the *Spring and Autumn*] will not grant that this is righteousness. (Queen and Major 2016: 313–14)

The text continues by highlighting the virtue of asymmetrically expecting more from oneself than from others:

> Righteousness does not refer to correcting [正] others but to correcting the self. When there are chaotic times and depraved rulers, everyone aspires

to correct others. Yet how can this be called "righteousness"? [. . .] Thus I say: Righteousness lies in correcting the self; it does not lie in correcting others. This is the standard. Now if we lack [some trait] but look for it in others, or if we have [some trait] and yet criticize it in others, this is something that no one will find acceptable; it is contrary to principles. How could this be called righteousness? (Queen and Major 2016: 315–16, my modifications)

The belief that rectifying the moral imperfections of the world comes only through self-improvement and that imposing one's morality or moral standards onto others is unvirtuous can also be found in the Daoist canon. In a conversation between Yan Hui and Confucius in the chapter "In the Human World" (人间世) of the *Zhuangzi*, Confucius (as a mouthpiece for Zhuangzi) similarly reiterates the priority of self-cultivation before moral castigation of others. The conversation begins with Yan Hui telling Confucius that he wishes to bring order to the state of Wei, as its ruler has been grossly derelict in carrying out his duties. Yan Hui tells Confucius, "I wish to take what I have learned from you and to derive some standards and principles [*ze*, 则] from it to apply to this situation. Perhaps then the state can be saved" (Ziporyn 2020: 34). Confucius responds by saying that only those who are already consummately virtuous themselves should worry about the failings of others:

The Consummate Persons of old made sure they had it in themselves before they tried to put it into others. If what is in yourself is still unstable, what leisure do you have to worry about some tyrant? (Ziporyn 2020: 34, my modifications)

In sum, the ideal of moral self-improvement as a panacea for rectifying the world's wrongs pervades the Chinese tradition. It is widely understood that imposing one's own moral standards onto others will hinder the amelioration of social ills rather than advance them, because ultimately all persons are sovereign agents in their own right, and any attempt to disabuse others of their preexisting form leads only to friction and resentment.

The Chinese Attitude of Non-interference with Animals

That the Chinese tradition of understanding non-Chinese as susceptible to and attracted by moral behavior, such that proper virtue itself is enough to influence others, should not be controversial given that they assumed that even animals are sensitive to moral virtue. Coherent with the processual holism that we discussed in chapter 3, the Chinese tradition did not see human culture as radically discontinuous with the rest of nature, nor human morality as supra-mundane. Thus, a pervasive view in the Chinese classics is that animals are in some ways sensitive to human virtue (again, understood as the ability to bring co-creative growth and flourishing) and that the proper ordering of the nonhuman world depends only on the perfection of virtue in human society, not on any violent and coercive campaign to organize and reconstitute the natural world.

It is worth briefly restating that the Chinese idea of non-interference with nature stands in stark contrast to the Greco-Christian conception. As the historian Keith Thomas writes in *Man and the Natural World*, for the English during the period of settler-colonialism in the "New World," "human civilisation indeed was virtually synonymous with the conquest of nature" (Thomas 1983: 25). Although not representative of all opinions, the typical attitude in the early modern period was that "the world was made exclusively for man, that nature was to be feared and subjugated, that the inferior species had no rights or that the differences between man and beast were unbridgeable" (50). Thus, "man's task, in the words of Genesis (i. 28), was 'to replenish the earth and subdue it'" (14–15), because "uncultivated land meant uncultivated men" (15). In contrast to this dualistic view of humans and the nonhuman natural world, with civilization on one side of the dualism dominating nature on the other, the Chinese tradition viewed the human as continuous with the nonhuman.

The Chinese tradition saw humans as continuous—rather than radically discontinuous—with animals, and it viewed human civilization (*wen*, 文) as a creative harmonization of the patterns (*wen*, 文) already present in nature (Xiang 2021a: 21–85, 109–24). Virtuous human conduct was understood to exert a transformational influence (*de hua*, 德化) on the animal world and on the cosmos as a whole (Sterckx 2002: 137). In the Chinese tradition, Roel Sterckx writes, the animal and the human coexisted within a continuous "moral cosmos" (Sterckx 2002: 153). One aspect of the assumption that the world is transformed through virtue was the related assumption that animals are not insensible to moral virtue; it was believed that they resonate with virtue, and that a sage-ruler's virtue can reach all animals. For example, after describing how humans and animals are essentially the same because both humans and animals wish to preserve their lives, have maternal bonds with their children, and are social with their kind, the *Liezi* says that in the age of sage-rule and human virtue, "men and animals lived together and walked side by side" (Graham 1990: 55):

> The divine sages of the most ancient times knew the habits of all the myriad things, and interpreted the cries of all the different species; they called them together for meetings and gave them instructions, as though they were human beings. So the fact that the sages would meet the spirits and goblins first, next summon the human beings of the eight quarters, and finally assemble the birds and beasts and insects, implies that there are no great differences in mind and intelligence between living species. The divine sages knew that this was the case, and therefore in teaching they left out none of them. (Graham 1990: 55)

The idea that the animal can be transformed by (human) virtue pervaded the tradition. As Sterckx explains, "the discourse on moral transformation was anchored in a doctrine which held that the human cultivation of virtue would cause animals to behave in a moral way" (Sterckx 2002: 124). Since no radical disjunction between animals and humans was perceived, it was also assumed that animals could be civilized and transformed into cultured beings (123).

Given that the Chinese tradition viewed human-made music as a more sophisticated refinement of preexisting sounds in the natural world (Xiang 2021a: 93–97), and certain forms of music as influencing moral-psychological disposition and so conduct, they also believed that music can help to cultivate human dispositions. Since all of nature forms a continuum, the Chinese tradition also thought that music could help to cultivate animal dispositions. Music was understood to civilize and tame the predatory instincts of wild animals.

In the same vein, one of the signs of the sociopolitical authority of a sage-ruler was his capacity to transform the animal world through his mastery of music (Sterckx 2002: 129–32). The *Book of Han* explains how the virtuous sage affects animals through his command of harmonious music:

> When all the sages harmonize in the courts, then the myriad creatures will harmonize in the fields. Therefore when the *shao* 韶 music of the pan-flutes is performed nine times, the phoenix will come and show its respect. When the music stones are struck and the chime stones are slapped, all the animals will lead each other in the dance. (quoted in Sterckx 2002: 132; Ban 1962: 1933)

Of course, passages like this one are mythic and fanciful, but these mythic fantasies still contrast meaningfully with their counterparts in the Greek tradition, the genre of myths about the taming of undomesticated beasts. In the Chinese instance, beasts are tamed through the deployment of meaningful natural patterns (music), that is, through a universal, cross-species, ameliorative, and symbolic medium. The Greek tradition, on the other hand, understood the taming of the beast in terms of their physical domination.

We see another example of the Chinese mythic understanding of how animals are tamed and influenced in the *Liezi*. In this Daoist text, we are told that when the sage-king Yao made Kui (夔) his director of music, all the animals responded to his music. When Kui performed the Xiao Shao (簫韶) music, the phoenix came to dance to its rhythm. The *Liezi* concludes:

> This is an example of attracting the beasts and birds by music. In what way, then, are the minds of beasts and birds different from man's? Since they differ from men in shape and voice, we do not know the Way to make contact with them, but the sage knows everything and understands everything, and that is why he succeeds in drawing them to him and making them his servants. (Graham 1990: 54)

Operative in this passage is the assumption that, because the most sublime music is universally able to affect all sentient beings, an important and efficacious way to influence other beings is through the mastery of music. The *Kong Family Master's Anthology* (*Kong Congzi*, 孔丛子) comments on the music master Kui leading the animals with music:

> These words refer to the transformatory effects of good government [*shan zheng zhi hua*, 鄯政治化]. When the emperors and kings of antiquity accomplished their deeds, they composed music. [. . .] If this music was harmonious, then heaven and earth would indeed respond to it. How much more so [was the reaction of] all animals. (quoted in Sterckx 133; Fu 2011: 22)

Here the sage's ability to influence animals and bring them into his service through the deployment of music is a metaphor for good government itself.

In fact, it was widely thought that animals behave immorally only because of a lack of virtue in the human realm, and that when there is correct virtue among humans, the animal world spontaneously becomes harmonious. Animals' predatory killings of humans, for example, were explained as the outcome of a lack of balance and virtue in the human realm (Sterckx 2002: 140–141). In the *Records of Ritual Matters by Dai the Elder* (*Da Dai Liji*; 大戴礼记; comp. 206 BCE–8 CE), for example, we read that when sages are ruling the state [. . .] rapacious beasts forget to attack, and [predatory] birds forget their spurs. Wasps and scorpions don't sting young babies. Mosquitoes and gadflies don't bite young foals. (quoted in Sterckx 2002: 140; Dai 1978: 351)

Sage-rule is understood as bringing order or harmony to the entire world without coercion. Whereas noncivilized behavior masters the world in a phys-ical and direct way through violent domination, the sage-ruler influences the world in an indirect, nonphysical way (*wuwei*) and acquires moral authority over animals through the medium of music and the cultivation of virtue (Sterckx 2002: 161). In the *Family Sayings of Confucius* (*Kongzi Jiayu*, 孔子家语; comp. third century CE), we read:

Confucius said: When Shun [a legendary sage-king; ca. twenty-third century BCE] was a ruler, in government he respected life and despised killing. In assigning offices he engaged worthies and dismissed the unwor-thy. His virtue was as tranquil and pure as heaven and earth. He could change like the four seasons and transform things. Therefore everything within the four seas was subject to his influence, which permeated the dif-ferent species [*yi lei*, 异类]. Phoenixes were soaring about, unicorns came, birds and beasts complied to his virtue. (quoted in Sterckx 2002: 147)

The sage's rule is non-aggressive. The animals of the world spontaneously order themselves and are drawn of their own accord to the virtue of the sage who embodies proper virtue.

In sum, traditional Chinese attitudes toward animals had the following dimen-sions: (1) the animal and the human formed a part of the same continuum; (2) animals were susceptible and responsive to morality and moral instruction through its pedagogical forms, such as music; (3) the animal world was harmoni-ously ordered when correct morality prevailed in the human realm; (4) as such, violent coercion of the animal world was a symptom of uncivilized behavior and an utmost lack of virtue; and (5) the utmost human virtue was shown when humans had no need to trespass on the animal world and when human virtue was enough, in a *wuwei* fashion, to bring harmony to all of the natural world.

These five points with regard to how the Chinese understood their relation-ship to the animal world parallel the Chinese attitude toward non-Chinese others. As Sterckx explains, "In the same way that animals who were susceptible to music and virtue would gather and perch within the central realm to figure as acolytes of the virtuous ruler, barbarians could be transformed to shed off their bestial instincts and trade their animal hides for Chinese clothing" (Sterckx 2002: 161). The traditional Chinese attitude towards the relationship between humans and animals (that they are compatible and not two antithetical realms. They can and should exist in harmony with each other) is likewise applicable to the Chinese and non-Chinese relationship. The Chinese understanding of efficacy is reflected in the relationship between both humans and animals and between humans and "barbarians." Since animals and non-Chinese are not mere matter without form, the efficacious way to have influence over them is through *wuwei*, noncoercive means.

The Ideal of Self-Cultivation in Chinese Foreign Policy Practice

The idea that one should not aggressively force one's vision on others because the virtue of the moral agent alone should be enough to attract the voluntary admiration of others pervades the Confucian canon. In the "Canon of Shun" chapter of the Book of Yu of the *Book of Documents* (one of the "five classics" that served as the foundation of Chinese political philosophy), for example, we read that through self-cultivation, others will be drawn to one like the North Star that Confucius spoke of:

> Be yielding to the distant [柔远], and look after the near. Respect the virtuous, trust the generous, disregard the artful. This is how the faraway tribes will lead on one another to make their compliant admiration [率服]. (Wang and Wang 2012: 22, my translation)

Similarly, in *Analects* 16.1 we read:

> This being the case, if those who are distant will not give their compliant admiration [服], simply refine your culture and virtue in order to attract them. Once you have attracted them, you should make them content. (Slingerland 2003: 192, my modifications)

For the Confucian, not judging others but instead making greater demands on oneself is the correct way to prove the validity of one's position. It cannot be overstated how persistent and pervasive this idea is in the Chinese tradition. "The Counsels of the Great Yu" chapter in the *Book of Documents* enjoins:

> Yi said, "Alas! be cautious! If you are cautious then you will not fall into error. Do not fail to observe the laws and ordinances. Do not find your

enjoyment in idleness. Do not go to excess hedonism. Trust meritorious men and do not be hesitant in your employment of them. Have no dealings with depraved men without hesitation. If you are indecisive, then your plans cannot come to fruition. Fully think through your plans and they will succeed. Do not go against what is right, to get the praise of the people. Do not oppose the people's wishes to follow your own desires. Attend to these things without idleness or omission, and the tribes all around will come and acknowledge your sovereignty [四夷来王]." (Wang and Wang 2012: 354–55, my translation)

The way to prove the "universality" of one's own values is thus to draw others to oneself through the superiority of one's conduct alone. It is for this reason that "the fundamental spirit of the traditional approach to the barbarian problem, therefore, was nongoverning and nonintervening" (Hsü 1960: 9). The historian Immanuel C. Y. Hsü (徐中约) writes:

It is these ideas and admonitions in the classical canons, which every scholar-statesman studied, that became the cornerstone of Chinese policy toward outlandish peoples. The basic tenet of such a policy was that the Chinese emperor should be virtuous and benevolent so that the barbarians, through spontaneous admiration, might voluntarily seek assimilation. It was not an active and aggressive policy of going out to convert the outlandish tribes, but rather a passive, "laissez-faire" policy of expecting them to come to obtain transformation of their own accord. (Hsü 1960: 8–9)

We see the lack of aggressive campaigns against foreign others at the end of a two-part biography of the Xiongnu in the *Book of Han*. According to Ban Gu, the ancient kings (ca. third millennium BCE) did not wage offensive campaigns against the Xiongnu (不就攻伐) and treated them as though they were operating in a different sphere because the Xiongnu had

different customs and food habits. Our languages are not mutually intelligible. They live far removed in the northern frontier wilderness following the grass and their flocks, maintaining their existence through hunting. [China and the Xiongnu] are separated by mountains and valleys and [we are] mutually obstructed by the desert. This is the way that the natural world defines inner and outer. (Ban 1962: 3834, my translation)

Ban Gu is saying that, as the Chinese and their northern neighbors were geographically separated from each and culturally different from each other, the ancient kings decided that it was best to let each people lead their separate lives. For the sage-kings of the past, Ban Gu concludes,

> government through education/government and instruction [政教] was not imposed on the people [the Xiongnu]. The changes in the calendar as promulgated by the emperor [正朔] were not imposed on them. To control them the sage-kings punished and resisted them when they came [to invade China] and prepared and guarded against them when then they left. If, attracted by China's civilization, they came to offer tribute, they would be treated with courtesy, and shown tenderness, and given indulgent treatment [*jimi*, 羈縻], without severing the relationship, so that the blame of being unrectified [*qu*, 曲] would always be on them. This was the constant way that the sage-kings ruled the Man and Yi. (Ban 1962: 3834, my translation)

The Chinese world knew of the existence of peoples different from themselves but found no reason in those differences to demonize other peoples as aberrant and then dominate them according to "Chinese" values.

Immanuel Hsü accurately summarizes the traditional Chinese foreign policy of non-intervention and winning over the other through the charismatic attraction of one's culture and virtue rather than military force:

> A corollary of the philosophy of nonintervention was the doctrine of non-exploitation of the barbarians. The Confucianists advocated China's not wearing herself out in endless warfare with the outer tribes, but winning their submission through a benevolent concern for their welfare. (Hsü 1960: 9)

This laissez-faire attitude toward foreigners has also been noted by the Sinologist Richard Smith:

> In theory, the Chinese world view was passive: foreigners were expected to gravitate to China solely out of admiration for Chinese culture. And indeed, the historical record abounds with praise for groups of foreigners as well as individuals who "admired right behavior and turned toward [Chinese] civilization" (*muyi xianghua*). Force was to be used only as a last resort in the conduct of China's foreign relations. (Smith 2015: 217)

This ideal is expressed in the "23rd Year of Lord Zhao" in the *Zuo Zhuan* (a historical text chronicling the period 722 to 468 BCE), where the ancient sage-kings are said to have reached such an acme of virtue and to have so tenderly cherished the outlying *yi* (夷) tribes in all four directions that these tribes actively protected the sage-kings (古者天子守在四夷) (Durrant, Li, and Schaberg 2016: 1625). Xu, the governor of Shen, employed this canonical example to admonish the chief minister of Chu, who had fortified the capital city against attack:

> What will Chu have to fear if it rectifies its borders, cultivates its territories and fields, builds up its frontier fortifications, wins the affection of its people and leading men, clarifies its system of neighborhood guards, establishes good faith with neighboring domains, uses caution in handling officials and defenders, and preserves the rituals for diplomatic exchanges, neither falling short nor asking for too much, showing neither weakness nor excessive force, and perfecting its defenses in order to be ready for the unexpected? As it says in the Odes,
>
> > Think on your ancestors;
> > Cultivate their virtue. (Durrant, Li, and Schaberg 2016: 1625)

Practices and phenomena that are perceived to be imperfect cannot be truly rectified through defeating them, but only through increasing one's own virtue. We can also see this worldview in the historical chronicles of Chinese engagement with the frontier tribes. In the *Book of Later Han*, we read:

> As it is said, if a Son of Heaven acts according to filial piety, the tribes of the four directions [*siyi*, 四夷] will become peaceful; nothing but filial piety can save the borders which, beset by rebellions, are contracting day by day. (Fan 1965: 1859, my translation)

The pervasive idea of refining the self as the only way to address external problems is reiterated here with regard to the relationship between the sovereign and the nomadic tribes that posed a political threat. In the *Book of Former Tang*, we read similar admonitions to increase one's own virtue in order to attract others to oneself:

> Where the state tax is fair, the instructions of the sovereign [王教] are complete, this is what is called "huaxia" [华夏, i.e., China]. The vast lands covered by the sky, with the extensive valleys and rivers, and with many people living among it, so innumerable that it cannot be comprehensively accounted for, these are the "dependent states" [蕃国]. The western and southern Man Yi are not few in number. Although [our] languages are not mutually intelligible, our likes and desires not the same, [they] can still

observe rules and yearn to pursue transformative teachings [瞻风], and maintain their offer of tribute from afar. [One should] be anxious [*huan*, 患] that oneself is without virtue and not be anxious [*huan*, 患] that people will not come. What is the proof for this? During the heyday of the Zheng-guan [of Emperor Taizong] and Kaiyuan [of Emperor Xuanzong] reigns, there were many who came to our country. (Liu 1975: 5286, my translation)

"China" (*huaxia*, 华夏) is, by definition, the place of correct education and fair taxes. As we have repeatedly seen, the Chinese understanding of efficacy and virtue is not concerned with the existence of practices antithetical to Chinese practices and the concomitant desire to voice disapproval of them. It is assumed by Confucians that all peoples have a moral nature (*liangzhi*, 良知), and so other peoples are not at fault when they do not turn to the moral agent. Other peoples' failure to appreciate one's eminence can only ever be caused by one's own shortcomings.

In the Chinese worldview, the empirical evidence of the validity of this assumption is the Tang dynasty at its height, when it was able to attract huge swathes of foreign peoples to China, including those who worked in the highest echelons of state power. Since the Chinese never made the assumption that some other persons are ontological barbarians and did genuinely think that nobody is without a moral nature, the expedient rationalization that others are not drawn to one's virtue because they are barbarians was not available to the Confucian-Chinese. The only possible reason for others not appreciating the moral agent, or for the existence of an imperfect world, was to look within.

Writing on the Northern Song's attitude toward its aggressive neighbors, Tao Jing-Shen (陶晋生, 1933–) describes the prevalent contemporary practice of attributing the vitality of its non-Chinese northern neighbors to the lack of virtue and governance within China itself. Even in this period of acute crisis,

> some officials continued to stress the cultivation of virtue by the Chinese emperor and the insignificance of "barbarian" disturbances. On the eve of the Jurchens' conquest of the Northern Sung, Ch'en Kung-fu, a censor, memorialized the throne that the most pressing priorities were the cultivation of virtue and some necessary political reforms. If the government implemented internal reforms, the "barbarians" would cherish Chinese virtue and fear Chinese military power. (Tao 1983: 76)

A popular belief in this period was that the non-Chinese northerners were "yin" whereas China was "yang," with the lack of harmony between them serving as a barometer of the lack of virtue on the part of the Chinese, the government, and the emperor (Tao 1983: 74–75). For example, Zhao Pu (赵普), who was prime minister to both Taizu and Taizong (the first and second emperors of the Song dynasty), opposed the use of military force against the non-Chinese northerners. He wrote in his memorials that since ancient times wise rulers pacified the non-Chinese and did not interfere in their affairs. Their policy was one of defense and cultivation of virtue (75). To show the pervasive attitude of resolving internal affairs in order to pacify external troubles, Tao pointed to a wide array of examples, from Shao Yong (邵雍; 1011–1077), the Cheng brothers, Zhao Ruyu (赵汝愚), Han Qi (韩琦; 1008–1075), Fan Zhongyan (范仲淹; 989–1052), Wang Anshi, Sima Guang, and Fan Zuyu's (范祖禹) *Mirror of the Tang* (唐鉴) to the introduction to the *Forgotten Events of the Xuan He Period* (大宋宣和遗事). When met with external threats, the consistent Chinese attitude was that one cannot simply impose a moral order on others and, relatedly, that the effective and virtuous way to resolve these external problems is through rectifying internal domestic order. As I have argued, the Chinese tradition held such a view owing to the metaphysical assumption that order is not a preestablished singularity. It follows that it is inefficacious for the moral agent to impose her form onto others on the assumption that she is the one with form.

The Inefficacy and Unsustainability of Colonialism

These ideas about what is efficacious in dealing with those of a different persuasion from oneself go a long way toward explaining why the Chinese tradition has no history of colonialism and never thought of colonialism or the imperium as a worthwhile pursuit or a mandate. Besides the inefficacy of imposing one's own form onto others, imperium is not a sustainable political model for another related reason. In practice, realizing an imperium requires that sovereign agents who were previously responsible for their own wellbeing be economically, politically, and culturally de-developed to the extent that they become the very barbarians of one's ideology. The practical realization of the metaphysics of colonialism is a self-fulfilling prophecy. Being the world's guardian comes with the responsibility of being perpetually responsible for previously self-sufficient peoples who have now been reduced to children who are politically and culturally dependent on the colonizer. Besides being unsustainable in the long run, this model arguably does not even produce that much value for the colonizer. For all the suffering that colonialism has brought to the world, previous colonial powers such as Portugal and Spain have little to show for it even just a few hundred years after their colonial heyday.

In the *Discourses on Salt and Iron,* which records the famous debate on the salt and iron monopoly policies of the state in 81 BCE, Confucian scholars condemned Qin and Han aggressions into foreign lands. Instead of aggressive expansion, the Confucian scholars advocated an inward-looking attitude based on pragmatic considerations. As they explained, military aggression did not improve the welfare of the domestic populace; instead, human lives were lost, the state's economic resources were depleted, and military forces were never able to conclusively drive away the nomads. Furthermore, because maintenance of Chinese control over the appropriated territories would drain China's economic, military, and political power, such control could never be permanently maintained. Rejecting the use of military force to subdue non-Chinese, they insisted on the Confucian idea found in *Analects* 16.1: "If remote people are not submissive, all the influences of civil culture and virtue are to be cultivated to attract them to be so" (quoted in Pan 1997: 30). The fact that colonizing the earth is arguably *counter* to one's pragmatic interests shows how much it is, in fact, an ideology. The Confucian scholars, who had no ideological view of colonialism and domination as inherently virtuous, pragmatically recognized the inefficacy of aggressive expansion.

The colonial domination of the earth is motivated by a non-empirical ideology of what constitutes virtue more than by desire to gain pragmatic advantage. In his book *Facing West: The Metaphysics of Indian-Hating and Empire-Building,* Richard Drinnon argues that the United States expanded its western frontier to encompass the whole globe. "True West had become a traveling shooting gallery. By engulfing the other cardinal points it had become global. It was everywhere and bound nowhere. It was ungrounded" (Drinnon 1997: x). If the western frontier is now "ungrounded," Drinnon asks, what would "winning" the West even mean (465)? Drinnon maintains that the American/Western ideal of dominating the globe was not rooted in some pragmatic goal of winning anything substantial, but rather in the ideology of the "white man's burden." That is, "winning the West" amounted to what Edward Said describes as a metaphysical obligation that, once achieved, confirms one's metaphysical worldview.

Having never entertained a metaphysics of colonialism, the Chinese tradition never saw the domination of the earth as a relevant or desirable ideal. As we have seen, two of the most significant episodes of territorial expansion in Chinese history were motivated by pragmatic concerns about defense, not by a desire for domination over others. It is worth noting that the later Confucian-Chinese tradition was highly critical of both Han Wudi's military campaign against the Xiongnu and the First Emperor of the Qin's unification of China. Violent expansion, even when motivated by defense, was met with moral stricture, as it was not seen as morally virtuous. As Patricia Ebrey writes, "Later Chinese historians did not celebrate the First Emperor as one of the greatest conquerors of all time (as one suspects Greek or Roman historians would have)" (Ebrey 2010: 61). Ebrey perhaps assumes that Greco-Roman historians would celebrate this kind of conquest because in the Western context violent domination of inferiors, as a metaphysical obligation, was inherently virtuous. There is strong reason to believe that the Confucian understanding of efficacy and virtue (self-improvement to increase one's moral gravitas so that others are drawn to one's example) helped to discourage the kind of colonizing and genocidal conduct given free rein in the Western world (where efficacy and virtue is shown in imposing one's moral paradigms on recalcitrant others). The Confucian model of efficacy and virtue, we could argue, informed the traditional Chinese ideal model of foreign policy.

Elsewhere (Xiang 2022), and borrowing from the insights of the historian William Appleman Williams, I have analyzed the psychology of colonialism as an exercise in evasion. Under the colonial mindset, instead of cultivating one's own value, both spiritual and economic, the colonizer's value subsists in the negation of the preexisting economic, cultural, moral, and spiritual value of the colonized. Racial ideology is thus inextricable from colonialism, since casting the colonized as a transgressive racial other justifies their economic disenfranchisement. By parsing exploitation of the racial-colonized other as punishment for that racial other's transgression, the colonizer gains cultural, moral, and spiritual value. The colonizer is virtuous through his punishment and exploitation of the transgressive racial other. In contrast, the Confucian worldview has no notion of moral value being gained through punishing a putative transgressor. In the sense of colonialism as an ideology through which value is gained by punishing the behaviors of others, Confucianism did not have an ideology of colonialism.

Harmony: The Chinese World Ordering

That the Chinese tradition lacked an aggressive ideology of expansion should not be controversial. As I have argued, the Chinese tradition of never dualistically conceiving of non-Chinese lands and peoples as formless matter onto which the Chinese form of civilization needed to be imprinted curbed the development of any such ideology. Citing the assimilation of non-Han Chinese during the Han dynasty, Yü Ying-Shih writes that after the northern tribes submitted to the Han, they were given the status of a dependent state (*shuguo*, 属国) and allowed to follow their own customs and way of life (Yü 1986: 383, 398). This practice is consistent with the treatment of non-Chinese as stipulated in the "Royal Regulations" (王制) chapter of the *Book of Rites*, which recommends that the emperor refrain from interfering with local customs:

> With regard to all the materials used for habitation, they must inevitably be influenced by the weather/climate, the nature of the land, the temperature and moistness of the climate. The wide valleys and the big rivers are different. Because people live in different places, thus their customs/ways of life [俗] are different. Hard [aggressive]-soft, lightness-heaviness, slowness-fastness [of their natures] are all different, their palates are different, their equipment/ weapons are different, their clothes are different. [One must] institute education [and not] change their customs/ways of life, all the rules [across the country] must be standardized, but one cannot diminish the local practices [which suit the locality]. [修其教, 不易其俗, 齐其政, 不易其宜]
>
> The people of those five regions—the central states, and the Rong, Yi, [and other tribes around them]—had all their several dispositions [*xing*, 性], which could not be altered. [...] The people of the central states, and of those Man, Rong, and Di, all had their dwellings, where they lived at ease; their flavors which they preferred; the clothes suitable for them; their proper implements for use; and their vessels which they prepared in abundance. In those five regions, the languages of the people were not mutually intelligible, and their likings and desires were different. To make what was in their minds apprehended, and to communicate their likings and desires, [there were officers]—in the east, called *ji* [寄]; in the south, *xiang* [象]; in the west, *di di* [狄鞮]; and in the north, *shi* [译]. (Wang 2016: 163–64, my translation)

We see a similar cosmopolitan sensitivity to local practices due to an appreciation for the different forms that cultures take in chapter 11 of the *Huainanzi* (second century BCE), "Placing Customs on Par" (*Qi Su Xun*, 齐俗训). There the reader is urged to understand that, as the translators explain, "the validity of any 'ritual' is contingent on its appropriateness to the time and place in which it is practiced, and the distinction between the tribal customs of the 'barbarians' living outside the Han domain and the rituals of the Han court is ultimately arbitrary" (Queen and Major 2010: 393). One of the key aspects of governance is recognizing the existing cultural forms of the peoples under one's rule. Trying to coerce others to be different will only result in resentment. Something of the spirit of the *Book of Rites* can be seen in the Tang governance of foreigners. Tang dynasty law stipulated that if foreigners from the same country commit a crime against each other, then the law of their homeland applies. If foreigners of different nationalities are involved, however, Chinese law applies, since they are on Chinese soil (Hansen 2012: 149). Again, we see an accommodating, perspectival understanding of cultural difference.

Instead of conceiving of non-Chinese and their lands as formless matter onto which the form of Chinese civilization should be imposed, Chinese civilization is instead conceived of as a kind of empty center that does not seek to impose itself but instead sustains the diverse growth of things according to their own particular needs. This empty center that sustains the growth of the myriad things around it can be understood in terms of the emptiness (*wu*, 无) that the *Daodejing* praises as the utmost in virtue and efficacy:

> The thirty spokes converge at one hub,
> But the utility of the cart is a function of the nothingness (*wn*) inside the hub.
> We throw clay to shape a pot,
> But the utility of the clay pot is a function of the nothingness inside it.
> We bore out doors and windows to make a dwelling,
> But the utility of the dwelling is a function of the nothingness inside it.
> Thus, it might be something (*you*) that provides the value,
> But it is nothing that provides the utility. (Ames and Hall 2003: 91)

The possibility of action or existence in the world is dependent on the emptiness or non-existence that stands at its center. The *Daodejing* also talks about the fecundity of the empty center through the imagery of the empty valley:

> The life-force of the valley never dies—
> This is called the dark female.
> The gateway of the dark female—
> This is called the root of the world.
> Wispy and delicate, it only seems to be there,
> Yet its productivity is bottomless. (Ames and Hall 2003: 85)

This very receptivity in the Chinese tradition is embraced in positive terms as a generative power. This view that all action in the world depends on a non-imposing center is at the heart of Chinese thinking about efficacy in social relationships.

We witness this same idea about efficacy, but reinterpreted for the sociopolitical context, in chapter 2 of the *Daodejing*, where the sage is able to let the myriad things flourish only because he acts in a non-imposing manner (*wuwei*) and is thus comparable to the empty center:

> It is for this reason that sages keep to actions that do not entail
>   coercion (*wuwei*)
> And disseminate teachings that go beyond what can be said.
> In all that happens (*wanwu*),
> The sages develop things but do not initiate them,
> They act on behalf of things but do not lay any claim to them,
> They see things through to fruition but do not take credit for them.
> It is only because they do not take credit for them that things do not
>   take their leave. (Ames and Hall 2003: 80, my modifications)

The sage is comparable to the empty center that stands at the heart of a wheel. By acting noncoercively (non-imposingly), the sage as empty center becomes the condition for the flourishing of others, and since all beings are dependent on him, they "do not take their leave." As this empty center that does not seek to impose itself, the Chinese civilizational center is understood in the same virtuous terms as those that are applied to the virtuous sage. The civilizational center can be likened to the sage in chapters 27 and 30 of the *Doctrine of the Mean*. He is tolerant, magnanimous, gentle, yielding and flexible, and capable of the forbearance to sustain the myriad things like an inexhaustible wellspring. Like Confucius's North Star model of the virtuous in *Analects* 2.1, and according to what Ames calls "centripetal harmony," (Ames 1993: 52) the sage/center is a fertile source that sustains all that comes into its orbit.

In the same way that a chef mixes different complementary ingredients to create a dish, so does harmony relate all particulars in a way that not only preserves their particularity but also maximizes them as a result of the order or coherence now created among all the parts. As we have already seen, a comparable idea underlies the Chinese account of efficacy in war. The mark of virtue is the ability to nurture the myriad things and so attract things to oneself, as well as to bring all particulars into coherence (harmony). The Chinese conception of world order sees the center—China—as the yielding, characterless center that sustains the diverse particulars in its environs in a way that, like nature itself, "shelters and supports everything that is without them causing injury to one another [万物并育而不相害]." (Ames and Hall 2001: 112, modified) Referring to what I have called the empty center, Hall and Ames describe what they call a "radial solar system":

> This radial solar system seems to be a signature of the Chinese world order. It is a centripetal order articulated outward from a central axis through patterns of deference. These concrete patterns "con-*tribute*" in varying degrees, and are themselves constitutive of the authority at the center. They shape and bring into focus the standards and values of the social and political entity. This determinate, detailed, center-seeking focus fades into an increasingly indeterminate and untextured field. The magnetic attraction of the center is such that, with varying degrees of success, it draws into its field and suspends the disparate, diverse, and often mutually inconsistent centers that constitute its world. (Hall and Ames 1995: 242–43)

Hall and Ames's concept of centripetal order is similar in some respects to Tingyang Zhao's concept of a whirlpool state pattern (Zhao 2019: 23). The German Sinologist Wolfgang Leander Bauer (1930–1997) also noticed this "whirlpool" or "centripetal order" paradigm in the Chinese relationship between center and periphery:

> This "middle," however, was not considered to be encircled as a ring, but rather as the center of a living, pulsating stream pouring outwards, which had to be kept free of all isolation in order to develop fully. On the other hand, the "middle" was also shaped by peripheral areas diametrically opposed to each other in their extremes; in it, these hostile opposites did not simply sublate [*aufgehoben*] but reached a harmonious development. (Bauer 1980: 7–8, my translation)

The center is thus not a static *archē* that imposes itself on difference in a unilinear fashion, but an organic one that requires change and diversity. There is, to an extent, a reciprocal exchange of identities between the center and the periphery. Present here is the understanding that the center depends on the periphery for its existence: the center is constituted by the periphery.

Albert Memmi has pointed out that colonialism seeks to maintain an unequal relationship between colonizer and colonized, whereby the colonizer gives form and the colonized receives form (see chapter 1). The Chinese relationship to the non-Chinese is not unidirectional in this way. Just as the lapidary (military strategist) factors in the existing patterns (forms) of the jade (battle), the virtuous agent likewise sees that peoples' existing patterns "con-*tribute*" and "are themselves constitutive of" the center. Ames and Hall eloquently describe the difference between the Western conception of efficacy as the imposition of form and the Chinese conception of efficacy as a co-creative harmonization of existing patterns in terms of "power" and "creativity":

> Power is to be construed as the production of intended effects determined by external causation. Real creativity, on the other hand, entails the spontaneous production of novelty, irreducible through causal analysis. Power is exercised with respect to and over others. Creativity is always reflexive and is exercised over and with respect to "self." And since self in a processive world is always communal, creativity is contextual, transactional, and multidimensional. Thus creativity is both *self*-creativity and *co*-creativity. Either everything shares in creativity, or there is no creativity. Indeed, it is this transactional, co-creative character of all creative processes that precludes the project of self-cultivation and self-*creation* from being egoistic. (Ames and Hall 2003: 17)

The efficacious agent is one who supports the existing patterns of things in a way that, like the work of the lapidary, brings all the existing patterns into coherence and makes the implicit order more prominent. In this process the agent is himself creatively reconstituted. It is important to stress that this view of the self or of China is not an exercise in self-sacrifice. Through the ability of the agent or of China to bring harmony to those that surround it, both the person and the political entity earn the esteem of others. This "soft power" then sustains the authority of the agent or the state as a *primus inter pares*.

Ganying and the Chinese Conception of Efficacy

The process that allows for the dynamic, mutually interactive relationship between particulars that constitutes harmony (coherence among diverse things) is "resonance" (*ganying*, 感应). The *Shuowen Jiezi* defines harmony as "responding to each other [相应也]." The term *ganying* literally means "stimulus" and "response." Some of the earliest analogies used in explaining harmony were culinary and musical metaphors, which illustrate the Chinese idea of harmony so well because the unity in diversity is not achieved by following a preestablished formula.[3] The particulars dynamically responding to and complementing each other are themselves the (emergent) order. We see this understanding of harmony as mutual responsiveness in *Zhouyu* C (周语下) of the *Discourses of the States* (国语), which uses a musical metaphor:

When instruments are played in accordance with their natures there is equilibrium [*yueji*, 乐极]. Bringing such equilibrium together is called tones [*sheng*, 声]. When tones mutually respond [*ying*, 应] and promote one another [*xiangbao*, 相保] it is called harmony. When low notes and high notes do not mutually trespass, it is called balance [*ping*, 平]. (Chen 2013: 137)

The musical metaphor also supports the idea that diverse particulars can be affirmed without redounding to chaos, and that order arises from the interaction of the parts. Here we see this idea in *Analects* 3.23:

The Master was discussing music with the Grand Music Master of Lu. He said, "What can be known about music is this: when it first begins, it resounds with a confusing variety of notes, but as it unfolds, these notes are reconciled by means of harmony, brought into tension by means of counterpoint, and finally woven together into a seamless whole. It is in this way that music reaches its perfection." (Slingerland 2003: 27)

Music that is in proper harmony enhances the parts of the whole that constitute it. As a dynamic interaction of various different parts, the harmony or "order" of a musical composition is not one that is externally imposed but is instead emergent from the parts. In forming a larger coherence, the whole becomes greater than the mere sum of its parts.

The West's (mis)understanding of the Chinese concept of harmony exemplifies the West's dualistic mode of thought. As Chenyang Li notes, the West has understood harmony as naive, passive agreement (Li 2014: 7–8). This "innocent harmony," as Li terms it, is contrasted with the West's preferred counterpart, "justice": the assertion by each person of his or her own rights, even if doing so leads to continuous conflict. In identifying harmony with the identity side of the identity-heterogeneity dichotomy, Western philosophy misses the point about the concept of harmony, as there is no harmony within either identity or mere heterogeneity. Under the harmony paradigm, difference is understood as enriching, so that without difference, there can be no order or harmony; difference is a prerequisite to order and harmony. Relatedly, the coherence between the particulars does not constitute a static order. As the particulars change, the coherence or order of the whole correspondingly changes.

As A. C. Graham noted, the terms *gan* and *ying* are roughly equivalent to the Western conception of causality. For example, it is the *ganying* of the different musical notes that results in (the form of) "music." If, under a Western model, order is understood as linear causation that presumes that all particulars are inert and "passively allow themselves to be pushed by 'causes'" (Graham 1992: 38), under the Chinese model order is understood to arise from the mutual responsiveness (*ganying*, 感应) of the parts. Under the Western conception of causality that Graham speaks of, all particulars are assumed to be not only inert but also identical with each other, and so an external, activating cause is needed to set them in motion. It is this dualistic understanding of causation that underlies the West's misunderstanding of Chinese harmony as "innocent harmony." In the Western understanding of harmony and causation, order and causation are understood to lie not in the particulars themselves, but in the activating cause. As each particular is assumed to be inert, they are also assumed to be identical, so that the cause acts in a predictable, linear way. By contrast, in the Chinese conception of causality that Graham alludes to, each particular is *ziran/sponte sua*, and order is understood as the coherence that emerges from the interaction of non-inert and non-identical particulars. Order is not external to the particulars but arises from their interactions.

Conclusion

The Chinese tradition's recognition of the preexisting form of all things leads to the awareness that imposing one's will onto others is inefficacious, as it results in psychological resentment. It is more efficacious to make one's own position so attractive that others are spontaneously drawn to it. This ideal view of how to conduct oneself around those of a different mind or culture, though imperfectly realized throughout Chinese history, is reflected in Chinese foreign policy and practice. Of course, a necessary precondition of this Chinese ideal about efficacy in dealings with others is the absence of any assumption that the other is the ontological barbarian of the Western imagination, which has been formative in Western foreign policy and practice. Instead, the Chinese conception of efficacy presupposes that all peoples are born with a moral knowing (or form, as one could also say). This conception of efficacy can be seen in China's historic relationships with its neighbors, which, because China assumes these others to already have form, are conducted with an eye to "resonance"—that is, mutual influence.

The Confucian-Chinese attitude to the non-Chinese and animals can be described as a passive ethnocentrism and anthropocentrism, respectively. What we find in the dominant Confucian tradition is the view that humans are the most numinous of all creatures and a cultural elitism that saw *huaxia* culture as eminently superior to the cultures of its neighbors.[4] However, a key element of the Chinese tradition's perceived sense of its own superiority to non-Chinese was its cosmopolitanism—that is, its syncretism and willingness to take on the best aspects of the behaviors, habits, and cultures of others.

If the Chinese tradition's chauvinism or sense of superiority arising from its cosmopolitanism strikes the Western reader as paradoxical, that impression shows how deeply embedded the idea of the GCB is in the Western consciousness, which assumes that any sense of superiority derives from one's dominance over all others. Implicit in European nationalism, for example, is the idea of the dominance of one's own nation over all other nations (for example, "Germany, Germany above all, above all in the world," as the German national anthem goes). In the Western understanding, superiority is achieved and displayed through the (violent) denigration of others as inferior. Superiority is a zero-sum game in which the alpha male has a monopoly position and all others are subjugated to him. Absent this idea of virtue as dominance, the Chinese sense of cultural superiority is premised on a cultural confidence in embracing the best aspects of other cultures and thus creating the most eminent culture. Enriched through difference, cosmopolitan *huaxia* culture does not subscribe to a machismo in which superiority is proven through dominance.

Relatedly, Confucian-Chinese anthropocentrism, unlike the Christian variety, does not see human superiority as proven by its dominance over the natural world, but rather in the ability to harmonize the world without physical domination.[5] Chinese culture is the functional law of the whole constituted by the particulars, which are always tacitly and holographically signaling toward this whole (see Xiang 2021a: 72–78).

Conclusion

THIS BOOK has presented a little-known story in the West, that of the historic cosmopolitanism of Chinese tradition and culture, which was produced through the deepening and coexistence of particulars. In the introduction I promised to explain the "killer apps" of Chinese cosmopolitanism and to thereby expose the (literal) "kill apps" of Western racism. That is, we can summarize the philosophical assumptions that historically contributed to Chinese cosmopolitanism from two perspectives: from the negative perspective of noting the absence of certain philosophical metaphysical assumptions that shaped Western practice, and from the positive perspective of describing the Chinese philosophical sources of cosmopolitanism. I will do both in what follows.

The "kill apps" of Western racism evolve as follows:

1. A psychological fear of the embodied nature of human existence—that is, fear of mortality and the fact of change—is central.
2. Those psychologically unable to accept the fact of their human condition invent an ontology of bivalent dualism under which the eternal and its perceived attributes, such as reason, spirit, and objectivity, are abstracted from the holistic flow of experience and posited as antithetical and inimical to the perceived opposite of the eternal: change and its perceived attributes, such as passion, flesh, and an inability to transcend one's perspective.
3. Those unable to accept the fact of human mortality can now associate themselves with the positive side of this bivalent dualism and project the negative side of the dualism onto the racial other: the "barbarian."
4. According to this ontology of bivalent dualism, the "race" with "form" embodies the attributes of the eternal and thus has an ontological

mandate to imprint form onto those who do not. This is the metaphysics of colonialism.

5. This racist system perpetuates itself ad infinitum. No matter how many
perceived barbarians this racist system annihilates or are colonized with
form, in practice, more barbarians will be created. This happens because
the "barbarian" is a figment of the imagination created to fulfill a psychological need, and as long as that need goes unfulfilled, the number of
barbarians who are purged will be irrelevant. This psychological need
can only be fulfilled through psychological rehabilitation of the sufferer
himself and not through the (creation and) destruction of barbarians.

For convenience, we can summarize the kill apps of Western racism as
(1) fear of change, (2) the ontology of bivalent dualism, (3) the invention of
the "barbarian" as the racial other, (4) the metaphysics of colonialism, and (5)
the insatiable nature of this racist psychology. Thus arises an escapist ideology
that is psychologically motivated by a desire for complete rationality and determinism but is ill equipped to deal with the empirical world. This ideology
is sustained by a gaze that dualistically reserves freedom for itself but determinism for all else in the natural world.[1] The psychology that underlies the
dualism between barbarism and civilization is one that remains unreconciled
to the embodied nature of the human condition. In this sense, Western racism
is rooted in the same world-denying typified by Parmenides, Orphism, and
Gnosticism, as well as in Christianity. This "schizophrenia," to borrow James
Baldwin's words, "in the mind of Christendom" and the Western tradition in
general has "rendered the domain of morals as chartless as the sea once was,
and as treacherous as the sea still is" (Baldwin 1998: 313–14).

We can summarize the sources of Chinese cosmopolitanism by way of the
contrasts between the Chinese and Western traditions:

1. The Chinese tradition was more empirical in that it accepted the fact
of change. Without the idea that only the unconditioned and eternal
is to be esteemed, the Chinese tradition did not repudiate humans'
embodied and contingent nature. As such, it did not suffer the West's
malaises and nightmares of its own making consequent upon the
psychological evasion of this fact, such as "barbarians."

2. On the premise that what *is* is change itself, the Chinese tradition did not
understand the structure of the world in terms of a static, ontological,
metaphysically determined hierarchy. The *Dao* that can be specified as
Dao is not the constant *Dao*.

3. The Chinese tradition therefore understood identity, whether at the level of the individual or of collective culture, as creatively indeterminate and always in process.

4. The Chinese tradition had an anti-representationalist account of experience and culture that was related to its acceptance that order in the world is not predetermined and static.

5. The Chinese tradition's empirical recognition that our identities are dynamic in nature and always changing and that the only meaningful difference between humans is not essential (racial) but cultural, combined with an anti-representationalist understanding of culture, led to a willingness to hybridize different cultures. The Chinese tradition from early on was more willing than the Western tradition to accept that cultures are not sacrosanct virgin territories whose value correlates with how pristine they are. As Anthony Appiah writes, "Cultural purity is an oxymoron" (Appiah 2007: 113). The Chinese tradition was more willing to acknowledge that "cultures are made of continuities *and* changes, and the identity of a society can survive these changes, just as each individual survives the alterations of Jacques's 'seven ages of man'" (107). Note that the willingness to hybridize cultures is directly contingent upon not seeing the culture of the other as inherently antithetical to civilization (barbaric).

6. The Chinese tradition understood that hybridization, which involves being pliant and accommodating (that is, being cosmopolitan), secures longevity by bringing different peoples into a hybrid whole. Unity and integrity cannot be secured through racial purity, which is unempirical and fictitious.

7. The Chinese tradition understood that dominating others—aggressively taking control of other peoples' lands and treating conquered peoples as inferiors—is not sustainable in the long term and thus is not efficacious. Instead, it understood that the most efficacious way to teach virtue is through example.

We can summarize these sources of Chinese cosmopolitanism as: acceptance of (1) the fact of change, (2) the changing nature of human order, and (3) (cultural) identity; (4) an anti-representationalist account of experience and culture; (5) embrace of the hybridization of cultures; and an understanding that (6) hybridization leads to longevity and that (7) dominating others is unsustainable. As we have said, all of these points can be attributed to the

Chinese tradition's greater empiricism as contrasted with the Western tradition's world-denying ideology. Elsewhere I have discussed *tian ren he yi*, which I translate as "a mutually participatory relationship between man and the cosmos," as one of the most cherished ideals in Chinese civilization (Xiang 2021a). Here I would argue that ultimately the Chinese tradition was cosmopolitan because of this ideal of *tian ren he yi*. With its inability to accept that the human being is a natural being like all the rest of nature, the West became obsessed with transcending the immanent world, an obsession that led to its racism. The collateral damage from this inability to be *tian ren he yi* has been borne by the racial other, the victim of the West's racism.

It is imperative that we fully understand that race and racial hierarchy are among the greatest obstructions to co-prosperity between the different peoples of this world. This book has shown that racism is a culturally specific phenomenon and ideology. Those who claim that Western-style racism is universal across all cultures bear the burden of proof to show that this is so, that the same philosophical ideas are found around the world. In showing the coherence between the West's racial ideology and its practice and the coherence between Chinese ideology and its actual practice, this book has demonstrated that any argument that European racial practice is a deviation from its ideals is simply indefensible. If the Chinese tradition had ever shared the metaphysically determined Western conception of race, which delimits the bounds of humanness, then we would find in Chinese culture as many pervasive and casual remarks about "the preference of the Oranootan [*sic*] for the black women over those of his own species" (Jefferson 1853: 149–50), and as much discourse revealing obsession with a dualistic other (barbarian), as we find in the Western tradition. We would be able to cite Chinese philosophers as eminent as Kant who often made racial remarks, such as "Americans and Blacks cannot govern themselves. They thus serve only for slaves," or "The white race [or any one race] possesses *all* motivating forces and talents *in itself*."[2] We could find Chinese philosophers as confident on behalf of their own "race" as Kant was that "all races will be extinguished [. . .] only not that of the Whites" (quoted in Mills 2005: 173–75). Indeed, we would find philosophers of any powerful Chinese dynasty frequently mentioning the racial inferiority of other races just as Enlightenment thinkers *overwhelmingly* did.

We would also find a consistent practice coherent with such a worldview. Neither in ideology (philosophy) nor in practice (history), however, is there anything in the Chinese tradition like the Western ideology of race, the Western practice of racial violence and genocide, or Western colonialism. The demonstrable coherence between Western ideology and practice, the demonstrable coherence between Chinese ideology and practice, and the contrast between them puts the cultural specificity of Western racism in a glaring light. As I have mentioned, for Sinologists of the early twentieth century and prior, it was a commonsense matter of fact that the Chinese tradition had a cultural conception of selfhood rather than a racial one. We should be critical of the shift in the consensus among Sinologists today, given that the Chinese textual tradition itself has not changed.[3]

An important reason for the West's difficulty in accepting that humans are not racist by nature is that the notion of the West's racialized history as culturally contingent challenges the idea of a universal human nature. There is no aspect of human nature, however, that is not shaped by the cultural. It is fallacious to posit that a putative "human nature" has a one-way causal efficacy, in the mode of the philosophical concept of an essence. An underlying argument of this book is that human behavior is radically formed through (cultural and social) environment, and thus a putatively stable human nature cannot be scapegoated as responsible for the crimes of history. Implicated instead are the agents and attitudes responsible for the prevailing culture that led to such barbarism.

Race-thinking and racism have explanatory power in elucidating some of the imperfections of the human experience, but they do not explain everything. What this book has *not* argued is that Chinese history was a utopistic model. Chinese history was created by flawed human beings who were capable of as much violence and cruelty as any other human being. The Chinese, however, never channeled their aggression toward a perceived racial other, as they did not have the constellation of ideas of barbarism, racism and ontological hierarchy that governed the Western tradition. The idea that one might hate another, not for any practical harm they have done one but because of their essence, is not within the Chinese horizon of relevance. Chinese history never demonstrated anything like the West's intolerance of difference. As has been shown, the psychological neurosis at the heart of the dualism between barbarism and civilization so foundational to Western racism arises from the inability to be reconciled to the embodied nature of the human condition. This dualism underlies Western ideas about personhood, the nature of the human being and human becoming, the ontological structure of the world, and the relationship of the human being to that order. As James Baldwin so profoundly understood, "What we really feel about him [the black man] is involved with all that we feel about everything, about everyone, about ourselves" (Baldwin 1998: 19).

In the introduction, I discussed the racist humanism that allows its practitioners to demand rigorous order for others while justifying disorder without responsibility for themselves. Another manifestation of this asymmetrical racist behavior is the Western academy's talk about its ideals, such as democracy, unqualified by any mention of the non-ideal practices carried out in the name of these ideals. Chinese ideals are not afforded this white privilege; instead, the fact that Chinese ideals have sometimes been accompanied by non-ideal practices is taken to be enough to prove their manifest falsity. Under this view, Confucianism is obviously corrupt as a political and moral ideal because historically a person, government, or other entity who called themselves "Confucian" committed abuses. Confucian ideas about the centrality of the family are obviously nonpracticable, as kinship ties often compromised the impartiality and integrity of governors in Confucian China. White privilege writes itself blank checks to cover all manner of baroque contortions to explain away its non-ideal practices in the name of its ideals, while the Chinese tradition is held to an impossible standard.

I have two responses to this racist standard stipulating that the precondition for the defensibility of the Chinese tradition's ideals is superhuman perfection: (1) As this book has shown, historical conflicts between China and its neighbors had nothing to do with race. At the risk of stating the obvious, the existence of violence in Chinese history does not disprove my thesis that China did not have a concept of race. (2) It is a (racist) fallacy to assume that China needs to have acted perfectly throughout its history for its ideals to be defensible.

I am keenly aware of another asymmetry: the asymmetry pervading comparative philosophy. The current state of the field strikes a Faustian bargain: Chinese philosophy is selectively amputated and ritually sacrificed as a particular that proves the universalism of Western paradigms in exchange for inclusion in "philosophy." Any exercise in comparative philosophy under the assumption that Western philosophy is the standard against which to assess the philosophy of the other perpetuates the very colonialism that holds us all captive. It is not comparative philosophy, but cultural appropriation of a tradition in service to a colonial philosophy and an anemic Western universalism that refuses to grow larger through exchange. Those who pick out elements of the Chinese tradition that conform to the European canon are furthering the project of Western intellectual and geopolitical colonialism. What they are not doing is broadening their own intellectual horizons by working through a different worldview.

It was partly out of a desire to break through this stalemate that I undertook this project. To make the point clear that comparative philosophy should be a discipline in which we learn from each other's philosophical traditions, I chose an aspect of the Chinese tradition from which the Western tradition could indubitably learn something. It is an incontrovertible fact of history that the Chinese tradition and Sino-sphere were less intolerant of difference than the Western tradition. In this regard, it is undeniable that the West has something to learn from "the Rest."

I know that critics will come for me because the imperium is ruthless toward those who challenge its continued existence. Before they come, I want my readers to be clear on what these critics are refusing to accept: that even in just one respect they have something to learn from another tradition, even though it is copiously borne out by the historical record. What they want is "civilization reduced to a monologue" (Césaire 2000: 74) because they are captive to an idea that will make captives of us all: the idea that "the Rest" of human civilization is made up of merely picturesque shells that spirit has cast aside in its progress toward the West as the end of humanity. The truth is that this idea is impracticable, simply because no one holds on to power forever. It is unspeakably sad to watch people cling to their captivity in a way that will ensure their destruction as well as ours. James Baldwin wrote:

> It is a terrible thing for an entire people to surrender to the notion that one-ninth of its population is beneath them. Until the moment comes when we, the Americans, are able to accept the fact that my ancestors are both black and white, that on that continent we are trying to forge a new identity, that we need each other, that I am not a ward of America, I am not an object of missionary charity, I am one of the people who built the country—until this moment comes there is scarcely any hope for the American dream. If the people are denied participation in it, by their very presence they will wreck it. (Baldwin 1998: 718–19)

Borrowing from Baldwin, I would say that it is a terrible thing for the West to surrender to the notion that the majority of the world's thought is beneath it. Until the moment comes when we are able to accept that world history is constituted by the brilliance of many civilizations, that we need to forge a new identity, that we need each other, that no culture is "a ward of the West" (or any other culture), that no civilization is an "object of missionary charity"—until this moment comes there is no hope for humanity. If people are denied participation in humanity, then "by their very presence," by the very fact of their very real difference, they will wreck it.

The West must accept that historically it irresponsibly used its power to genocidally eradicate the pluralism of the world's peoples and substituted its own self-serving version of sameness. It needs to reassess its long-held idea of turning the world into its image and learn to be cosmopolitan, to accept that difference is enriching. Doing so will require that the West confront its innermost demons: the fear of mortality and of change that drove it to invent the "barbarian" in the first place and then treat other peoples as the barbarian of its imagination.

In *The Fire Next Time*, James Baldwin wrote, "If the concept of God has any validity or any use, it can only be to make us larger, freer, and more loving. If God cannot do this, then it is time we got rid of Him." What Baldwin means by this is that if the idea of God has only made us more violent and more intolerant as opposed to more loving and tolerant, then we should give up the idea of God. Paralleling this, if Eurocentric universalism, the West's insistence that they are at the end of history and that they have the greatest access to truth has always been complicit with the mass murder of the racial other, then it's time we got rid of these ideas. If the West's particular version of moral universalism is inextricable from racial violence and genocide, then for the sake of humanity, we need to get rid of it. Humanity can do without the oppressive ideal of civilization reduced to a monologue, a zero-sum game in which only one people represents the end of humankind. In its stead, on the *dao* that we all must walk in the company of others, we can learn from one another and, in so doing, embrace a larger, freer and more loving humanity.

GLOSSARY

Barbarism/barbarian

Closely related to the concept of race and racism is the concept of the barbarian. "Barbarism" means something very specific in Western philosophy and history. By no means does it refer merely to a perceived uncouthness. Instead, the barbarian is the Manichean other, antithetical to civilization and eternally savage.

The concept of the barbarian serves the purpose of dialectical self-definition. That is, the Western self is defined negatively through the rejection of everything embodied by the barbarian, the dualistic other. The Western idea of race, I argue, grew out of the idea of the barbarian in that all non-Western peoples were understood in terms of the Greek paradigm of the barbarian.

China/Chinese

Although the term "China" is used in many languages, it does not have an exact correspondence in the Chinese tradition. The *Qing* government, for example, referred to itself as *daqingguo*, "the great Qing state." It would be erroneous to assume that the way we use the term "China," that is, as a nation-state, applies to its various near-equivalents throughout history. In the pre-Qin period, for example, *zhongguo* would have meant "the central states." Another near-equivalent, *huaxia*, according to *The Rectified Interpretation of Zuo's Spring and Autumn Annals*, refers to the domains that enjoy great ritual propriety (*liyi*, 礼仪) and ceremonial dress (*fuzhang*, 服章).[1] The *Rectified Interpretation of the Book of Documents* explains that illustrious clothing and headwear are called *hua* and the large state is called *xia*.[2] I have often placed "China" in quotation marks to alert the reader to the anachronism of thinking about "China" in contemporary terms.

Colonization/colonialism

I use "colonization" not in the weak sense of territorial expansion but in the sense of enacting the ideology of racial hierarchy. Within a colony, the colonizer makes an effort to maintain the hierarchical and racial distinction between the colonizer and the colonized. Race is inextricable from colonialism and subjugation.

The American historian Reginald Horsman sees the ideology of racial hierarchy at the heart of American expansionism. Even though it "used the rhetoric of redemption," white supremacism, or "Anglo-Saxonism," was "no benign expansionism" (Horsman 1981: 303). Its underlying assumption was that "one race was destined to lead, others to serve—one race to flourish, many to die." In the face of this expansionism, whereby "Anglo-Saxons sought out the most distant corners of the globe" and replaced "a variety of inferior races" (303),

> most of the world's peoples were condemned to permanent inferiority or even to extinction. General world progress was to be accomplished only by the dominating power of a superior race, and a variety of lesser races were accused of retarding rather than furthering world progress. (Horsman 1981: 297)

Horsman's point that a racial ideology motivated American expansionism is also applicable to European expansionism since the "Age of Discovery." The white race has long believed itself in possession of a mandate to overwhelm the rest of the world and its peoples. As W.E.B. Du Bois wrote, "Whiteness is the ownership of the earth forever and ever" (Du Bois 1999: 18).

There is a pervasive epistemology of ignorance in the Western academy with regard to what colonialism actually entailed. This ignorance has often led many to falsely equate "colonialism" with any kind of warfare between different political entities, but it is important not to do so. "Colonialism" is the geopolitical manifestation of racial ideology, accompanied by racial violence and racial genocide to achieve race supremacy. Contrary to the mainstream opinion epitomized by John Robert Seeley's comment that the British empire was acquired in a fit of absentmindedness, empire grew out of a vast, sophisticated, and preexisting ideological framework. A crucial element of that framework was racial hierarchy. Colonialism is a geopolitical ordering of the world and its resources in accordance with ideas about racial order.

Given the white denial, epistemology of ignorance, and myth of innocence in the West, I am not at all confident that most people reading this book know what (Western) colonialism entailed. A great hurdle for sincere and often well-meaning Western scholars in acknowledging the racial other's grievances and perspectives on colonialism and racism is their unawareness of the extent of the West's historical racial violence. To avoid the possibility that some readers may think I am unfairly critical of the West here and too sympathetic to China, I will provide a brief survey of the facts.

As noted in the introduction, Western colonialism ultimately led to the decimation of the native populations of three of the world's six inhabitable continents and enslaved and halved the population of Africa. In *American Holocaust: The Conquest of the New World*, David Stannard writes that by the end of the nineteenth century native Americans had undergone the "worst human holocaust the world had ever witnessed, roaring across two continents non-stop for four centuries and consuming the lives of countless tens of millions of people" (Stannard 1992: 146). By Stannard's count, close to 100 million people were killed during the "American Holocaust." Revising the conventional rationalization that many Amerindians died from disease after European expansion, Stannard shows that European designs upon the Amerindians were deliberately genocidal—hence the title of his work (xii). Despite the myths that Europeans told about their presence on the American continent, their settlement there in fact necessitated "the most extensive and most violent programs of human eradication, that this world has ever seen" (54). Stannard reports on recent scholarship's upward revision in the total number of Amerindian deaths, from 8 million for the hemisphere as a whole and fewer than 1 million for the region north of Mexico to as many as 145 million and 18 million, respectively (11).

For forty thousand years, hundreds of millions of the Americas' native peoples had lived and built civilizations on a land mass that was one-quarter of the earth's surface. (Stannard 1992: 55) Post-Columbian depopulation rates are now known to have been between 90 and 98 percent with such consistency that an overall decline of 95 percent is now used as a working rule of thumb (Stannard 1992: x). On Stannard's account, this was the worst demographic disaster in the history of humankind. According to the recent research of a group of geographers, the European genocide of the native Americans caused death on so a massive scale that the global climate was changed. The researchers estimate that the death of fifty-six million people over a period of one hundred years in South, Central, and North America led to a drop in carbon levels enough to cool the earth by 1610, precipitating what is known as the "Little Ice Age" (Koch et al. 2019). Similarly for Enrique Dussel, European settlement in the Americas led to the "first holocaust of the violent myth of modernity" (Dussel 1995: 122). The "second holocaust" was the subjection of "thirteen million Africans" (122). When Aimé Césaire writes in *Discourse on Colonialism* that "Europe is responsible before the human community for the highest heap of corpses in history" (Césaire 2000: 45), this is no hyperbole.

Within the first three decades of the French conquest of Algeria (1830–1860), the French military massacred between half a million and one million people out of an Algerian population of three million (Jalata 2016: 92). The Algerian League for the Defense of Human Rights estimates that a total of ten million Algerians perished as victims of French colonial rule (Maymouni 2019). In the "Scramble for Africa" (1881–1914), almost 90 percent of the African continent came under European control. During King Leopold II's reign over the Congo (1885–1908), the native population was enslaved to harvest rubber. Those who could not meet their quotas were dismembered. Adam Hochschild states that half the population—ten million people—died during this time (Hochschild, n.d.). In *The Origins of Totalitarianism*, Hannah Arendt writes that the Congo population of between twenty and forty million people was reduced to eight million in this period (Arendt 2017: 241). During the 1950s, around one and a half million Kikuyu—nearly the entire Kikuyu population—were locked up in detention camps (Elkins 2005: xiv). In the Tasmanian genocide (1826–1829), the British settlers wiped out nearly all the people of Tasmania. When the lawyer Raphael Lemkin formulated the idea of "genocide" after World War II, he included Tasmania as a case study in his history of the concept (Lawson 2014: 9).

The United States, Canada, Australia, New Zealand, Rhodesia, and South Africa were all founded on the extermination, displacement, and/or herding onto reservations of aboriginal populations. By 1914, colonialism had brought 85 percent of the earth under European rule as colonies, protectorates, dependencies, dominions, and commonwealths. The global economy is dominated to this day by the former colonial powers and their offshoots and its international financial institutions (the International Monetary Fund, the World Bank).[3] It has been estimated that the reparations the United States owes for its historical use of slave labor, in 2009 dollars, range from $5.9 trillion to $14.2 trillion (Craemer 2015: 639). To put this number in perspective, the size of the American economy was $19.39 trillion in 2017. Taking into consideration the fact that United States was built on land illegitimately expropriated from the native Americans, it is feasible to say that the entire American GDP is not sufficient to cover the reparations that it owes.

The Chinese were drugged into submission through what John Fairbank has termed "the most long-continued and systematic international crime of modern times" (Fairbank 1978: 213). By 1850, the British opium trade in China accounted for 15 to 20 percent of the British empire's revenue (Bradley 2015: 17). Opium was the single largest commodity trade in the nineteenth century (14); indeed, "the entire commercial infrastructure of European trade in Asia was built around opium" (Trocki 1999: 52).

Since the founding of the European Union in 1957, Europe has enjoyed the greatest period of peace in over two thousand years (Hennigan 2017). Since its founding in 1776, the United States has been at war 225 out of 243 years. The Filipino historian Epifanio San Juan has argued that 1.4 million Filipinos died during the Filipino-American War, which constitutes an act of genocide (San Juan 2005). The Vietnamese government estimates that 3.4 million Vietnamese (civilians included) died during the Vietnam War (Appy 2016: 242). In a now-infamous 1996 interview, US Ambassador to the United Nations (later Secretary of State) Madeleine Albright, when asked whether the US sanctions on Iraq that led to the death of 567,000 children was worth it, responded that it was. The United States now has thirty-eight overseas naval bases and over eight hundred military bases. As late as 2014, President Obama proclaimed that he "believed in American exceptionalism with every fiber of his being."[4] According to a Council on Foreign Relations survey, in 2016 alone Obama dropped 26,171 bombs, or 72 bombs daily in Afghanistan, Libya, Yemen, Somalia, Syria, Iraq, and Pakistan. At a 2008 campaign interview, Hillary Clinton told the American public that she could "totally obliterate" Iran. In seventy-one countries (more than one-third of the world) since 1945, the United States has overthrown or interfered in the government, assassinated the leaders, dropped bombs, or suppressed a populist or nationalist movement, ending the lives of millions of people in the process while condemning many millions more to lives of misery (Blum 2013: 2). The political scientist Lindsay O'Rourke notes that during the Cold War alone, the United States covertly supported six regime change operations that directly or indirectly replaced democratically elected leaders with authoritarian regimes: Iran (1952–1953), Guatemala (1953–1954), Congo (1960), British Guiana/Guyana (1961–1971), Brazil (1964), and Chile (1964–1973) (O'Rourke 2018: 25). Further, throughout the Cold War, the United States backed authoritarian leaders in its covert regime changes more than 70 percent of the time (30). She notes that during the Cold War US administrations

attempted overt regime change in North Korea (1950), Lebanon (1958),*
Dominican Republic (1965),* Libya (1986), Grenada (1983),* and Panama
(1989)* and covert regime change in France (1947–1952),* Italy (1947–1968),*
Albania (1949–1956), Belarusian SSR (1949–1956), Bulgaria (1949–1956),
Czechoslovakia (1949–1956), East Germany (1949–1956), Estonian SSR
(1949–1956), Hungary (1949–1956), Latvian SSR (1949–1956), Lithuanian
SSR (1949–1956), Poland (1949–1956), Romania (1949–1956), Soviet Union/
Russian SSR (1949–1959), Ukrainian SSR (1949–1956), China (1949–1968),
North Korea (1950–1953), Iran (1952–1953),* Guatemala (1952–1954),* Japan
(1952–1968),* Indonesia (1954–1958), Syria (1955–1957), Lebanon (1957–1958),*
Tibet (1958–1968), Laos (1959–1973), Congo (1960),* Cuba (1960–1961),
Dominican Republic (1960–1961),* Dominican Republic (1961–1962),*
Cuba (1961–1968), North Vietnam (1961–1964), British Guiana/Guyana
(1961–1971),* Chile (1962–1973),* Haiti (1963), South Vietnam (1963),* Bolivia
(1963–1966),* Brazil (1964),* Somalia (1964–1967), Mozambique (1964–1968),
Angola (1964–1972), Dominican Republic (1965–1968),* Haiti (1965–1969),
Thailand (1965–1969), South Vietnam (1967–1971),* Bolivia (1971),* Italy
(1972–1973),* Iraq (1972–1975), Portugal (1974–1975),* Angola (1975–1976),
Grenada (1979), Nicaragua (1979–1980), South Yemen (1979–1980), Afghanistan (1979–1989),* Nicaragua (1980–1989),* Chad (1981–1982),* Ethiopia
(1981–1983), Poland (1981–1989),* Suriname (1982–1985), Cambodia (1982–
1989), Libya (1982–1989), Liberia (1983–1988), Philippines (1984–1986),* Chile
(1984–1989),* Haiti (1986–1988), Angola (1985–1988), and Panama (1987–1989)
(O'Rourke 2018: 3; *denotes that US-backed forces assumed power).

According to the dramatist Harold Pinter, between the end of World War II
and 2005, the United States supported or engendered every military dictator-
ship in the world (Indonesia, Greece, Uruguay, Brazil, Paraguay, Haiti, Turkey,
the Philippines, Guatemala, El Salvador, and Chile) (Pinter 2015). Although
"the magnitude of US aggression puts it historically into a league all by itself"
(Blum 2013: 3), it is motivated by the same logic behind European aggression:
white supremacism. As the historian Dylan Rodríguez puts it, "White supremacy and racist genocide are the mobilized global logics of US nation
building" (Rodríguez 2010: 1). Indeed, the twenty-seventh president of the
United States, William H. Taft, declared this intention in 1912: "The day is
not far distant," he said, when "the whole hemisphere will be ours in fact as,
by virtue of our superiority of race, [it] is already ours morally" (quoted in
Chomsky 1993: 158).

The West/Westerner

By the "West" I refer specifically to all those countries that, beginning with the "Age of Discovery," colonized—that is, subjugated—peoples they deemed to be inferior to themselves. This colonization of "the inferior" was motivated by the ideology of race and racial hierarchy. "Westerners" are thus defined as those colonizers who adhered to a philosophy of race and racial hierarchy.

This definition of "the West" converges geographically with the Western European countries and the Anglo-Saxon countries (the United States, Canada, Australia, and New Zealand) that Europeans appropriated through colonization, and "Westerner" as defined here overlaps to a great extent with those who were formed by a Greco-Christian heritage. The charge that I am "essentializing" the West is specious considering that the West has long essentialized itself as racially and culturally superior and antithetical to the non-West. In fact, it was the West that invented the idea of "the West." I am merely repeating the West's own (dualistic) definition of itself.

As Charles Mills has written in *The Racial Contract*, a central characteristic of the racialized world that we live in is that the creators and beneficiaries of a racialized system espouse, to their advantage, systematic ignorance of their role in creating, sustaining, and benefiting from it. The term that Mills coined to characterize such ignorance, "inverted epistemology," applies to the West's discomfort with and disavowal of the term "West" today.

NOTES

Introduction

1. Franklin Perkins argues that comparative philosophy is fundamentally about comparative metaphysics. "Changes on the level of metaphysical theory," he writes, "can bring about changes in practices" (Perkins 2016: 189).

2. As the authors of "Introducing Confluence: A Thematic Essay" write, a true comparative philosophy "will enable one to shed light and make explicit the tacit and unexamined presuppositions of one's own tradition, and in so doing, reflect upon these presuppositions" (Kirloskar-Steinbach, Ramana, and Maffie 2016: 46).

3. A good example of uncritically and arbitrarily misapplying Western theoretical paradigms is Magnus Fiskesjö's work on Chinese imperial understandings of the "barbarian." His application of Alexandre Kojève's master-slave dialectic to the Chinese relationship to non-Chinese is random and arbitrary, as is his description of the Chinese relationship to the non-Chinese in terms of Carl Schmitt's idea of the "exception," that is, "the radical crisis of every possibility of clearly distinguishing between membership and inclusion, between what is outside and what is inside, between exception and rule" (Fiskesjö 1999: 153–54). Western paradigms of subjectivity cannot simply be grafted onto the Chinese context without providing an account of why and how they are applicable. At the risk of stating the obvious, Western experiences are not universal.

4. Walter Mignolo writes eloquently about this problem of comparative philosophy in "Philosophy and the Colonial Difference." He describes the "double bind" in which non-Western "philosophy" finds itself: when non-Western philosophy is presented as too different, it is dismissed as not genuine philosophy, but when it is presented as similar to Western philosophy, it is dismissed as making no distinctive contribution to "philosophy" (Mignolo 1999: 37).

5. Elsewhere (Xiang, forthcoming[d]) I have framed the recent phenomenon of sinologists portraying racism and colonialism as internal to the Chinese tradition as motivated by important psychological, economic, and geostrategic influences that can be understood in terms of the "epistemology of ignorance." Through their weaponization of the discourse of race, sinology is complicit in the project of upholding the white supremacist status quo.

6. This recent vogue is an about-face on the consensus among the previous generation of eminent sinologists such as John K. Fairbank (1907–1991; Fairbank 1942: 130), Joseph R. Levenson (1920–1969; Levenson 1964), James Townsend (1932–2004; Townsend 1992: 97), and Herrlee Creel (1905–1994; Creel 1970: 197). In lieu of the idea of race and nation, the prior consensus was that the Chinese thought of the world in terms of *tianxia* (all under heaven). All peoples in

the world could become part of both the cultural and the political sphere that is *huaxia* (civiliza-tion) as long as they were acculturated in certain norms. However, by the mid-1990s we began to witness publications such as *Cultural Encounters on China's Ethnic Frontiers*, in which Stevan Har-rell, in his introduction entitled "Civilizing Projects and the Reaction to Them," (mis)appropri-ates Edward Said's concept of "orientalism" to define the historical Confucian attitude toward peoples beyond China's historical jurisdiction as "inferiors" to be "civilized" (Harrell 1995: 3–36, 8). Harrell assumes that the Confucian and Christian practices were equivalent. Another example of how casually Western racism is projected onto the Chinese tradition can be seen in James Hargett's introduction to Fan Chengda's *Treatises of the Supervisor and Guardian of the Cinnamon Sea* (桂海虞衡志), in which he states, "It is general knowledge that the Chinese regarded all foreign people, including members of indigenous tribes within China itself, as racially and cultur-ally inferior" (Hargett 2010: L). Within the space of a few decades then, the view that the Chinese tradition was one without a notion of race and nationhood was replaced with one in which a (supposed) Han "race," in a proto-European version of settler-colonialism, murderously expanded its frontiers to make *Lebensraum* for its Han ethno-state.

7. It is worth remembering that while it is today common to translate *yidi* (夷狄) as "barbarian," the sinologist James Legge was translating it in the late nineteenth century as "rude tribes of the east and north" (Legge 1861: 20) or "rude, uncultivated tribes" (Legge 1861: 135). Reading Western racism into the Chinese tradition is a very recent phenomenon. I hazard that there are two reasons for this new trend. First, China's rise and what is now perceived as its threat to Western hegemony reminds us of the very real connection between funding for area studies and the needs of the American national security state. For example, after 9/11, President George W. Bush issued a Na-tional Security Language Initiative to increase the linguistic capabilities of Americans in Arabic, Chinese, Hindi, Persian, Russian, and Central Asian languages (Engerman 2009: 338). (For an account of how "Soviet studies" was created to meet the needs of the Cold War, see Engerman 2009.) Second, a younger generation of sinologists tend to make their work relevant by relating the Chinese tradition to whichever way the academic wind is currently blowing. As the issue of race is such a relevant one in the West, there has been an attempt to bring Western discussions on race to bear on the Chinese tradition. There is nothing inherently wrong in doing so, except that many of these sinologists know little about the nature and history of race in the West.

8. For another example of how casually Western paradigms are applied to the Chinese ex-perience, see Spencer Tucker's description of the Han's relationship to what is modern-day Vietnam as a "civilizing mission" that was "not unlike that of the French in the nineteenth century" (Tucker 1999: 7). The paradigm of reading Western racism and colonialism into the Chinese tradition was so well established by the twenty-first century that, in his (otherwise brilliant) work *Between Winds and Clouds: The Making of Yunnan*, Yang Bin applies Frederick Jackson Turner's idea of the American western frontier to the Chinese southern frontier (Yang 2008: 5, 108). These works reveal a fundamental lack of understanding of the nature of the American frontier with the native Americans, and so the inapplicability of the Western experi-ence to the Chinese context.

9. The reader should be informed that Dikötter is a well-known revisionist historian. One of his revisions is to reject the conventional consensus that the Western opium trade in China was an act of colonial immorality. As one reviewer of his book *Narcotic Culture* has written, "*Narcotic Culture* appears to be one of the revisionist histories of which there have been several

lately that have aimed at convincing us that imperialism wasn't all that bad, or at least that we should not blame the imperialists, in this case the opium traders who made vast fortunes from the trade, for the social problems they created" (Lodwick 2005: 76). Another Dikötter revision has been to equate the Great Famine of 1958–1961 under Mao Zedong with the Jewish Holocaust under Nazism. As one of his critics, the postcolonial scholar Pankaj Mishra (2011), has written, "A crucial nuance is lost on Dikötter, and should be highlighted again: that people exposed to early death mostly as a result of terrible decisions, crop failures and food shortages belong to a different order of victimhood than those singled out for being Jewish or homosexual and then gassed to death or shot. To imply otherwise is to cheapen the extraordinary and unprecedented crime of the Holocaust." Dikötter's revisions of the previous scholarly consensus that the concept of race and the phenomenon of racism is absent in the Chinese tradition should be seen as a continuation of the type of revision called out by Mishra.

10. In the 2015 edition, Dikötter writes, "For our purposes, it will suffice to point out that some form of racial categorisation, however unsystematic, existed well before the arrival of Europeans in the nineteenth century" (Dikötter 2015: 2).

11. First published in 1992 by C. Hurst & Company and Hong Kong University Press, then by Stanford University Press in 1994, *The Discourse of Race in Modern China* was reissued in a revised and expanded second edition by Oxford University Press in 2015. The reviews of the first edition overwhelmingly hailed it as pioneering and a classic. The *New York Review of Books* called it "a provocative [...] groundbreaking work." Roy Porter, the director of the Wellcome Institute for the History of Medicine at University College, London, declared that "Frank Dikötter's luminous study should be essential reading." The *Times Literary Supplement* wrote, "Frank Dikötter's important pioneering work establishes that ideas and perceptions of race in the 'Middle Kingdom' have been no less ethnocentric than in Europe." The *International Herald Tribune* asserted, "In *The Discourse of Race in Modern China* Dikötter shatters conventional notions about China's being relatively free of racism," while *Asian Affairs* found the work to be "careful and dispassionate [...] firmly grounded in attention to detail and a sensitivity to Chinese ideas and nuances of language." Similar accolades were given by William T. Rowe of Johns Hopkins University, Fredrick Wakeman of the University of California at Berkeley, Sir G.E.R. Lloyd of Cambridge University, Nathan Sivin of the University of Pennsylvania, *Far Eastern Economic Review*, *Australian Journal of Chinese Affairs*, *Journal of Communist Studies*, Gregor Benton of *SOAS Bulletin*, *English Historical Review*, *Journal of the Social and Economic History of the Orient*, *Ethnic and Racial Studies*, *Journal of Asian History*, *Anthropology Today*, and *Asian Studies Review*. More recently, the book was cited by Ron Mallon as evidence that "race-like ideas played a historic role" in imperial China (Mallon 2016: 33).

12. One exception to this critical reception was the negative review by the American-Turkish historian Arif Dirlik, who called Dikötter's work "orientalist" (Dirlik 1993: 70).

13. As a point of contrast, the main text of Benjamin Isaac's attempt to prove that racism existed in the Greco-Roman world, *The Invention of Racism in Classical Antiquity*, runs for 516 pages. It should strike any scholar as highly dubious that Dikötter's 10 pages could be sufficient to establish an argument about the existence of racism in China when Isaac needed 516 to make a similar argument. Isaac's study covers a comparable span of history and was focused on another cradle of civilization likewise rich in textual sources. In addition, both studies adopt theses that are politically sensitive in today's geopolitical context. That this asymmetry is allowed to

pass without comment testifies to the double standard that is still applied to the Chinese tradition in the Western academy.

14. I have many personal anecdotes on how Eurocentrism joins ignorance in justifying and morally legitimizing Western colonialism.

(1) I received a review of a piece that I submitted to a journal (and that forms chapter 5 of this book) that argued that China did not colonize other countries because its unique metaphysics shaped practice, as I had argued, but because China did not have "capitalism":

> It is of course a large and unsettled historiological question why capitalism did not develop in China. But had it done so, I hazard that China would have projected its military and economic power to the rest of the world, regardless of Chinese metaphysical traditions. Chinese ideologists would then doubtless have been able to find in their own metaphysical and ethical traditions the means of justifying it after the fact. That is just what people do. In this alternate world, one could imagine an essay like the present one arguing that the roots of Chinese colonialism are to be found in Chinese metaphysics. It would be precisely as plausible as the thesis of this essay.

"Capitalism" is an ill-defined term. Is it (1) privately owned enterprises, (2) exchanging goods and services on the free market, or (3) a few oligarchs organizing production at the top? Any one of these definitions define human activity throughout human history, but not all "capitalist" cultures then also rapaciously seek to dominate world resources as "Western" colonialism/imperialism has done since the fifteenth century. As is well known, already in the Western Han 81 BCE, a debate (recorded in *The Discourses on Salt and Iron*, 盐铁论) was held at the imperial court on economic policy regarding agriculture, commerce, and industry and the wisdom of state monopolies on iron and salt. As is also well known, the traditional Chinese social hierarchy gave last place to the merchants. It would seem that traditional China not only did have "capitalism"—or at least something that approximated it—but was aware of the dangers of leaving it unchecked. However one defines "capitalism," it is worth bearing in mind that China (along with India) had the biggest share of world GDP throughout the majority of world history (Desjardins 2017). I suspect that a more insightful distinction is that in Chinese history, for various reasons, we do not see a merchant "liberal" class coming to dominate political life as we see in Western Europe. On the relationship between colonialism, the rise of liberalism, and the interests of the merchant class, see Losurdo 2011.

(2) In a submission to another journal, my reviewer rebuked me that Western colonialism was made possible because "the successes of science played a key role in making European colonialism possible, and to deny them would be to reject the possibility of understanding the modern world at all." This reviewer espoused the common view that the West's history of committing genocides is not a moral issue worthy of reflection, but rather a consequence of superior virtue—that is, the technological sophistication of the West. Quite perversely, the Western responsibility for the greatest loss of human lives in history becomes a virtue and is attributed to Western superiority. I explain the thinking behind the idea that domination is a virtue in chapter 4. I also debunk the (racist) idea that historical China did not have the technological wherewithal to conduct colonizing campaigns in the European mode in chapter 5. As will be seen, at the time of Columbus's travels, China was a greater maritime power than Europeans.

(3) In another submission to the top journal in the field of Chinese comparative philosophy, my reviewer compared the "extermination campaigns of Tang and Qing dynasties [. . .] of Tibet, Vietnam and Korea" to the Spanish conquest of the Americas.

15. If this sounds hyperbolic, remember that, "in 2011, President Obama announced the 'pivot to Asia'—which meant that two-thirds of US naval and air forces would concentrate in the Asia-Pacific, the biggest build-up of military forces since World War II. This was aimed, clearly, at China. [...] China is surrounded by 400 US military bases; US naval forces are on the doorstep of China. US missiles are pointed at China from Okinawa and southern Korea." At the same time, there is "no demonstrable Chinese military threat to the US." John Pilger, "John Pilger Q&A: 'US Missiles Are Pointed at China,'" *Al Jazeera*, December 6, 2017, https://www.aljazeera.com/indepth/features/2017/11/john-pilger-qa-missiles-pointed -china-171129123444414.html.

16. On his website (https://www.frankdikotter.com/), Dikötter talks of having received over $2 million from US and UK institutions to fund his research.

17. This term, used ironically here, comes from Martti Koskenniemi's *The Gentle Civilizer of Nations: The Rise and Fall of International Law 1870–1960* (Cambridge: Cambridge University Press, 2002).

18. John Stuart Mill, for example, thought that only Europeans were civilized enough to be capable of self-governance. The darker peoples of other civilizations, in their immaturity, needed to receive proper instruction by European civilization. Since European rule was needed to bring these other cultures out of their immaturity, it was incumbent on Europe to rule these cultures, for their own good. See Bogues 2005.

19. As Enrique Dussel says, "Europe's centrality reflects no internal superiority" but is instead "the outcome of its discovery, conquest, colonization, and integration of Amerindia—all of which give it an advantage over the Arab world, India, and China." Europe later permitted itself to "exult in its values, inventions, discoveries, technology, and political institutions as its exclusive achievement. But these achievements result from the displacement of an ancient interregional system born between Egypt and Mesopotamia and found later in India and China" (Dussel 1995: 11).

20. As Edith Hall writes, "It was the Persian wars which first produced a sense of Panhellenic identity and the notion of the barbarians as the universal 'other.'" (Hall 1989: 6)

21. Elsewhere I reconstruct a Chinese version of "cosmopolitanism" that resonates with Césaire's definition of the universal via the Chinese concepts of *qing* (情), *gan* (感), and *tong* (通) (Xiang, forthcoming a and b). I have also reconstructed the Chinese ideal of cosmopolitanism, or *tianxia*, with a stress on the characteristically non-essentialist conception of personhood and the premium placed on relationality in the Chinese tradition (Xiang, forthcoming c). Here I argue that the logic of "Chinese-ness" is the embrace and harmonization of difference.

22. A sample of readers on the subject of racism establishes this belief. The Hackett reader, *The Idea of Race* (Bernasconi and Lott 2000), for example, begins with François Bernier (1620–1688). The *Oxford Handbook of Philosophy and Race* starts its historical account with Locke (Zack 2017). Ivan Hannaford argues that a conscious idea of race has existed only since the Reformation (Hannaford 1996: 187 ff.). In the *locus classicus* introduction to this field, *Racism: A Short Introduction*, George Fredrickson writes, "It is the dominant view among scholars who have studied conceptions of difference in the ancient world that no concept truly equivalent to that of 'race' can be detected in the thought of the Greeks, Romans, and early Christians" (Fredrickson 2002: 17).

23. My definition of racism is coherent with that of Robert Wistrich, a leading historian of anti-Semitism:

If we define racism in its most basic sense as *heterophobia* (hatred of the other) and the attempt to "essentialize" real or perceived differences so that *fixed* attributes are henceforth applied to human groups, then the consequences are bound to be far-reaching. Race theory not only assumes the existence of distinct, identifiable races each with their own separate "essence" or "character," but it also presupposes a hierarchy of differences. There are "superior" and "inferior" races which supposedly embody higher and lower values. In the racist typology, motivated as it had been since the mid-1850s by anti-egalitarian doctrines, these differences are deemed to be hereditary, immutable, and "eternal." They serve to justify and rationalize the will to exclusion of the "collective other," defined as alien, different, more primitive, or inferior. (Wistrich 1999: 2)

24. In this informed account of the ethnic dynamics in Xinjiang, Yan Sun argues that the ethnic tensions in Xinjiang and Tibet in contemporary China stem from the incomplete transition from an empire to a nation-state. Under the imperial model, "Confucian universalism" did not ethnicize identities. For Sun, under the "cultural universalism (*tianxia*)" of imperial China, "culture (as a way of life) was more fundamental than nationalism or race" and allowed for ethnic acculturation and both localized and hybrid identities (Sun 2020: 26). China's contemporary tensions with ethnic minorities result from China's adoption of Western concepts. As Sun shows, the fifty-five ethnic minorities in China today are an artificial creation of the ethnic policy agenda of the Communist Party of China (CPC). The concept of "ethnicity" would have been alien to traditional China, and thus the classification of the different peoples inhabiting China engineered many identities that had not existed before, or had existed only weakly (37–39). As Sun points out, it was this classification project that created the "Han people," as the "Han" were just those who did not identify with any particular group. The project of ethnic classification artificially fixed identities that historically had always been fluid (42). Sun notes that before the 1930s there was no collective ethnic Uyghur identity, and the various Uyghur groups would have identified themselves by the oases they came from. Indeed, even the appellation "Uyghur" appeared only after the Soviet Union revived the ninth-century ethnonym (from the Uyghur Khaganate of the eighth and ninth centuries) and applied it to all non-nomadic Turkic Muslims of Xinjiang (43). Arguably, it was nation-state assumptions about ethnicity and the taxonomic project of CPC policy in the 1950s that created the Uyghur identity. In Sun's view, the motive behind CPC ethnic taxonomizing was to secure class universalism for all groups (47). However, the policy the CPC used to realize this ideal created fixed ethnic groups where there had been dynamic, overlapping, heterogeneous identities, with the (unintended) consequence of politicizing ethnic identities (48). During the Mao era, the state pursued a universalizing ideology of class struggle as a means of ensuring national unity. Under this ideology, ethnic masses were rallied against their coethnic oppressors. Despite working well at the beginning of the nation's founding, this socialist ideology could not provide long-term stability (298). In the current system, there are autonomous regions, such as the Xinjiang and Tibet autonomous regions.

We can see from Sun's study that ethnic tensions are directly correlated with the many challenges faced by China in the twentieth century, and with the policy responses to these challenges. For example, after the reform and opening-up policies of the 1970s, Tibetan and Uyghur youth were disadvantaged in the new market economy owing to their lack of Mandarin language competence (300). This new economic model has further exacerbated land-based economic tensions as the hinterland is increasingly turned into resource reservoirs for the inland (301).

Sun's study shows that the sources of ethnic tensions in contemporary China are manifold and deeply complex. What is clear, however, is that race is not the main explanation for these tensions. This absence of a clear racial basis in ethnic tensions shows that my thesis about the absence of racial ideology in premodern China arguably applies to the contemporary period as well. On a more abstract and philosophical level, the central tension in ethnic policies that Sun points to can be construed as a problem between the particular and the universal. The Maoist period's universalizing approach, which emphasized equality, and the centralizing tendencies of today stand in tension with the particularism of identities and tendencies toward local government. I would suggest that one solution that contemporary China might countenance is increasing its promotion of cultural syncretism as a civilizational identity.

The universalistic ideology of class struggle cannot do justice to the important particularity of cultural identities. However, valorizing cultural identity alone leads to an inability to share in a wider vision of the whole. Cultural ghettoization should not be seen in positive terms. If the state promoted a version of Chinese culture, history, and identity that is plural in origins and enriched by many different peoples and cultures, then "Chinese" identity would be intrinsically inclusive of minority groups. Arguably, China historically was just such a cosmopolitan melting pot, and its historical logic is to increasingly syncretize the cultures within its orbit. Perhaps it is this aspect of the historic Chinese experience that will become more useful for the continuing experiment that is contemporary China.

Chapter 1. A Brief History of Chinese Cosmopolitanism

1. By the close of the eighteenth century, the population of 300 million people under Qing rule (Mitter 2008: 104) constituted 30 percent of the world's population, which stood at around 1 billion people (United Nations, "The World at Six Billion," https://web.archive.org/web/20160305042439/http://www.un.org/esa/population/publications/sixbillion/sixbilpart1.pdf). By 1850, when China had a population of 450 million (Elman 2000: 237) and the world population was around 1.2 billion ("Estimates of Historical World Population," Wikipedia, (https://en.wikipedia.org/wiki/Estimates_of_historical_world_population#cite_note-Richard_Jones_1978-21), that figure had increased to about 40 percent.

2. This fact was noticed by Liang Qichao as early as 1905 in his article "Observations on the Chinese People in History [历史上中国民族之观察]": "The Chinese people were not originally one race, but a mixture of many races" (Liang 2015: 4. my translation).

3. I have problematized this tendency to deconstruct China as a coherent historical entity as a "hermeneutics of suspicion" (Xiang 2018b). One of the examples I provide (28–29) of the kind of scholarship that seeks to undermine the coherence of historical China is the editorial introduction to *Remapping China: Fissures in Historical Terrain* (Hershatter et al. 1996).

4. The earliest literatures of the Greek tradition presupposed the importance of autochthony. (Isaac 2004: 114; Loraux 1984: 46) A preoccupation with autochthony is a reflection of the premium attached to substance purity that also underlies thinking about eugenics (explored later). The idea of Athenian autochthony—and thus superiority to all other people of the world—is "firmly rooted in the Greek conceptual world" (Isaac 2004: 132) and pervades its

literature, from Lysias's *Epitaphios*, Isocrates's *Pangyricus*, the Iliadic catalog, Thucydides, Pseudo-Xenophon, Aristophanes's *Wasps*, and Euripides's *Ion* to Plato in the *Menexenus* and in the noble lie he told in the *Republic*. For Plato, in Law 693a, one of the disastrous consequences of a defeat by Persia would have been mixed marriages and so the end of a separation between Greek and non-Greek (Plato 1997: 1382). The Athenian idea of pure descent was carried over into the Roman period, and "the view that pure lineage is better than mixed ancestry occurs frequently in the Latin literature" and can be seen in Tacitus, Plutarch, and Pompeius Trogus (Isaac 2004: 114–32). The term "Autochthones" itself comes from the ancient Greek *autos* (αὐτός, "self") and *khthon* (χθών, "soil"), which literally means "people sprung from earth itself" and refers to the original inhabitants of a country (as opposed to settlers) and their descendants who have kept themselves free from an admixture of foreign peoples. As I understand it, the premium placed on racial purity in the Greek tradition was a means to resolve the question of political solidarity. To convince the inhabitants of a city-state that they were connected by blood was a way of ensuring a common sociopolitical will or solidarity. As Isaac explains, autochthony was associated with the idea of mutual solidarity and absence of internal political strife. (Isaac 2004: 115).

5. For more examples of how China/Chinese culture/Chinese history is a hybrid product of "interactive recomposition" whereby different ethnic groups were "coinventors," see Zhao 2019: 34–36.

6. Throughout this project, I have mostly used literatures from Western historians and sinologists or works published in English instead of literatures from Chinese historians so as to avoid the cynical rebuke that Chinese historians are apologists and so their works are unreliable.

7. Smithsonian National Museum of Natural History, "What Does It Mean to Be Human?," https://humanorigins.si.edu/evidence/genetics (last updated August 15, 2022).

8. I am grateful to an archaeology student in my critical philosophy of race class of 2020, Deepthi Hewa Dewage, for bringing my attention to the innovations in this field.

9. Although I cite Reich's work. I am also aware of the open letter signed by sixty-seven scientists and researchers reprimanding Reich for not making clear that genetic variation does not follow the lines of socially constructed racial groups (Kahn et al. 2018).

10. Indeed, I have written on how scientists today are *still* beholden to the idea of race (Xiang 2021b). As the sociologist Catherine Bliss writes, "Since the mapping of the human genome, racial research has reemerged and proliferated to occupy scientific concerns to an extent unseen since early twentieth-century eugenics," such that genomics is now "devoted" to understanding race (Bliss 2012: 2). The scientific community's obsession with genetics bleeds into how sinologists understand Chinese identity.

11. For a more systematic account of the similarities, premised on the metaphysics of the organism, between Chinese thinking about pluralism and the postcolonial thought of prominent decolonial thinkers such as Aimé Césaire, see Xiang, forthcoming(c).

12. Isaac is here talking about Aristotle's theory of natural slavery and his advice to Alexander the Great that he treat the subjugated peoples of his empire "like plants and animals" (Isaac 2004: 181). Because later European colonialism is so indebted to Aristotle's theory of natural slavery, I have used Isaac's description of Aristotle's view of colonialism to describe later European colonization.

13. Elsewhere I argue that the distinguishing feature of (American) colonialism can be understood as the noncreation of value and the simultaneous extraction of value through destruction. Colonialism's parasitic relationship to value is both material and psychological. On the material level, colonizers exploit the resources and labor of the colonized without making creative use of their own resources or laboring themselves. On the psychological level, the racist colonizer castigates the colonized as a barbarian other to be defeated. The American empire, for example, reaps revenues from undermining the economies of noncompliant states through the disaster-capitalist industries that profit from the resulting chaos, as well as from the arms industry, which relies on the economy of destruction. This behavior is motivated and justified by the assumption that the states to be imperialized are the bivalent other, a view that allows the colonizer to evade self-critique and ignore the need to cultivate its own value (Xiang 2022).

14. These peoples were the Xiongnu, Xianbei, Di, Qiang, and Jie (Gernet 1982: 186).

15. Readers might object that historically much of the conduct of Chinese international relations was indeed hierarchical and thus problematic. It needs to be made clear that there are different types of hierarchies. What made the hierarchy of the Western colonial world order so pernicious was that it was ultimately a racial hierarchy. A racial hierarchy is ontological. That is, in this hierarchy certain groups of people are forever deemed to be inferior to others. The hierarchy that governed the political relationship between the historical Chinese state and neighboring states was sociopolitical. In the Confucian social-political understanding of hierarchy, the sovereign fulfills his social role as a sovereign, the minister his social role as a minister, the father his social role as a father, and the son his social role as a son (*Analects* 12.11). Intrinsic to the Confucian tradition is a meritocracy in which no one has a birthright to their place in a hierarchy. The sovereign is a sovereign only because he fulfills his duties as such. If he neglects the duties of the sovereign role, he is no longer considered a sovereign, even if he was born into the ruling family. Likewise, a father cannot claim to be a father solely by virtue of being the biological progenitor of his offspring. A father is defined not by his biological or ontological contribution, but by his fulfillment of the social role of a father, such as providing for his children. That the Chinese view of hierarchy is based on such social roles distinguishes it from the ontological/racial hierarchy of the Great Chain of Being that motivated and underlay Western colonialism. Under racial ontology, the higher-born races are essentially superior and by natural law can and should dominate the lower born. They need do nothing to prove their superiority, which is proven by their race. Under the Confucian view of hierarchy—and arguably in the hierarchical relationship between China and its neighbors—a more elevated place in the social hierarchy comes with responsibilities toward those lower in the hierarchy. A teacher is obligated to ensure the flourishing of her students, and a father the well-being of his child. Likewise, China's historically central position in the East Asian world order came with duties of care toward its neighbors. See Bell and Pei (2020: 106–42) for a more detailed exposition of the Chinese understanding of hierarchy between states.

16. This trope persisted throughout European history. In his *Lectures on the Philosophy of World History*, for example, Hegel writes, "The Chinese [. . .] empire is the realm of *theocratic despotism*. [. . .] The head of state in China is a despot, and he leads a systematically constructed government with a numerous hierarchy of subordinate members" (Hegel 1975: 200; see also Hegel 1975: 121–22).

17. Tao Jing-Shen reminds us that the Han relationship with the Xiongnu was initially based on equality, and that diplomatic parity characterized the relationship of the Northern Wei (368–532) with the Southern dynasties. Sino-Turkish and Sino-Tibetan relationships during the Tang were often marked by equality. In sum, China has a "long tradition of conducting relations with neighbouring countries on a basis of equality" (Tao 1983: 67–68).

18. The European fear of the nomadic invasion is to some extent racist because what was feared was not only the geographical invasion itself but also the threat of racial miscegenation with an "Asiatic" race. The Slavic population of Europe, such as the Russians, are often condescendingly referred to as "Mongols." See Shlapentokh (2013) for an account of how depictions by nineteenth-century France presented Russians as brutish Asiatics and a mortal threat to civilized Europe. A recent *Wall Street Journal* op-ed, "Russia's Turn to Its Asian Past," was accompanied by an image of Putin dressed as a Mongolian, playing on this deep-seated racist idea (Trofimov 2018). https://www.wsj.com/articles/russias-turn-to-its-asian-past-1530889247.

19. The army that King Wu used in the conquest of the Shang is described in the *Bamboo Annals* (古本竹书纪年) and was composed of "Western Yi" (Fang and Wang 2005: 42).

20. For another account of the process of mutual borrowings between the different states in the pre-Qin period, please see Pines 2005: 79–90.

21. For a book-length treatment of this issue, see Xiang 2021a.

22. I develop these ideas on the similarity of racial thinking's explanation of causality to a substance ontology in my article "The Persistence of Scientific Racism" (Xiang 2021b). There I argue that the obsession with biologically determinist explanations for the irreducibly complex process of human becoming can be better understood through Ernst Cassirer's analysis of science's gradual liberation from the concept of substance and replacement by the concept of function—that is, by a processual-relational description of causality. I also show that Cassirer's concept of function, when applied to personhood, became his famous "symbolic animal," that is, a cultural conception of selfhood.

23. On this issue, see McCumber 1999, 46–47, 58.

24. A recent Sinological work that problematizes the widespread assumption that the Confucians had a cultural conception of personhood and thus made the status of "Chinese" available to all who took on Chinese culture is Shao-yun Yang's *The Way of the Barbarians*. In his introduction, Yang problematizes the cultural assimilation model on two counts: (1) The traditional Chinese did not have a concept of "culture" in the modern sense and so could not have had a cultural conception of personhood (Yang 2019: 11). To this I would say that there need not have been a term before the practice could exist. For example, the practice of birth control did not rely on Margaret Sanger's invention of the term. Similarly, although the modern terms *zhexue* (philosophy) and *wenxue* (literature) did not traditionally exist, it is not the case that premodern China had neither philosophy or literature. Yang's definition of culture "in the broad anthropological sense of the shared values, beliefs, and practices of people living in a given community" is also problematic. First of all, when one speaks of the Confucians having a cultural definition of personhood, one means that culture modifies human "nature" in important ways and that human difference is cultural as opposed to ontological. The anthropological definition of culture bears no relevance to what is meant by a cultural definition of personhood. Second, the discipline of anthropology is indebted to European colonialism. The anthropological sense of culture is thus irrelevant to the Chinese context. (2) The Chinese distinguished *fengsu*

(customs) from *liyi* (ritual propriety). Non-Chinese were without *li* and had only *fengsu*. In Yang's interpretation, *liyi* is equated with morality in such a way that the assertion in premodern Chinese texts that non-Chinese have *fengsu* but not *liyi* is tantamount to saying that the non-Chinese are without morality (15, 21). The bifurcation here between customs and morality strikes me as reading Christian-Western ideas into the Chinese canon. The Western bifurcation between customs and morality is even enshrined in Western language: see Allen Wood's summary of Kant's distinction between *Sittlichkeit* and *Moralität* (Wood 2019: 239–40). Again, Sinologists do themselves and the Chinese tradition a great disservice when they uncritically read Western paradigms into the Chinese tradition.

25. It was conventionally assumed in the classical period that genetic inheritance is the sole determinant and constituent of latter-day ability (Isaac 2004: 109–33). For the classicist Benjamin Isaac, there can be no doubt that the modern eugenics movement was inspired by these ancient ideas (128). Plato believed that there are different grades of soul and that without the right eugenics, the quality of the soul deteriorates. For example, in *Phaedo* 91c–95a (Plato 1997: 79–82), Plato reasons that some souls are better than others. In *Timaeus* 41e–42d (1245), we learn that although all souls were originally created equal, there has subsequently been a steady change. As such, it is important that "the best men must have sex with the best women as frequently as possible, while the opposite is true of the most inferior men and women, and, second, that if our herd is to be of the highest possible quality, the former's offspring must be reared but not the latter's" (*Resp.* 459d–e; Plato 1997: 1087). For Plato, such selective breeding would safeguard the preservation of the city. Mixed marriages, on the other hand, would produce degenerate offspring who would ruin the city. Similar eugenicist ideas can be seen in *Timaeus* 19a (1227) and *Resp.* 546d–547a (1159). For more examples of eugenicist ideas in Plato, see Isaac 2004: 124–26.

26. It should be stressed that the cultural and anti-essentialist conception of personhood is shared by all the other major philosophical schools. The Daoists would not disagree that culture plays a decisive role in shaping who we are. They would agree that we have capacities that would not exist if we did not have cultural forms, and that our capacities are different according to the different cultures in which we find ourselves. Implicit in the *Zhuangzi's* perspectivism on the arbitrariness of certain socially conventional norms is the assumption that the very norms we take to be sacrosanct and see as naturalistic are in fact merely cultural. Please see the *Liezi's* understanding of variation in social customs (Graham 1990: 104) and the cosmopolitan exhortation in the *Huainanzi* that the plurality of different customs be accepted (Queen and Major 2010: 406–7). This conception of customs as forming differences among peoples can also be seen in the "Prevailing Atmosphere and Customs" (风俗篇) chapter of the sixth century CE Daoist text *Liuzi* (刘子): "Prevailing atmosphere [风] is *qi* and customs [俗] are habits [习]. The earth and the spring, whether *qi* is slow or fast, whether sounds are high or low, are all prevailing atmosphere. When people inhabit this particular land, habit becomes their nature [性] and we call it custom [习以成性, 谓之俗焉]" (Liu 1998: 443). The embrace of such varied practices is evidence of the Daoist position that there is no one way in which human nature manifests itself, nor, by implication, only one stable nature, as it is custom that forms nature. For Daoists as for Confucians, human nature is formed by culture.

An operative assumption in the argument of the Mohists (another major philosophical school of early China) for their moral system of "universal love" is the malleability of human nature. In response to skepticism about the practicality of universal love, Mozi (the founder of the Mohist school) answered that people do many things contrary to their original desires, such as besieging cities, fighting in wars, and dieting for slender waists. They achieve these things if there is enough impetus and enticement to do so, because human nature is ultimately amenable to external cultural demands. From this response it can be seen that the Mohists also assumed the malleability of human nature and so held a similarly a culturalist understanding of personhood (Mo Zi 2015: 128–29) and believed that culture plays the determinative role in forming the human being. There is a strong basis for arguing that the Chinese tradition *as a whole* assumed that culture is largely responsible for forming the adult human being. Confucius himself said in *Analects* 7.1 that he was a transmitter, not a creator, and one of the values he transmitted and elaborated upon was the idea that the human being is a human becoming. We can see the legacy of the idea that custom has a major role in constituting human nature in Xuanzang's *The Great Tang Dynasty Record of the Western Regions* (大唐西域记): "Human beings are of different dispositions [性], stubborn [刚] or pliable [柔], and speak different languages. This is caused by climatic conditions and by customary usage [俗]" (Xuanzang 1996: 15).

27. "Daoism," Stanford Encyclopedia of Philosophy, last revised June 28, 2007, https://plato .stanford.edu/entries/daoism/ .

28. For a list of Indian monks who came to China and translated Buddhist scripture from 67 CE to 980 CE, see Chang 1957: 80–82. For lists of Indian and Central Asian translators, Buddhist scriptures, and fascicles of the scriptures, see Chang 1957: 82. For a list of Chinese monks who went to India, see Chang 1957: 83.

29. Semu (色目) is the name of a caste established by the Yuan dynasty. The Mongols established permanent legal definitions of status based on ethnic identity. In the highest-level group were the Mongols themselves; next was the Semu, or "people of varied categories." These were Western Asians, Central Asians, and Inner Asians. Numerically, the Uyghurs were the most important members of this group, but it also included other Turkic peoples, Persians, Arabs, and even Europeans. The rest of the population was divided between the inhabitants of northern China and the Chinese inhabitants of the Southern Song territories conquered after 1273. The Semu group was most heavily drawn upon to fill civil administrative posts. "The Mongols and the Semu were the two privileged groups within Yuan society, the Mongols holding power and the Semu exercising both policy making and day-to-day supervision in the interests of their employer" (Mote 2003: 489–90).

To promote trade to their courts and keep them supplied, the Mongol rulers introduced an institution: the Ortaq (斡脱), from the Turkic word *ortak* ("partner"). The khans, their wives, princes, members of the Mongol elite, and even government officials would enter into a commercial, contractual partnership with a merchant (Ortaq). Most of these merchants were Turkic, either Uyghurs or West Turkistanis (Biran and Fiaschetti 2020: 175–76; Findley 2005: 84).

30. For an account of the synthesis of Islam and Chinese learning and the creation of Chinese Islam, see the works of Sachiko Murata, particularly *The Sage Learning of Liu Zhi: Islamic Thought in Confucian Terms, The First Islamic Classic in Chinese: Wang Daiyu's Real Commentary on the True Teaching*, and *Chinese Gleams of Sufi Light: Wang Tai-yü's Great Learning of the Pure and Real and Liu Chih's Displaying the Concealment of the Real Realm*.

31. For an account of the indigenization process in Yunnan, see Yang 2008: 5, 74–107.

32. Bei (裴) for migrants from Shule (疏勒), Bai (白) for Kucha (龜兹), Kang (康) for Samarkand, An (安) for Anguo (安國), Cao (曹) for Caoguo (曹國), Shi (石) for Shiguo (石國),

Mi (米) for Miguo (米國), and He (何) for migrants from Heguo (何國). Twenty-eight ethnicities were Sinicized during the Tang dynasty, including migrants from Xianbei (鮮卑), Xiongnu (匈奴), and Gaoli (고려) and migrants of Turkish (突厥), Anguo, and Samarkand descent (Jeong 2016: 946).

33. During the Tang, goods and peoples from many foreign countries were given the epithet *hu* and designated "Westerners," especially Iranians, and sometimes Indians, Arabs and Romans. (Schafer 1963: 4)

34. Other sources for this region include Yi Jing's (义净; 635–713) *A Record of Buddhist Practices Sent Home from the Southern Sea* (西域南海寄归内法传) and Hui Chao's (慧超; 704–787) *An Account of Travel to the Five Indian Kingdoms* (往五天竺国传).

35. Da Qin (大秦) refers to countries of the west, probably Persia or Syria, or even the Roman empire (Bays 2012: 7). The historian John Foster defined it as "the Roman Empire, or rather that part of it which alone was known to the Chinese, Syria" (Foster 1939: 3). Scholars have also variously argued that Da Qin could refer to Macedonia, Syria, Egypt, or Arabia (Yu 2013: 1).

Chapter 2. The Barbarian in the Western Imagination and History

1. Sinologists who use the term *oikumene* as a translation of *tianxia*, or "the Chinese world," are thus either not understanding what *oikumene* means in the Western context or what *tianxia* means in the Chinese context. See, for example, Joachim Gentz, "Long Live the King! The Ideology of Power between Ritual and Morality in the *Gongyang zhuan* 公羊传," in which he writes that "the Son of Heaven ruled over his oecumene (*tianxia*, 天下)" (Gentz 2015: 77; see also Pines 2012: 15).

2. Williams seems to use "savage" in contradistinction to "barbarian" to refer to mythical, monstrous creatures. He uses "barbarian" to refer to the empirically existing racial other who was perceived as monstrous by the Western imagination.

3. In *Nicomachean Ethics*, Aristotle describes tribes from the Black Sea who eat "raw meat" and "human flesh" as well as each other's children (*NE*, 1148 b 22–23; Aristotle 2007: 1814). In *Politics*, he speaks of many foreign races being inclined to murder and cannibalism, such as the tribes of the Black Sea, the Achaeans and Heniochi, and others of the mainland races (*Politics* 1338b 20; Aristotle 2007: 2124).

4. Cannibalism was one of the signifiers of an antithetical other. Herodotus, for example, describes the people in the Pontus areas as "Man-eaters": "Their customs are utterly bestial [. . .] they alone of these peoples, eat human flesh" (quoted in Isaac 2004: 208). For Herodotus, Williams notes, cannibalism was "an effective and readily recognized categorical marker for identifying the most extreme forms of the barbarian's degeneracy from the civilized norms and values of the Greeks." Moreover, cannibalism was *assumed* to exist among distant (and therefore savage) parts of the world (Williams 2012: 65). Cannibalism became the ascription *non plus ultra* throughout European history for reducing the racial other to the role of barbarian. The Amerindians, for example, were described by contemporary Europeans as cannibals, although scholars have been unable to find any evidence of the practice (Pagden 1982: 225–26n154).

5. This is why caution is required when equating descriptions of mythical beings in Chinese texts such as the *Shanhaijing* (山海经) to these proto-ethnographical and geographical works

in the Western canon. In the Western context, the monstrous races are identified with actual existing ethnic others, whereas mythical creatures in texts like the *Shanhaijing* remain mythical creatures. As Wolfgang Bauer writes about the *Shanhaijing* (山海经), "only occasionally are there indications that seem to refer to real information about faraway peoples" (Bauer 1980: 10, my translation). It should be stressed that the *Shanhaijing* is not a work of geopolitical ethnography like Herodotus's *Histories* and Hippocrates's *Airs, Waters, Places*, both of which *were* making claims about existing ethnic groups and for this reason have been interpreted as the beginnings of Western racism. The *Shanhaijing* cannot be compared with Greek and Roman texts making stereotyped statements, however fanciful they may be, about actual ethnic groups such as the Phoenicians, Carthaginians, Syrians, Egyptians, Persians, Gauls, Germans, and Jews. Racist stereotyping is inextricable from the justification for dominating a group of people, but nowhere in the *Shanhaijing* is there any suggestion that these peoples are free game for domination because they do not look like Chinese peoples. As the Sinologist Richard Strassberg writes, the creatures described in the *Shanhaijing* are understood, in line with the "traditional Chinese worldview," as "an intimate part of the natural environment" or "[a] part of the ecology within the cosmos of heaven and earth." As such, "they dwelled elusively alongside humankind, which was obliged to learn how to recognize them and to employ the appropriate strategies for coexisting with them" (Strassberg 2002: 2, xiii).

6. In "White Racism or World Community," Baldwin writes: "There is a sense in which it can be said that very long ago, for a complex of reasons, but among them power, the Christian personality split itself into two, split itself into dark and light, in fact, and it is now bewildered, at war with itself" (Baldwin 1998: 754).

7. Baldwin expresses this point beautifully: "They require a song of me less to celebrate my captivity than to justify their own" (Baldwin 1998: 842).

8. "Professor Arens [1979] maintains that it is rarely, if ever, possible to substantiate accusations of cannibalism," Pagden writes. "[. . .] No European account of cannibalism will, he claims, stand up to critical examination. Either the supposed witness turns out not to have been present at the crucial moment when the victim was eaten or his account is, on internal evidence, unreliable as an ethnographical report. Although Professor Arens's argument is based solely on printed sources which are easily available in English, his hypothesis, in so far as it applies to the Amerindians, also holds true for the large body of documentary material on cannibalism. I, at least, have not found a single eye-witness account of a cannibal feast nor, indeed a single description which does not rely on elements taken from classical accounts of anthropophagy" (Pagden 1982: 225–26n154).

9. Slotkin explains: "Almost from the moment of its literary genesis, the New England Indian captivity narrative functioned as a myth, reducing the Puritan state of mind and world view, along with the events of colonization and settlement, into archetypal drama. In it a single individual, usually a woman, stands passively under the strokes of evil, awaiting rescue by the grace of God. The sufferer represents the whole, chastened body of Puritan society; and the temporary bondage of the soul to the flesh and to the temptations arising from original sin, and of the self-exile of the English Israel from England. In the Indian's devilish clutches, the captive had to meet and reject the temptation of Indian marriage and/or the Indian's 'cannibal' Eucharist. To partake of the Indian's love or of his equivalent of bread and wine was to debase, to un-English the very soul" (Slotkin 2000: 94).

10. As Slotkin writes, "Looking at the culture of the New World in which they had come to live, the Puritans saw a darkened and inverted mirror image of their own culture, their own mind. For every Puritan institution, moral theory and practice, belief and ritual there existed an antithetical Indian counterpart. Such analogies were never lost on the Puritans, who saw in them metaphors of God's will. Clearly the Indian cultures were the devil's city on a hill, emblematic opposites to their own Bible commonwealth" (Slotkin 2000: 57).

11. A recent work by Yaqing Qin on constructing a Chinese theory of international relations also points out that the fundamental Western worldview when it comes to self and other is premised on negating the other, with conflict being the natural relationship between them (Qin 2018, 162).

12. George W. Bush, "Commencement Address at the United States Military Academy in West Point, New York," June 1, 2002, American President Project, https://www.presidency.ucsb .edu/documents/commencement-address-the-united-states-military-academy-west-point-new -york-1.

13. As Roel Sterckx reminds us: "No one single denotative definition that summarizes the essential ontological properties of a being that approximates the Greek or Western notion of an animal can be found in early Chinese writings" (Sterckx 2002: 17).

Chapter 3. Chinese Processual Holism and Its Attitude toward "Barbarians" and Nonhumans

1. My use of "anomalous" indicates the lack in the Chinese tradition of any conception of the transcendent or a supernatural entity that can supervene in the natural order. That is, I am arguing that there is no specifically theistic notion of the anomalous in the Chinese tradition. However, the tradition does have a conception of that which deviates from the norm. For example, there are passages from the *Zhuangzi* in which people develop extraordinary skills, such as catching cicadas, drawing perfect circles, or cutting up oxen. I use "anomalous" in the former as opposed to the latter sense. I thank one of the reviewers for urging me to clarify this point.

2. I am not using "organism" in the sense of the biological determinism of the early twentieth century, which effectively redounds to a metaphysical determinism because of its stress on the subordination of the part to the whole (as opposed to an interactive process of mutual influence), teleology, and purpose. Under Spengler's *Decline of the West*, for example, the human being has no creative agency, as she is merely a part that is subordinated to the supra-organism of the whole that is human history. That is, the most pernicious aspects of the "organicism" that underlay the fascistic discourse of the early twentieth century were Aristotelian conceptions of biology. My use of "organism" has no similarities to the teleological, Aristotelian understanding of the organism, in which the part has a telos mandated by the whole. Arguably, the Aristotelian understanding of the organism merely applies to the biological realm a mechanistic relationship between the part and the whole. In fact, the process interpretations of biology that I reference are deliberately trying to overcome these Aristotelian habits of thought. For more on what I mean by "organism" and "organic harmony," see my account of "organic holism" in Xiang 2019a.

3. For clarification, see Xiang 2019a: 262. Here I describe the organic, or "functional," whole by contrasting it with the idea of wholeness found in a substance ontology.

4. Contra Philip Ivanhoe and his colleagues, who equate the Chinese idea of oneness with the idea of the Great Chain of Being (Ivanhoe et al. 2018: 4), the Chinese conception of the whole is *not* this metaphysical determinism of medieval Western ontology.

5. A term coined by the process philosopher A. N. Whitehead.

6. These points are reiterated by E. N. Anderson and Lisa Raphals in their essay "Daoism and Animals": "The Daoists did not see a sharp barrier between people and animals, or, more generally, between humanity and nature. In fact, they saw humans and animals as mutually dependent, and, indeed, regularly prone to change into each other. Change and transformation are seen in Daoism as universal and necessary [. . .] in a deep and basic sense, *dao* unites humans and animals" (Anderson and Raphals 2006: 286).

7. I develop this argument in Xiang 2021a. See also the section "The 'Symbolic Idealism' of the *Yijing*" in Xiang 2018a: 178–80, and the section "Human Agency: Difference as Cultural, Not Ontological" in Xiang 2019c: 3–5.

8. Zhu Xi also spoke of spirits (神) as "the essence [精英] of *qi*" (Zhu 1986: 9, my translation), the place where *qi* is 'essential [精] and subtle [妙]'" (2422, my translation) and "the essential and bright [明] [portion] of *qi*" (3343, all translations here my own). For this section on Zhu Xi, I have consulted Kim 2015: 132, and Kim 2000: 93.

9. See Mencius 1A7: "Thus, if one extends his kindness it will be enough to protect all within the four seas, whereas if one fails to extend it, he will have no way to protect his wife and children" (Mencius 2009: 9–10).

10. In Chinese, the pits of peaches and apricots are referred to as *taoren* (桃仁) and *xingren* (杏仁). On a linguistic level, the potential for growth and germination in the pits of peaches and apricots is related to the concept of "humaneness" (*ren*, 仁).

11. As Roel Sterckx writes, "Despite the substantial volume of material on animals preserved in writings from the Warring States and Han China, these texts rarely sought to analyze the living species following a systematic biology, zoology, theology, or anthropology" (Sterckx 2002: 5). This stark contrast has prompted the celebrated Sinologist J.J.M. De Groot to argue that "Chinese authors have roundly avowed themselves altogether unable to discover any real differences between men and animals" (De Groot 1964: 4:157). This particular characteristic of Chinese thought has also been remarked upon by the Sinologist Marcel Granet, who writes that the Chinese "have no taste for classifying things in terms of genus and species" (Granet 1934: 125). It has been said that this inability to see humans as clearly distinct from animals is due to the Chinese tradition's tendency not to appeal to an essential property common to all members of a class (see Hall and Ames 1995: 253; Ames 1993: 39).

12. Bruya 2022: 7.

13. The same analogy of Qin with animals—specifically wolves and tigers—is frequently repeated in the *Records on the Warring States*. See Zhai 2008: 53, "On Western Zhou," in "Qin Sent Chu Liji to West Zhou with One Hundred Chariots" (秦令樗里疾以车百乘入周); Zhai 2008: 841, "Third Volume on Zhao," in "Qin Attacks Zhao's Changping" (秦攻赵于长平); Zhai 2008: 575, "First Volume on Chu," in "Su Qin Advocated Hezong on Behalf of Zhao and Went to Persuade King Wei of Chu" (苏秦为赵合从说楚威王); Zhai 2008: 957, "First Volume on Wei," in "On Behalf of Zhao, Su Qin Persuaded Wei's King to Join Hezong" (苏子为赵合从).

14. Thus, when Chinese texts do draw a line between Chinese and non-Chinese, they do not necessarily mean to say that there is an ontological dualism between Chinese and non-Chinese.

I would argue that any difference noted by the early Chinese can be understood as provisional and temporary, a view consistent with Chinese processual holistic metaphysics.

15. This genre arose during the Six Dynasties (220–589 CE).

16. In connection with the Chinese folkloric assumption that nothing is beyond moral concern, including ghosts and demons, it is worth pointing out (as I have in Xiang 2015) that the overwhelming motif of nineteenth-century anti-Semitic discourse is the metaphor of the Jew as a ghost. Whereas in Western discourse the Jew-as-ghost cannot be rehabilitated for civilization because he is ontologically other and antithetical, in Chinese discourse we see a starkly different attitude toward ghosts.

17. In Xiang 2015, I use this story to illustrate the Confucian processual understanding of selfhood, arguing that this understanding of how human status is achieved explains why the Confucian tradition fears the other far less than the Western tradition does, since it sees the other as not eternally other but capable of being made familiar. This processual understanding of selfhood contributed to the Chinese historical assimilation of initially foreign peoples throughout the millennia, creating what we now know as the Han people.

18. 漠漠孤城落照间, 黄榆白苇满关山, 千枝羌笛连云起, 知是胡儿牧马还, https://www .gushixiu.net/momoguchengluozhaojianhuangyubaiweimangu-c/.

19. 营州少年厌原野, 狐裘蒙茸猎城下. 虏酒千钟不醉人, 胡儿十岁能骑马.

20. 石国胡儿向碛东, 爱吹横笛引秋风, 夜来云雨皆飞尽, 月照平沙万里空.

21. An early "Age of Discovery" tradition was to see the Amerindian as having been so spontaneously generated (Pagden 1982: 23). Some, notably Paracelsus (1493/1494–1541, whose burying place became a Catholic shrine), Andrea Cesalpino, and the French Huguenot Isaac de la Peyrère, believed that the Amerindians (the "wild men," *sylvestres homines*), along with other humanoids such as nymphs, satyrs, and pygmies, "might be soulless men descended from another 'Adam' or created spontaneously from the earth" (22).

Chapter 4. Race, Metaphysical Determinism, and the Great Chain of Being

1. Related to this point, Robert Bernasconi has argued that Kant's hierarchical theory of race emerged out of a desire to explain the apparent diversity of human beings in nature. The regulative and reflective concept of race, like that of the purposiveness of nature, serves a role in our understanding of nature. For Kant, predecessors such as Leibniz and Bonnet, in "proposing what came to be known as the chain of being," were proposing an excellent regulative principle of reason (Bernasconi 2001: 29).

2. I refer to the famous statement in the *Physics* that since all material bodies in the universe are in motion, each must be moved by a more powerful body. The entire chain of bodies is set in motion by an unmoved Prime Mover, who alone is unmoved (*Physics* 258b10–259a20; Aristotle 2007: 432).

3. Alexander Pope, "Essay on Man," in *The Library of the World's Best Literature: An Anthology in Thirty Volumes*, compiled by C. D. Warner et al. (1917), available at Bartleby.com, https://www .bartleby.com/library/poem/4123.html.

4. It was held as obvious to Francisco de Vitoria (1483–1546), the father of international law, that the Indians were mentally incapacitated: "The Indians have neither laws nor magistrates

that are adequate (*convenientes*); nor are they capable of governing the household (*rem famili-arem*) satisfactorily" (quoted in Pagden 1982: 80). In *Libellus de insulanis oceanis* (*Book on the Oceanic Islands*), the jurist Palacio Rubios observed that, as the Indians formed matrilineal societies, they were not real communities but mere hordes (52–54). On the basis of these customs, he declared them to be "so inept and foolish that they do not know how to rule themselves." "Broadly speaking," he concluded, they could "be called slaves as those who are almost born to be slaves" (quoted in Pagden 1982: 54). Nicolás Monardes (1493–1588) dismissed the evident wealth of Amerindian metal workmanship in gold and silver as insufficient evidence of material culture because they did not practice metalwork in the "true" metal—iron (92). Dr. Diego Alvarez Chanca, a physician on Columbus's voyages, similarly wrote that the natives were barbarous creatures whose "degradation is greater than that of any beast in the world." Among his reasons for this claim was that they laid out their towns in a particular way, and they ate iguanas (quoted in Stannard 1992: 204).

5. On the European tradition of using ontological hierarchy to justify social inequality, see Powers 2021: 73–98.

6. Under a logic comparable to Aristotle's theory of natural slavery, Hegel, in his *Lectures on the Philosophy of World History*, defended African slavery, as it brought Africans into contact with (European) culture and thus allowed Africa to enter into history (Bernasconi 2005: 144). As Hegel writes in his *Philosophy of Subjective Spirit*, "The question of racial variety bears upon the rights one ought to accord people; where there are various races, one will be nobler and the other has to serve it" (Hegel 1978: 47). As Michael Hoffheimer remarks, "Passages [in Hegel's oeuvre] that asserted the natural proclivity of Negroes for slavery could be, and in fact were, read as race-based justifications for slavery" (Hoffheimer 2005: 207). Long passages of Hegel's descriptions of Negroes were read by a proponent of American slavery in a congressional hearing in 1860 (215n81).

Chapter 5. The Metaphysics of Harmony and the Metaphysics of Colonialism

1. The *Zhu Fan Zhi* was written by the commissioner of foreign trade at Quanzhou in Fujian in 1226 CE. This work is acknowledged to be "perhaps the most important historical text available to date offering a Chinese perspective on the Southeast Asian trade during the Southern Song period" (Soon 2001: 134).

2. For an account that details the extensive trade networks between the Song and its neighbors, see Yoshinobu 1983: 89–115.

3. Zheng He's voyages are also recorded in Arabic sources; see Jost 2019.

4. Mote suggests that this stereotype might have arisen from the sixteenth-century European encounter with the Qing. The Europeans "scoffed at the myopic delusions" of the "rigidities of the 'Chinese world order'" (Mote 2003: 376).

5. Sima Qian's *Shiji* contains fascicles on the Xiongnu (匈奴), Southern Yue (南越), Eastern Yue (东越), Korea (朝鲜), Yi of the southwest (西南夷), and Dayuan (大宛). Dayuan refers to a country that is in present-day Kazakhstan. The capital of Dayuan, Guishancheng (贵山城), is in present-day Uzbekistan (Sima 2010: 7271n1). The fascicle on Dayuan mentions more than twenty countries west of China (7270).

6. The *Book of Han* contains fascicles on the Xiongnu (匈奴), Southwestern Yi, Two Yue and Korea (西南夷两粤朝鲜), Southwestern Yi (西南夷), Southern Yue (南粤), Min-Yue (闽粤), Korea (朝鲜), and city-states of the Western Territories (西域传).

7. The *Book of the Later Han* contains fascicles on the Eastern Yi (东夷, which comprises Fuyu (夫余), Yilou (挹娄), Gaogouli (高句骊), Dong Woju (东沃沮), Hui (濊), Sanhan (三韩), and Wo (倭); the Southern and Southwestern Yi (南蛮西南夷), the Western Qiang (西羌), the Western Territories (西域), the Southern Xiongnu (南匈奴), and the Wuhuan and Xianbei (乌桓鲜卑).

8. Edwin Pulleyblank takes it to be phonetically derived from Seleukia (Pulleyblank 1999: 73–74). Yu takes it to be the Seleucid Syrian Kingdom to the west of Anxi i.e. Parthian Persia (Yu 2013: 5). As David Graf writes, "It is now generally accepted that *Tiaozhi* represents the area of southernmost Babylonia and that the name may be derived from the 'Tigris'" (Graf 2018: 453).

9. For an account of the relations between China and India during the Han dynasty, see Yang 2013.

10. For an account of the Silk Road in Chinese, Arabic, and Persian sources, see Hua 2016.

11. This kind of description would be repeated in other dynastic histories. The *Jin Shu*—written in the early seventh century CE about the period 265–419 CE—also describes *Daqin*, its political institutions, its trade with India and Parthia in exotics such as frankincense, coral, and amber, the tallness of its habitants, and their facial resemblance to the Han, though they wore Western dress (Fang 1974: 2544; Hirth 1885: 43–45; Yu 2013: 114–21). The *Liang Shu*—written ca. 629 CE about the period 502–556 CE—describes India, *Daqin*, and Parthia as well as the exotic products they produced (Yao 1973: 797–98; Hirth 1885: 47–48; Yu 2013: 118–21). The *Wei Shu*—written before 572 CE about the period 386–556 CE—describes Andu (安都, Antioch), the capital of *Daqin* and how to get there from Tiaozhi (条支, Babylonia) and Jiaozhi (交趾, a prefecture whose seat of government was to northwest of present-day Hanoi) (Wei 1974: 2275–76; Hirth 1885: 48–51; Yu 2013: 121–26). The *Song Shu*—written ca. 500 CE about the period 420–478 CE—also describes *Daqin* and India, as well as the trade that flowed in from these regions, such as rhinoceros horns (Shen 1974: 2399; Hirth 1885: 45–46; Yu 2013: 126–27).

12. These kingdoms were Alexandria (Zesan, 泽散), Propontis (Lüfen, 驴分), Palmyra (Qielan, 且兰), Jerusalem (Xiandu, 贤督), Damascus (Sifu, 氾复), and Hatra (Yuluo, 于罗) (Chen 1982: 861–62; Yu 2013: 95–96).

13. This description of Byzantium includes its cityscape, its political system, the king's palace, how the inhabitants dressed, and the country's natural resources, as well as an account of the city of Constantinople (Liu 1975: 5313–14; Hirth 1885: 51–56). A similar account is given in the *New Book of Tang*, which describes Constantinople, its customs and people, the Arab takeover of the city, and the tributes it offered to China (Ouyang and Song 1975: 6260–61; Hirth 1885: 56–61).

14. For translations of names into their modern-day equivalents, I have consulted Paul Halsall's work, "East Asian History Sourcebook: Chinese Accounts of Rome, Byzantium, and the Middle East, c. 91 BCE–1643 CE," https://depts.washington.edu/silkroad/texts/romchin1.html.

15. Similar accounts appear in Ma Duanlin's (马端临) *Comprehensive Investigations Based on Literary and Documentary Sources* (文献通考; Ma 2011: 9377–79; Hirth 1885: 77–91), Zhao Ru-kuo's (赵汝适) *Records of Foreign People* (诸蕃志; written in the thirteenth century; Zhao 2000: 81–85; Hirth 1885: 92–96), and the *History of Ming* (明史; concluded 1739 CE, about the period 1368–1643 CE; Zhang 1974: 8457–58; Hirth 1885: 64–67).

16. For an account of the wealth of written sources available to the Song government through returning envoys and foreign envoys, see Franke 1983: 116–48.

17. There are 898 annotations on Columbus's copy of d'Ailly's *Imago Mundo* (Watts 1985, 80n12). For more on the medieval worldview that Columbus would have shared, see Pauline Watts's "Prophecy and Discovery: On the Spiritual Origins of Christopher Columbus's 'Enterprise of the Indies.'" Watts argues that d'Ailly, among others, "must be considered a principal source of Columbus's apocalypticism" (Watts 1985: 92). As David Stannard has written, Columbus was "obsessed" with the eschatological idea that the second coming was imminent (Stannard 1992: 192). Watts concludes that what motivated Columbus's travels was his desire to liberate the Holy Land (Watts 1985: 99).

18. Incidentally, Jews in the Middle Ages were identified with the Cynocephaly (Hannaford 1996: 127).

19. Cf. Hanke 1959: 130–31n 14; Stannard 1994: 197–98. Anthony Pagden writes that cannibalism was a standard description of non-European cultures "ever since the first Greeks ventured out into the western Mediterranean" (Pagden 1982: 80–81). He notes that this obsession can be seen as early as Homer's *Odysseus*, Pliny, Saint Jerome's description of the insatiable craving for human flesh of the Irish and Scottish, Christian encyclopedists such as Saint Isidore of Seville, and Tertullian's ascription of cannibalism to the Tartars, Thracians, and Mongols. By the end of the fifteenth century, anthropophagi had become a "regular part of the topography of exotic lands." Europeans attributed cannibalism to non-Western cultures because "cannibalism, sodomy and bestiality all offended man's rational nature" (86). Under this worldview, non-Westerners, considered irrational by nature, were understood to be cannibals by nature.

20. See Littlefield and Parrins 2011. For a record of the evolution of the legal discourses of Amerindian land dispossession, see Williams 1990: 227–317.

21. "Its nature is to be available for anything to make its impression upon, and it's modified, shaped and reshaped by the things that enter it" (*Timaeus* 50c; Plato 1997: 1253).

22. This thing (*chora*) upon which imprints are made is "itself devoid of any of those characters that it is to receive from elsewhere" (*Timaeus* 50d–e; Plato 1997: 1253). It is "totally devoid of any characteristics" (*Timaeus* 50e; Plato 1997: 1253).

23. "And the third type is space, which exists always and cannot be destroyed. It provides a fixed state for all things that come to be" (*Timaeus* 52b; Plato 1997: 1225).

24. For the very strong association of Dao—the order of the world—with the female in Daoist-Chinese metaphysics and its positive overtones, see the very eloquent summary in "Dao as Female Body" in Wang 2012: 55–58. Relatedly, in her work on metaphors in early Chinese philosophy, Sarah Allan argues that "the ancient Chinese turned directly to the natural world—to water and the plant life that it nourishes—for the root metaphors of their philosophical concepts" (Allan 1997: xii). The structural metaphors of the Chinese philosophic tradition are premised on the ability of nature—for example, water—to accommodate and nurture all things.

25. The idea that the greatest efficacy in the world is an ability to support the diversity of growth pervades the *Doctrine of the Mean*. Further examples are found in passages 1 and 16.

26. See *Doctrine of the Mean* 22 and 25.

27. *Doctrine of the Mean* 31 and 32 also exhort human beings to follow the all-accommodating nature of nature.

28. See my account in chapter 2 of Xiang 2021a; see also Xiang 2018a.

29. See Mattice 2014: 26–28 for a similar account of the importance of harmony in Chinese accounts of military strategy.

Chapter 6. The Metaphysics of Harmony in Practice

1. In the *Records on the Warring States Period* (战国策), for example, the term *de* (德) is often used to denote the distribution of honors, the paying of tribute, the gifting of land, enticements of others with favors, the paying of respects, or the honoring of somebody. For example, in "Someone Had a Talk with Qin's King" (谓秦王) in the *Fifth Volume on Qin*, an adviser cautions the king of Qin to distribute equal honors among the different states because maintaining these relations will help him secure long-term hegemony. "Now Your Majesty has given many generous favours to the states of Han and Wei. However, you don't pay any attention to damaging relations with the state of Qi" (今王广德魏、赵、而轻失齐) (Zhai 2008: 291). In "The Troops of Chu and Those of Wei Engaged in Battle Near Mount Xing" (楚魏战于陉山) in the *Fourth Volume on Qin*, an adviser to the Qin seeks a gift of land himself from the king: "Your majesty will also do me a big favor by forcing Wei to cede me the land" (是王以魏地德寡人) (262–63). Similarly, in "Third Year of Lord Cheng" of the *Zuo Zhuan*, we see an exchange between King Gong of Chu (楚共王) and Zhi Ying (知罃), a captive Jin commander who is about to be released. King Gong asks Zhi Ying whether he is grateful (*de*, 德) to him for his release (然则德我乎) (Durrant, Li, and Schaberg 2016: 741). For an account of *de* meaning "to care for and help others to gain benefit" in the pre-Qin texts, see Zhao 2021: 94–95.

2. It needs to be borne in mind that the Confucian tradition has a place for the idea that some times even the elite culture needs to learn from others. As recorded in the "17th Year of Lord Zhao" chapter of the *Zuo Zhuan*, Confucius famously said, "I have heard that 'when the Son of Heaven has lost his officials [when they neglect proper knowledge and execution of their duties], knowledge is preserved among the tribes of the four quarters'" (Durrant, Li, and Schaberg 2016: 1545, my modifications). As I have stressed, the Chinese (and Confucian) tradition was highly syncretic in practice, reflecting its readiness to learn from others, including other traditions.

3. The "Shaogong 20th Year" chapter of the *Zuozhuan* discusses harmony in terms of balancing different flavors.

4. To be fair to the Chinese tradition, unlike the Greek attitude toward the Persians (whom they viewed as barbarians), there is a case to be made that Confucian attitudes toward border peoples were more empirically informed.

5. "The fear of you and the dread of you shall be upon every beast of the earth, and upon every fowl of the air, upon all that moveth upon the earth, and upon all the fishes of the sea; into your hand are they delivered. Every moving thing that liveth shall be meat for you" (Genesis, ix. 2–3).

Conclusion

1. This projection of freedom for the West and determinism for the non-West is seen in the refusal of certain European philosophers to acknowledge that the non-West has "philosophy." For Hegel, only the Caucasian race has the subjective capacity for freedom (Hegel 1978: 57). In the appendix to the introduction of his *Lectures on the Philosophy of World History*, for example, Hegel talks of the oriental realm as still immersed in external nature and thus unable to "attain the inward conditions of subjective freedom" (Hegel 1975: 202). Within this oriental realm, "ethical life has an immediate and lawless character" (198). In assuming that philosophy arose

only in Greece with the historical dawning of self-consciousness, Hegel follows Kant in excluding Asia from the philosophical canon (Park 2013: 114).

2. Kant, who is commonly regarded as the "father of the modern concept of race" (Mills 1997: 70), dedicated "the largest period of his career to research in, and teaching of, anthropology and cultural geography" (Eze 1997: 2). From the 1770s until his retirement in 1796, Kant formulated and defended a (pseudo-) scientific concept of race and published three essays on race: "Of the Different Races of Human Beings" (1775; republished 1777), "Determination of the Concept of a Human Race" (1785), and "On the Use of Teleological Principles in Philosophy" (1788) (Park 2013: 93).

3. In my forthcoming paper, "Decolonizing Sinology: On Sinology's Weaponization of the Discourse of Race" (Xiang, forthcoming[d]), I frame Sinology's change in consensus on the matter of race in China in terms of its complicity with white supremacy, imperialism, and the military-industrial-academic complex. Specifically, this change in consensus is located within the post–cold war dynamics of international relations.

Glossary

1. 夏, 大也。中国有礼仪之大,故称夏; 有服章之美,谓之华.

2. 冕服华章曰华, 大国曰夏.

3. As a *Financial Times* headline put it, "The Fall of the Soviet Bloc Has Left the IMF and G7 to Rule the World and Create a New Imperial Age" (quoted in Chomsky 1993: 61).

4. Jaffe 2015.

WORKS CITED

Alcoff, Linda Martín. "Philosophy and Philosophical Practice: Eurocentrism as an Epistemology of Ignorance." In *The Routledge Handbook of Epistemic Injustice*, edited by Ian James Kidd, José Medina, and Gaile Pohlhaus Jr., 397–408. London: Routledge, 2017.

Allan, Sarah. *The Way of Water and the Sprouts of Virtue*. Albany: State University of New York Press, 1997.

Ames, Roger. *Sun-Tzu: The Art of War*. New York: Ballantine Book, 1993.

Ames, Roger T., and David L. Hall. *Focusing the Familiar: A Translation and Philosophical Interpretation of the* Zhongyong. Honolulu: University of Hawai'i Press, 2001.

———. *Dao De Jing: A Philosophical Translation*. New York: Ballantine Books, 2003.

Anderson, E. N., and Lisa Raphals. "Daoism and Animals." In *A Communion of Subjects: Animals in Religion, Science, and Ethics*, edited by Paul Waldau and Kimberley Patton. New York: Columbia University Press, 2006.

Appiah, Anthony. *Cosmopolitanism: Ethics in a World of Strangers*. London: Penguin, 2006.

Appy, Christian G. *American Reckoning: The Vietnam War and Our National Identity*. New York: Penguin, 2016.

Arendt, Hannah. *The Origins of Totalitarianism*. London: Penguin, 2017.

Arens, W. *The Man-Eating Myth: Anthropology and Anthropophagy*. New York: Oxford University Press, 1979.

Arrighi, Giovanni. *Adam Smith in Beijing: Lineages of the Twenty-First Century*. London: Verso, 2007.

Aristotle. 2007. *The Complete Works of Aristotle: The Revised Oxford Translation*, edited by Jonathan Barnes, vols. 1 and 2. Princeton, NJ: Princeton University Press.

Bai, Tongdong. *Against Political Equality: The Confucian Case*. Princeton, NJ: Princeton University Press, 2020.

Baldanza, Kathlene. *Ming China and Vietnam: Negotiating Borders in Early Modern China*. Cambridge: Cambridge University Press, 2016.

Baldwin, James. *James Baldwin: Collected Essays*. New York: Library of America, 1998.

Baldwin, James, and Pratt D. Darnell. *Conversations with James Baldwin*, edited by Fred L. Standley and Louis H. Pratt. Jackson: University Press of Mississippi, 1989.

Barisitz, Stephan. *Central Asia and the Silk Road: Economic Rise and Decline over Several Millennia*. Cham, Switzerland: Springer International Publishing, 2017.

Bauer, Wolfgang, ed. *China und die Fremden: 3000 Jahre Auseinandersetzung in Krieg und Frieden*. Munich: C. H. Beck, 1980.

Bayley, C. A. *The Birth of the Modern World 1780–1914: Global Connections and Comparisons.* Malden, MA: Blackwell Publishing, 2004.

Bays, Daniel H. *A New History of Christianity in China.* Chichester, UK: Wiley-Blackwell, 2012.

Bell, Daniel A., and Wang Pei. *Just Hierarchy: Why Social Hierarchies Matter in China and the Rest of the World.* Princeton, NJ: Princeton University Press, 2020.

Benite, Zvi Ben-Dor. *The Dao of Muhammad: A Cultural History of Muslims in Late Imperial China.* Cambridge, MA: Harvard University Asia Center, 2005.

Bernasconi, Robert. "Who Invented the Concept of Race? Kant's Role in the Enlightenment Construction of Race." In *Race,* edited by Robert Bernasconi, 11–36. Oxford: Blackwell, 2001.

———. "Why Do the Happy Inhabitants of Tahiti Exist?" In *Genocide and Human Rights: A Philosophical Guide,* edited by John K. Roth, 139–48. New York: Palgrave Macmillan, 2005.

———. "A Most Dangerous Error: The Boasian Myth of a Knock-Down Argument against Racism." *Angelaki* 24, no. 2 (2019): 92–103.

Bernasconi, Robert, and Tommy Lee Lott. *The Idea of Race.* Indianapolis: Hackett Publishing, 2000.

Bernheimer, Richard. *Wild Men in the Middle Ages: A Study in Art, Sentiment, and Demonology.* Cambridge, MA: Harvard University Press, 1952.

Biran, Michal, Jonathan Z. Brack, and Francesca Fiaschetti. *Along the Silk Roads in Mongol Eurasia: Generals, Merchants, and Intellectuals.* Oakland: University of California Press, 2020.

Bliss, Catherine. *Race Decoded: The Genomic Fight for Social Justice.* Stanford, CA: Stanford University Press, 2012.

Blum, William. *America's Deadliest Export: Democracy—The Truth about US Foreign Policy and Everything Else.* New York: Zed Books, 2013.

———. "Overthrowing Other People's Governments: The Master List." William Blum (website), n.d. https://williamblum.org/essays/read/overthrowing-other-peoples-governments -the-master-list.

Bogues, Anthony. "John Stuart Mill and 'The Negro Question': Race, Colonialism, and the Ladder of Civilization." In *Race and Racism in Modern Philosophy,* edited by Andrew Valls, 217–34. Ithaca, NY: Cornell University Press, 2005.

Bradley, James. *The China Mirage: The Hidden History of American Disaster in Asia.* New York: Little, Brown and Co., 2015.

Bresciani, Umberto. *Reinventing Confucianism: The New Confucian Movement.* Taipei: Taipei Ricci Institute for Chinese Studies, 2001.

Brown, Dee. *Bury My Heart at Wounded Knee: An Indian History of the American West.* London: Vintage, 1991.

Bruya, Brian. *Ziran: The Philosophy of Spontaneous Self-Causation.* Albany: State University of New York Press, 2022.

Bryce, James. *Impressions of South Africa.* Frankfurt am Main: Outlook Verlag GmbH, 2020.

Bucher, Bernadette. *Icon and Conquest: A Structural Analysis of the Illustrations of de Bry's Great Voyages,* translated by Basia Miller Gulati. Chicago: University of Chicago Press, 1981.

Bury, J. B. *The Ancient Greek Historians (Harvard Lectures).* New York: Macmillan, 1909.

Cañizares-Esguerra, Jorge. *Puritan Conquistadors: Iberianizing the Atlantic, 1550–1700.* Stanford, CA: Stanford University Press, 2006.

Casale, Giancarlo. *The Ottoman Age of Exploration.* Oxford: Oxford University Press, 2010.

Castriota, David. *Myth, Ethos, and Actuality: Official Art in Fifth-Century BC Athens*. Madison: University of Wisconsin Press, 1992.

Césaire, Aimé. *Discourse on Colonialism*, translated by Joan Pinkham. New York: Monthly Review Press, 2000.

———. "Letter to Maurice Thorez." *Social Text* 28, no. 2 (2010): 145–52.

Chang, Carsun. *The Development of Neo-Confucian Thought*. New Haven, CT: College and University Press, 1957.

Chang, Dongsun. "A Chinese Philosopher's Theory of Knowledge." *Review of General Semantics* 9, no. 3 (1952): 203–26.

Chen, Sanping. *Multicultural China in the Early Middle Ages*. Philadelphia: University of Pennsylvania Press, 2012.

Chen Yan et al. *The Maritime Silk Road and Cultural Communication between China and the West*. New York: Lexington Books, an Imprint of The Rowman & Littlefield Publishing Group, 2020.

Chomsky, Noam. *Year 501: The Conquest Continues*. Boston: South End Press, 1993.

Christopoulos, Lucas. "Hellenes and Romans in Ancient China (240 BC–1398 AD)." *Sino-Platonic Papers* 230 (August 2012).

Clausewitz, Carl von. *On War*, translated by Michael Howard and Peter Paret. Oxford: Oxford University Press, 2007.

Cornford, Francis MacDonald, trans. *Plato's Cosmology: The Timaeus of Plato*. Indianapolis: Hackett Publishing, 1997.

Cosmo, Nicola Di. *Ancient China and Its Enemies: The Rise of Nomadic Power in East Asian History*. Cambridge: Cambridge University Press, 2002.

Cosmo, Nicola Di, and Don J. Wyatt. "Introduction." In *Political Frontiers, Ethnic Boundaries, and Human Geographies in Chinese History*, edited by Nicola Di Cosmo and Don J. Wyatt. London: Routledge, 2003.

Craemer, Thomas. "Estimating Slavery Reparations: Present Value Comparisons of Historical Multigenerational Reparations Policies." *Social Science Quarterly* 96, no. 2 (2015): 639–55.

Creel, Herrlee G. *The Origins of Statecraft in China*, vol. 1, *The Western Chou Empire*. Chicago: University of Chicago Press, 1970.

Davis, H. R. *Yunnan: The Link between India and the Yangtze*. Cambridge: Cambridge University Press, 1909.

De Groot, J.J.M. *The Religious System of China*, 6 vols. Taipei: Literary House, 1892–1910; reprint, 1964.

Desjardins, Jeff. "2,000 Years of Economic History in One Chart." Accelerating a Net-Zero Future, September 8, 2017. https://www.visualcapitalist.com/2000-years-economic-history-one-chart/.

Dewey, John. *Early Works*, vol. 1, *1882–98*, edited by Jo Ann Boydston. Carbondale: Southern Illinois University Press, 1969.

Dikötter, Frank. *The Discourse of Race in Modern China*. Hong Kong: Hong Kong University Press, 1992.

——. *The Discourse of Race in Modern China*, fully revised and expanded 2nd ed. Oxford: Oxford University Press, 2015.

Dirlik, Arif. "The Discourse of Race in Modern China." *China Information* 7, no. 4 (1993): 68–71.

Douglas, Mary. *Purity and Danger: An Analysis of the Concepts of Pollution and Taboo*. London: Routledge, 2001.

Drinnon, Richard. *Facing West: The Metaphysics of Indian-Hating and Empire-Building*. Norman: University of Oklahoma Press, 1997.

Du Bois, W.E.B. *Darkwater: Voices from within the Veil*. New York: Dover Publications, 1999.

Dupré, John, and Daniel J. Nicholson. "A Manifesto for a Processual Philosophy of Biology." In *Everything Flows: Towards a Processual Philosophy of Biology*, edited by Daniel J. Nicholson and John Dupré, 3–45. Oxford: Oxford University Press, 2018.

Durrant, Stephen W., Li Wai-yee, and David Schaberg, trans. *Zuo Tradition: Commentary on the "Spring and Autumn Annals."* Seattle: University of Washington Press, 2016.

Dussel, Enrique. *The Invention of the Americas: Eclipse of "the Other" and the Myth of Modernity*. New York: Continuum, 1995.

Ebrey, Patricia Buckley. *China: A Cultural, Social, and Political History*. Cambridge: Cambridge University Press, 2010.

Eddo-Lodge, Reni. *Why I'm No Longer Talking to White People about Race*. New York: Bloomsbury Publishing, 2017.

Eliade, Mircea. *The Myth of the Eternal Return: Cosmos and History*, translated by Willard R. Trask. Princeton, NJ: Princeton University Press, 1971.

Eliav-Feldon, Miriam, Benjamin Isaac, and Joseph Ziegler, eds. *The Origins of Racism in the West*. Cambridge: Cambridge University Press, 2009.

Elkins, Caroline. *Imperial Reckoning: The Untold Story of Britain's Gulag in Kenya*. New York: Henry Holt and Co., 2005.

Elman, Benjamin A. *A Cultural History of Civil Examinations in Later Imperial China*. Berkeley: University of California Press, 2000.

Engerman, David C. *Know Your Enemy: The Rise and Fall of America's Soviet Experts*. Oxford: Oxford University Press, 2009.

Eze, Emmanuel Chukwudi. *Race and the Enlightenment: A Reader*. Malden, MA: Blackwell, 1997.

Fairbank, John K. "Tributary Trade and China's Relations with the West." *Far Eastern Quarterly* 1, no. 2 (1942): 129–49.

———, ed. *The Cambridge History of China*, vol. 10, *Late Ch'ing, 1800–1911, Part I*. Cambridge: Cambridge University Press, 1978.

Fairbank, John King, and Merle Goldman. *China: A New History*. Cambridge, MA: Harvard University Press, 2006.

Fanon, Frantz. *The Wretched of the Earth*, translated by Constance Farrington. New York: Grove Press, 1963.

Feitlowitz, Marguerite. *A Lexicon of Terror*. New York: Oxford University Press, 2011.

Ferguson, Niall. *Civilization: The West and the Rest*. New York: Penguin, 2011.

Fernández-Armesto, Felipe. *Millennium: A History of Our Last Thousand Years*. London: Black Swan, 1996.

Finkielkraut, Alain. *The Imaginary Jew*. Lincoln: University of Nebraska Press, 1994.

Findley, Carter V. *The Turks in World History*. New York: Oxford University Press, 2005.

Fiskesjö, Magnus. "On the 'Raw' and the 'Cooked' Barbarians of Imperial China." *Inner Asia* 1, no. 2 (1999): 139–68.

Ford Campany, Robert. *Strange Writing: Anomaly Accounts in Early Medieval China*. Albany: State University of New York Press, 1996.

Foster, John. *The Church of the T'ang Dynasty*. London: Macmillan, 1939.

Franke, Herbert. "Sung Embassies: Some General Observations." In *China among Equals: The Middle Kingdom and Its Neighbours, 10th–14th Centuries*, 116–48. Berkeley: University of California Press, 1983.

Fredrickson, George M. *Racism: A Short History*. Princeton, NJ: Princeton University Press, 2002.

Freeburg, Christopher. *Melville and the Idea of Blackness: Race and Imperialism in Nineteenth-Century America*. Cambridge: Cambridge University Press, 2012.

Friedländer, Saul. "Europe's Inner Demons." In *Demonizing the Other: Antisemitism, Racism, and Xenophobia*, edited by Robert S. Wistrich, 210–22. New York: Routledge, 1999.

Füredi, Frank. *The Silent War: Imperialism and the Changing Perception of Race*. New Brunswick, NJ: Rutgers University Press, 1998.

Ge, Zhaoguang. *What Is China? Territory, Ethnicity, Culture, and History*, translated by Michael Gibbs Hill. Cambridge, MA: Belknap Press of Harvard University Press, 2018.

Gentz, Joachim. "Long Live the King! The Ideology of Power between Ritual and Morality in the *Gongyang zhuan* 公羊传." In *Ideology of Power and Power of Ideology in Early China*, edited by Yuri Pines, Paul Goldin, and Martin Kern, 69–117. Leiden: Brill, 2015.

Gernet, Jacques. *A History of Chinese Civilization*, 2nd ed., translated by J. R. Foster and Charles Hartman. Cambridge: Cambridge University Press, 1982.

Gobineau, Arthur de. *The Inequality of Human Races*, translated by Oscar Levy. London: Heinemann, 1915.

Godwin, Todd R. *Persian Christians at the Chinese Court: The Xi'an Stele and the Early Medieval Church of the East*. London: I. B. Tauris, 2018.

Gordon, Lewis R. *Bad Faith and Antiblack Racism*. New York: Humanity Books, 1995.

Gould, Stephen Jay. *The Mismeasure of Man*, revised and expanded ed. New York: W. W. Norton & Co., 1996.

Graf, David F. "The Silk Road between Syria and China." In *Trade, Commerce, and the State in the Roman World*, edited by Andrew Wilson and Alan Bowman, 443–530. Oxford: Oxford University Press, 2018.

Graham, A. C., trans. *The Book of Lieh-tzŭ: A Classic of the Tao*. New York: Columbia University Press, 1990.

———. *Two Chinese Philosophers: The Metaphysics of the Cheng Brothers*. La Salle, IL: Open Court, 1992.

Granet, Marcel. *La pensée chinoise*. Paris: Albin Michel, 1934; reprint, 1999.

Hall, David L., and Roger T. Ames. *Anticipating China: Thinking through the Narratives of Chinese and Western Culture*. Albany: State University of New York Press, 1995.

Hall, Edith. *Inventing the Barbarian: Greek Self-Definition through Tragedy*. Oxford: Clarendon Press, 1989.

Hanke, Lewis. *Aristotle and the American Indians: A Study in Race Prejudice in the Modern World*. Chicago: Henry Regnery Co., 1959.

Hannaford, Ivan. *Race: The History of an Idea in the West*. Baltimore: Johns Hopkins University Press, 1996.

Hansen, Mogens Herman. "The *Polis* as an Urban Centre: The Literary and Epigraphical Evidence." In Hansen, *The Polis as an Urban Centre and as a Political Community*, 9–96. Copenhagen: Det Kongelige Danske Videnskabernes Selskab, 1997.

Hansen, Valerie. *The Silk Road: A New History*. Oxford: Oxford University Press, 2012.

Hargett, James M. "Introduction." In Fan Chengda, *Treatises of the Supervisor and Guardian of the Cinnamon Sea*, translated by James M. Hargett, xix–lxvi. Seattle: University of Washington Press, 2010.

Harrell, Stevan. "Introduction: Civilizing Projects and the Reaction to Them." In *Cultural Encounters on China's Ethnic Frontiers*, edited by Stevan Harrell. Seattle: University of Washington Press, 1995.

Harris, Robert. *Fatherland*. New York: HarperCollins, 1992.

Hedges, Chris. *America: The Farewell Tour*. New York: Simon & Schuster, 2019.

Hegel, Georg Wilhelm Friedrich. *The Philosophy of History*, translated by Joseph Sibree. New York: Dover Publications, 1956.

———. *Lectures on the Philosophy of World History: Introduction: Reason in History*, edited by Maurice Cowling, E. Kedourie, G. R. Elton, J. R. Pole, and Walter Ullmann, translated by H. B. Nisbet. Cambridge: Cambridge University Press, 1975.

———. *Hegel's Philosophy of Subjective Spirit*, vol. 2, *Anthropology*, translated and edited by Michael J. Petry. Boston: Reidel, 1978.

Hennigan, Michael. "EU at 60—The Longest Period of Peace in Europe in over 2,000 Years." FinFacts, March 29, 2017. https://finfacts.ie/Irish_finance_news/articleDetail.php?EU-at-60---the-longest-period-of-peace-in-Europe-in-over-2-000-years-775.

Herman, John E. *Amid the Clouds and Mist: China's Colonization of Guizhou 1200–1700*. Cambridge, Mass: Harvard University Asia Center: Distributed by Harvard University Press, 2007.

Hershatter, Gail, Emily Honig, Jonathan N. Lipman, and Randall Stross, eds. *Remapping China: Fissures in Historical Terrain*. Stanford, CA: Stanford University Press, 1996.

Hirth, F. *China and the Roman Orient: Researches into Their Ancient and Mediaeval Relations as Represented in Old Chinese Records*. Shanghai and Hong Kong: Kelly & Walsh, 1885.

Hochschild, Adam. "Leopold II: King of Belgium." *Britannica*, n.d. https://www.britannica.com/biography/Leopold-II-king-of-Belgium.

Hoffheimer, Michael H. "Race and Law in Hegel's Philosophy of Religion." In *Race and Racism in Modern Philosophy*, edited by Andrew Valls, 194–216. Ithaca, NY: Cornell University Press, 2005.

Holcombe, Charles. *In the Shadow of the Han: Literati Thought and Society at the Beginning of the Southern Dynasties*. Honolulu: University of Hawai'i Press, 1994.

———. "Immigrants and Strangers: From Cosmopolitanism to Confucian Universalism in Tang China." *Tang Studies* 20/21 (2002): 71–112.

Horsman, Reginald. *Race and Manifest Destiny: The Origins of American Racial Anglo-Saxonism*. Cambridge, MA: Harvard University Press, 1981.

Hourani, George F. *Arab Seafaring in the Indian Ocean in Ancient and Early Medieval Times*, edited by John Carswell, rev. ed. Princeton, NJ: Princeton University Press, 1995.

Hulsewé, A.F.P., and M.A.N. Loewe. *China in Central Asia: The Early State: 125 BC–AD 23*. Leiden: Brill, 1979.

Human Science Research Network. "Four Professors: A Manifesto for Chinese Culture to the World." June 16, 2020. http://renxueyanjiu.com/index.php?m=content&c=index&a=show&catid=78&id=3206&page=2.

Hsü, Immanuel C. Y. *China's Entrance into the Family of Nations: The Diplomatic Phase, 1858–1880.* Cambridge: Cambridge University Press, 1960.

Hung Hing Ming. *Li Shi Min, Founding the Tang Dynasty: The Strategies That Made China the Greatest Empire in Asia.* New York: Algora Pub, 2013.

Impey, Oliver. *Chinoiserie: The Impact of Oriental Styles on Western Art and Decoration.* New York: Charles Scribner's Sons, 1977.

Isaac, Benjamin. *The Invention of Racism in Classical Antiquity.* Princeton, NJ: Princeton University Press, 2004.

Ivanhoe, Philip J., Owen J. Flanagan, Victoria S. Harrison, Hagop Sarkissian, and Eric Schwitzgebel. *The Oneness Hypothesis: Beyond the Boundary of Self.* New York: Columbia University Press, 2018.

Jaffe, Greg. "Obama's New Patriotism." *Washington Post*, June 3, 2015. https://www.washingtonpost.com/sf/national/2015/06/03/obama-and-american-exceptionalism/.

Jäger, Johannes. "Foreword." In *Everything Flows: Towards a Processual Philosophy of Biology*, edited by Daniel J. Nicholson and John Dupré, xi–xv. Oxford: Oxford University Press, 2018.

Jalata, Asafa. *Phases of Terrorism in the Age of Globalization: From Christopher Columbus to Osama Bin Laden.* New York: Palgrave Macmillan, 2016.

James, William. *The Varieties of Religious Experience: A Study in Human Nature.* Penguin Books, 1985.

Jefferson, Thomas. *Notes on the State of Virginia.* Richmond, VA: J. W. Randolph, 1853.

Jennings, Francis. *The Invasion of America: Indians, Colonialism, and the Cant of Conquest.* New York: W. W. Norton & Co., 1975.

Jeong, Su-il. *The Silk Road Encyclopedia.* Irvine, CA: Seoul Selection, 2016.

Jin, Ha. *The Banished Immortal: A Life of Li Bai.* New York: Vintage, 2019.

Jonas, Hans. *The Phenomenon of Life: Toward a Philosophical Biology.* Evanston, IL: Northwestern University Press, 2001.

Jost, Alexander. "He Did Not Kiss the Earth between His Hands: Arabic Sources on the Arrivals of the Zheng He Fleet in Aden and Mecca (1419–1431)." In *Early Global Interconnectivity across the Indian Ocean World*, vol. 1, *Commercial Structures and Exchanges*, edited by Angela Schottenhammer, 79–95. Cham, Switzerland: Palgrave Macmillan, 2019.

Jullien, François. *A Treatise on Efficacy: Between Western and Chinese Thinking.* Honolulu: University of Hawai'i Press, 2004.

Kahn, Jonathan, et al. "How Not to Talk about Race and Genetics," *BuzzfeedNews*, March 30, 2018, https://www.buzzfeednews.com/article/bfopinion/race-genetics-david-reich.

Kang, David C. *East Asia before the West: Five Centuries of Trade and Tribute.* New York: Columbia University Press, 2010.

Kant, Immanuel. *Lectures on Ethics*, translated by Louis Infield. New York: Harper Torch Books, 1963.

Kim, Yung Sik. *The Natural Philosophy of Chu Hsi (1130–1200).* Philadelphia: American Philosophical Society, 2000.

———. "Zhu Xi on Scientific and Occult Subjects: Defining and Extending the Boundaries of Confucian Learning." In *Returning to Zhu Xi: Emerging Patterns within the Supreme Polarity*, edited by David Jones and Jinli He, 121–46. Albany: State University of New York Press, 2015.

King, William. *An Essay on the Origin of Evil*, translated from Latin by Edmund Law. Cambridge: printed for W. Thurlbourn & J. Woodyer, 1732.

Kirloskar-Steinbach, M., Geeta Ramana, and J. Maffie. "Introducing Confluence: A Thematic Essay." *Confluence: Journal of World Philosophies* 1 (2016). https://scholarworks.iu.edu/iupjournals/index.php/confluence/article/view/513.

Kissinger, Henry. *On China*. London: Allen Lane, 2011.

Koch, Alexander, Chris Brierley, Mark M. Maslin, and Simon L. Lewis. "Earth System Impact of the European Arrival and Great Dying in Americans after 1492." *Quaterney Science Reviews* 207 (2019): 13–36.

Kroll, Paul W. *A Student's Dictionary of Classical and Medieval Chinese*. Leiden: Brill, 2015.

Lang, Olga. *Chinese Family and Society*. New Haven, CT: Yale University Press, 1946.

Lattimore, Owen. "China and the Barbarians." In *Empires in the East*, edited by Joseph Barnes. New York: Doubleday, 1934.

Lauren, Paul Gordon. *Power and Prejudice: The Politics and Diplomacy of Racial Discrimination*, 2nd ed. New York: Routledge, 2018.

Lavan, Myles P. "Devastation: The Destruction of Populations and Human Landscapes and the Roman Imperial Project." In *Reconsidering Roman Power: Christian Perceptions and Reactions*, edited by Katell Berthelot, 179–205. Rome: L'École Française de Rome, 2020.

Lawson, Tom. *The Last Man: A British Genocide in Tasmania*. London: I. B. Tauris & Co., 2014.

Lee, Pauline C. *Li Zhi* 李贽, *Confucianism, and the Virtue of Desire*. Albany: State University of New York Press, 2012.

Lee, Ji-Young. *China's Hegemony: Four Hundred Years of East Asian Domination*. New York: Columbia University Press, 2016.

Lee, Robert G. *Orientals: Asian Americans in Popular Culture*. Philadelphia: Temple University Press, 1999.

Legge, James. *The Chinese Classics*, vol. 1, *Confucian Analects, The Great Learning, and the Doctrine of the Mean*. London: Trübner & Co., 1861.

———. *The Nestorian Monument of Hsî-An Fû in Shen-Hsî, China*. London: Trübner & Co., 1888.

Levathes, Louise. *When China Ruled the Seas: The Treasure Fleet of the Dragon Throne 1405–1433*. New York: Simon & Schuster, 1994.

Levenson, Joseph R. *Modern China and Its Confucian Past: The Problem of Intellectual Continuity*. Garden City, NY: Doubleday, 1964.

Lewontin, Richard C. "The Apportionment of Human Diversity." In *Evolutionary Biology*, edited by Theodosius Dobzhansky, Max K. Hecht, and William C. Steere. New York: Springer, 1972.

Li, Chenyang. *The Confucian Philosophy of Harmony*. New York: Routledge: 2014.

Li. 2016. "Local Histories in Global Perspective: A Local Elite Fellowship in the Port City of Quanzhou in Seventeenth-Century China." *Frontiers of History in China* 11, no. 3 (2016): 376–99.

Lipman, Jonathan N. *Familiar Strangers: A History of Muslims in Northwest China*. Seattle: University of Washington Press, 1997.

Littlefield, Daniel, Jr., and James W. Parins, eds. *Encyclopedia of American Indian Removal*, 2 vols. Santa Barbara, CA: Greenwood, 2011.

Liu, Lydia H. *The Clash of Empires: The Invention of China in Modern World Making*. Cambridge, MA: Harvard University Press, 2004.

Lodwick, Kathleen L. "Narcotic Culture: A History of Drugs in China." *China Review International* 12, no. 1 (Spring 2005): 74–76.

Loraux, Nicole. *The Children of Athena: Athenian Ideas about Citizenship and the Division between the Sexes*, translated by Caroline Levine. Princeton, NJ: Princeton University Press, 1984.

Losurdo, Domenico. 2011. *Liberalism: A Counter-History*. New York: Verso.

Lovejoy, Arthur O. *The Great Chain of Being: A Study of the History of an Idea*. Cambridge, MA: Harvard University Press, 1964.

Lynn, Richard J. *The Classic of Changes: A New Translation of the I Ching as Interpreted by Wang Bi*. New York: Columbia University Press, 1994.

———. *The Classic of the Way and Virtue: A New Translation of the Tao-Te-Ching of Laozi as Interpreted by Wang Bi*. New York: Columbia University Press, 1999.

Majumdar, Ramesh. *Champa: History and Culture of an Indian Colonial Kingdom in the Far East 2nd–16th Century AD*. New Delhi: Gyan Publishing House, 1985.

Mallon, Ron. *The Construction of Human Kinds*. Oxford: Oxford University Press, 2016.

Marks, Jonathan M. *Human Biodiversity: Genes, Race, and History*. New Brunswick, NJ: Transaction Publishers, 1995.

Mattice, Sarah A. *Metaphor and Metaphilosophy: Philosophy as Combat, Play, and Aesthetic Experience*. New York: Lexington Books, 2014.

Maymouni, Abbas. "France's Colonial-Era Crimes 'Unforgotten' in Algeria." Anadolu Agency, May 11, 2019. https://www.aa.com.tr/en/africa/frances-colonial-era-crimes-unforgotten-in-algeria/1635943#:~:text=1.5%20million%20martyrs&text=Algerians%20accuse%20France%20of%20using,rule%20at%20over%2010%20million.

McCumber, John. *Metaphysics and Oppression: Heidegger's Challenge to Western Philosophy*. Bloomington: Indiana University Press, 1999.

Memmi, Albert. *The Colonizer and the Colonized*. London: Earthscan Publications, 2003.

Mencius. *Mencius*, translated by Irene Bloom. New York: Columbia University Press, 2009.

Mignolo, Walter D. "Philosophy and the Colonial Difference." *Philosophy Today* 43, supp. (1999): 36–41.

Miller, Harry. *The Gongyang Commentary on the Spring and Autumn Annals*. New York: Palgrave Macmillan, 2015.

Mills, Charles. *The Racial Contract*. Ithaca, NY: Cornell University Press, 1997.

———. "Kant's *Untermenschen*." In *Race and Racism in Modern Philosophy*, edited by Andrew Valls, 169–193. Ithaca, NY: Cornell University Press, 2005.

Mishra, Pankaj. "Interview: Frank Dikötter, Author of 'Mao's Great Famine' [UPDATED]," Asia Society, November 15, 2011, https://asiasociety.org/blog/asia/interview-frank-dik%C3%B6tter-author-maos-great-famine-updated.

———. *Bland Fanatics: Liberals, Race, and Empire*. London: Verso, 2021.

Mitter, Rana. *Modern China: A Very Short History*. Oxford: Oxford University Press, 2008.

Morgan, David. "Clinton Says US Could 'Totally Obliterate' Iran." *Reuters*, April 22, 2008. https://www.reuters.com/article/us-usa-politics-iran/clinton-says-u-s-could-totally -obliterate-iran-idUSN2224332720080422.

Mote, F. W. *Imperial China, 900–1800*. Cambridge, MA: Harvard University Press, 2003.

———. *Intellectual Foundations of China*. New York: Alfred A. Knopf, 1971.

Murata, Sachiko. *Chinese Gleams of Sufi Light: Wang Tai-yü's* Great Learning of the Pure and Real *and Liu Chih's* Displaying the Concealment of the Real Realm. Albany: State University of New York Press, 2000.

———. *The Sage Learning of Liu Zhi: Islamic Thought in Confucian Terms*. Cambridge, MA: Harvard University Asia Center, 2009.

———. *The First Islamic Classic in Chinese: Wang Daiyu's Real Commentary on the True Teaching*. Albany: State University of New York Press, 2017.

Needham, Joseph. *Science and Civilization in China*, vol. 2, *History of Scientific Thought*. Cambridge: Cambridge University Press, 1956.

Nelson, Eric S. "The *Yijing* and Philosophy: From Leibniz to Derrida." *Journal of Chinese Philosophy* 38, no. 3 (2011): 377–96.

———. "Recognition and Resentment in the Confucian *Analects*." *Journal of Chinese Philosophy* 40, no. 4 (2013): 287–306.

Nylan, Michael. "Talk about 'Barbarians' in Antiquity." *Philosophy East and West* 62, no. 4 (2012): 580–601.

O'Rourke, Lindsey A. *Covert Regime Change: America's Secret Cold War*. Ithaca, NY: Cornell University Press, 2018.

Pagden, Anthony. *The Fall of Natural Man: The American Indian and the Origins of Comparative Ethnology*. Cambridge: Cambridge University Press, 1982.

———. *The Burdens of Empire: 1539 to the Present*. Cambridge: Cambridge University Press, 2015.

Pan, Yihong. *Son of Heaven and Heavenly Qaghan: Sui-Tang China and Its Neighbors*. Bellingham: Center for East Asian Studies, Western Washington University, 1997.

Park, Peter K. J. *Africa, Asia, and the History of Philosophy: Racism in the Formation of the Philosophical Canon, 1780–1830*. Albany: State University of New York Press, 2013.

Parrish, Susan Scott. "The Female Opossum and the Nature of the New World." *William and Mary Quarterly* 54, no. 3 (1997): 475–514.

Perkins, Franklin. "Metaphysics and Methodology in a Cross-Cultural Context." In *The Bloomsbury Research Handbook of Chinese Philosophy Methodologies*, edited by Sor-hoon Tan, 183–98. London: Bloomsbury Academic, 2016.

Peters, F. E. *Greek Philosophical Terms: A Historical Lexicon*. New York: New York University Press, 1967.

Pines, Yuri. "Beasts or Humans: Pre-Imperial Origins of the 'Sino-Barbarian' Dichotomy." In *Mongols, Turks, and Others: Eurasian Nomads and the Sedentary World*, edited by Reuven Amitai and Michal Biran, 59–102. Leiden: Brill, 2005.

———. "Biases and Their Sources: Qin History in the 'Shiji.'" *Oriens Extremus* 45 (2005/2006): 10–34.

———. *Envisioning Eternal Empire: Chinese Political Thought of the Warring States Era*. Honolulu: University of Hawai'i Press, 2009.

———. *The Everlasting Empire: The Political Culture of Ancient China and Its Imperial Legacy.* Princeton, NJ: Princeton University Press, 2012.

Pinter, Harold. "Harold Pinter's Nobel Acceptance Speech: Art, Truth, and Politics." October 5, 2015. https://www.transcend.org/tms/2015/10/nobel-acceptance-speech-art-truth-politics.

Plato. *Plato: Complete Works,* edited by John M. Cooper. Indianapolis: Hackett Publishing, 1997.

Pollak, Michael. *Mandarins, Jews, and Missionaries: The Jewish Experience in the Chinese Empire.* New York: Weatherhill, 1998.

Powers, Martin. *Art and Political Expression in Early China.* New Haven, CT: Yale University Press, 1991.

———. "What Is Authority Made Of?" *Journal of World Philosophies* 6, no. 1 (2021): 73–98. https://scholarworks.iu.edu/iupjournals/index.php/jwp/article/view/4546.

Pulleyblank, Edwin G. "Reviewed Works: The Roman Empire as Known to Han China." *Journal of the American Oriental Society* 119, no. 1 (1999): 71–79.

Qin, Yaqing. *A Relational Theory of World Politics.* Cambridge: Cambridge University Press, 2018.

Queen, Sarah A., and John S. Major. *Luxuriant Gems of the Spring and Autumn; Attributed to Dong Zhongshu,* edited and translated by Sarah A. Queen and John S. Major. New York: Columbia University Press, 2016.

Reich, David. *Who We Are and How We Got Here: Ancient DNA and the New Science of the Human Past.* Oxford: Oxford University Press, 2018.

Rodzinski, Witold. *The Walled Kingdom: A History of China from 2000 BC to the Present.* London: Flamingo, 1984.

Rodríguez, Dylan. *Suspended Apocalypse: White Supremacy, Genocide, and the Filipino Condition.* Minneapolis: University of Minnesota Press, 2010.

Roosevelt, Theodore. *The Strenuous Life: Essays and Addresses.* Mineola, NY: Dover Publications, 2009.

Rose, Paul Lawrence. *German Question/Jewish Question: Revolutionary Antisemitism in Germany from Kant to Wagner.* Princeton, NJ: Princeton University Press, 1990.

Rossabi, Morris, ed. *China among Equals: The Middle Kingdom and Its Neighbors, 10th–14th Centuries.* Berkeley: University of California Press, 1983.

Said, Edward. *The Question of Palestine.* New York: Vintage Books, 1980.

———. *Culture and Imperialism.* London: Vintage Books, 1994.

———. *Orientalism.* London: Penguin, 2003.

Sakurai, Yumio. "Eighteenth-Century Chinese Pioneers on the Water Frontier of Indochina." In *Water Frontier: Commerce and the Chinese in the Lower Mekong Region, 1750–1880,* edited by Nola Cooke and Li Tana. Lanham, MD: Rowman & Littlefield, 2004.

San Juan, Epifanio. "US Genocide in the Philippines: A Case of Guilt, Shame, or Amnesia?" March 22, 2005. https://web.archive.org/web/20090622095234/http://www.selvesand others.org/article9315.html.

Sardar, Ziauddin, Ashis Nandy, and Merryl Wyn Davies. 1993. *Barbaric Others: A Manifesto on Western Racism.* London: Pluto Press.

Sartre, Jean-Paul. *Anti-Semite and Jew: An Exploration of the Etiology of Hate.* translated by George J. Becker. New York: Schocken Books, 1995.

Schafer, Edward H. *The Golden Peaches of Samarkand: A Study of T'ang Exotics*. Berkeley: University of California Press, 1963.

Schwartz, Benjamin I. "The Chinese Perception of World Order, Past and Present." In *The Chinese World Order: Traditional China's Foreign Relations*, edited by John King Fairbank, 276–288. Cambridge, MA: Harvard University Press, 1968.

Shapiro, Sidney, ed. and trans. *Jews in Old China: Studies by Chinese Scholars*. New York: Hippocrene Books, 1984.

Shlapentokh, Dmitry. "Russians as Asiatic: Memory about the Present." *European Review* 21, no. 1 (2013): 41–55.

Sigal, Samuel. "It's Disturbingly Easy to Buy Iraq's Archeological Treasures." *Atlantic*, March 19, 2018. https://www.theatlantic.com/international/archive/2018/03/iraq-war-archeology -invasion/555200/.

Skaff, Jonathan Karam. *Sui-Tang China and Its Turko-Mongol Neighbours*. Oxford: Oxford University Press, 2012.

"Slicing Soup." *Natura Biotechnology* 20 (2002).

Slingerland, Edward, trans. *Confucius Analects*. Indianapolis: Hackett Publishing, 2003.

Slotkin, Richard. *Regeneration through Violence: The Mythology of the American Frontier 1600–1860*. Norman: University of Oklahoma Press, 2000.

Smith, Richard J. *The Qing Dynasty and Traditional Chinese Culture*. Lanham, MD: Rowman & Littlefield, 2015.

Snodgrass, Mary Ellen. *Encyclopedia of the Literature of Empire*. New York: Facts on File, 2010.

Soon, Derek Heng Thiam. "The Trade in Lakawood Products between South China and the Malay World from the Twelfth to Fifteenth Centuries AD." *Journal of Southeast Asian Studies* 32, no. 2 (2001): 133–49.

Sorabji, Richard. *Animal Minds and Human Morals: The Origins of the Western Debate*. London: Duckworth, 1993.

Stannard, David E. *American Holocaust: The Conquest of the New World*. New York: Oxford University Press, 1992.

Sterckx, Roel. *The Animal and the Daemon in Early China*. Albany: State University of New York Press, 2002.

Strassberg, Richard E., ed. *A Chinese Bestiary: Strange Creatures from the Guideways through Mountains and Seas*. Berkeley: University of California Press, 2002.

Sun, Yan. *From Empire to Nation State: Ethnic Politics in China*. Cambridge: Cambridge University Press, 2020.

Sussman, Robert Wald. *The Myth of Race: The Troubling Persistence of an Unscientific Idea*. Cambridge, MA: Harvard University Press, 2014.

Tao, Jing-Shen. "Barbarians or Northerners: Northern Sung Images of the Khitans." In *China among Equals: The Middle Kingdom and Its Neighbors, 10th–14th Centuries*, edited by Morris Rossabi, 66–86. Berkeley: University of California Press, 1983.

Thomas, Keith. *Man and the Natural World: Changing Attitudes in England 1500–1800*. London: Allen Lane, 1983.

Thompson, Leonard. *The Political Mythology of Apartheid*. New Haven: Yale University Press, 1985.

Tibebu, Teshale. *Hegel and the Third World: The Making of Eurocentrism in World History*. New York: Syracuse University Press, 2011.

Tillyard, E.M.W. *The Elizabethan World Picture*. London: Chatto & Windus, 1943.

Todorov, Tzvetan. *The Conquest of America: The Question of the Other*, translated by Richard Howard. New York: HarperPerennial, 1984.

Togan, Isenbike. "Court Historiography in Early Tang China: Assigning a Place to History and Historians at the Palace." In *Royal Courts in Dynastic States and Empires: A Global Perspective*, edited by Jeroen Duindam, Tülay Artan, and Metin Kunt, 171–98. Leiden: Brill, 2011.

Townsend, James. "Chinese Nationalism." *Australian Journal of Chinese Affairs* 27 (1992): 97–130.

Trevor-Roper, Hugh. *The Rise of Christian Europe*. New York: Harcourt, Brace & World, 1965.

Trocki, Carl A. *Opium, Empire, and the Global Political Economy: A Study of the Asian Opium Trade, 1750–1950*. New York: Routledge, 1999.

Trofimov, Yaroslav. "Russia's Turn to Its Asian Past," *Wall Street Journal*, July 6, 2018. https://www.wsj.com/articles/russias-turn-to-its-asian-past-1530889247.

Tu, Wei-ming. *Centrality and Commonality: An Essay on Confucian Religiousness*. Albany: State University of New York Press, 1989.

Tucker, Spencer C. *Vietnam*. Lexington: University Press of Kentucky, 1999.

Turner, Frederick. *Beyond Geography: The Western Spirit against the Wilderness*. New Brunswick, NJ: Rutgers University Press, 1992.

Vaissière, Étienne de la. "Central Asia and the Silk Road." In *The Oxford Handbook of Late Antiquity*, edited by Scott Fitzgerald Johnson, 142–69. Oxford: Oxford University Press, 2012.

———. "The Steppe World and the Rise of the Huns." In *The Cambridge Companion to the Age of Attila*, edited by Michael Maas, 175–92. Cambridge: Cambridge University Press, 2015.

Wang, Robin. *Yinyang: The Way of Heaven and Earth in Chinese Thought and Culture*. Cambridge: Cambridge University Press, 2012.

Wang, Yangming. *Instructions for Practical Living and Other Neo-Confucian Writings*, translated by Wing-tsit Chan. New York: Columbia University Press, 1963.

Watts, Pauline Moffitt. "Prophecy and Discovery: On the Spiritual Origins of Christopher Columbus's 'Enterprise of the Indies.'" *American Historical Review* 90, no. 1 (1985): 73–102.

White, Hayden. "The Forms of Wildness: Archaeology of an Idea." In *The Wild Man Within: An Image of Western Thought from the Renaissance to Romanticism*, edited by Edward Dudley and Maximillian E. Novak. Pittsburgh: University of Pittsburgh Press, 1972.

Williams, Robert A., Jr. *The American Indian in Western Legal Thought: The Discourse of Conquest*. Oxford: Oxford University Press, 1990.

———. *Savage Anxieties: The Invention of Western Civilization*. New York: Palgrave Macmillan, 2012.

Wistrich, Robert S., ed. *Demonizing the Other: Antisemitism, Racism, and Xenophobia*. Amsterdam: Harwood Academic Publishers, 1999.

Wong, Roy Bin. *China Transformed: Historical Change and the Limits of European Experience*. Ithaca, NY: Cornell University Press, 1997.

Wood, Allen W. *Kant's Ethical Thought*. Cambridge: Cambridge University Press, 2019.

Wolin, Sheldon. *Democracy Incorporated: Managed Democracy and the Specter of Inverted Totalitarianism*. Princeton, NJ: Princeton University Press, 2008.

Xiang, Shuchen. "The Ghostly Other: Understanding Racism from Confucian and Enlightenment Models of Subjectivity." *Asian Philosophy* 25, no. 4 (2015): 205–22.

———. "Freedom and Culture: The Cassirerian and Confucian Account of Symbolic Formation." *Idealistic Studies* 47, no. 3 (2018a): 175–94.

———. "Orientalism and Enlightenment Positivism: A Critique of Anglophone Sinology, Comparative Literature, and Philosophy." *The Pluralist* 13, no. 2 (2018b): 22–49.

———. "Organic Harmony and Ernst Cassirer's Pluralism." *Idealistic Studies* 49, no. 3 (2019a): 259–84.

———. "Why the Confucians Had No Concept of Race (Part I): The Anti-Essentialist Cultural Understanding of Self." *Philosophy Compass* 14, no. 10 (2019b): e12628.

———. "Why the Confucians Had No Concept of Race (Part II): Cultural Difference, Environment, and Achievement." *Philosophy Compass* 14, no. 10 (2019c): e12627.

———. *A Philosophical Defense of Culture: Perspectives from Confucianism and Cassirer.* Albany: State University of New York Press, 2021a.

———. "The Persistence of Scientific Racism: Ernst Cassirer on the Myth of Substance." *Critical Philosophy of Race* 9, no. 1 (2021b): 126–50.

———. "Chinese Processual Holism and Its Attitude towards 'Barbarians' and Nonhumans." *SOPHIA* 60 (2021c): 941–64. https://doi.org/10.1007/s11841-020-00781-w.

———. "Sinophobia, Imperialism, Disorder without Responsibility." *Sartre Studies International* 28, no. 2 (2022). 42–66.

———. "*Qing* (情), *Gan* (感), and *Tong* (通): Decolonizing the Universal from a Chinese Perspective: Part 1." *Comparative and Continental Philosophy*, forthcoming(a).

———. "*Qing* (情), *Gan* (感), and *Tong* (通): Decolonizing the Universal from a Chinese Perspective: Part 2." *Comparative and Continental Philosophy*, forthcoming(b).

———. "*Tianxia* and Its Decolonial Counterparts: 'China' as Civilization, Not Ethnicity." *China Review*, forthcoming(c).

———. "Decolonizing Sinology: On Sinology's Weaponization of the Discourse of Race." *Social Dynamics*, forthcoming.

Xu, Xin. *The Jews of Kaifeng, China: History, Culture, and Religion.* Jersey City, NJ: Ktav Publishing House, 2003.

Xuanzang. *The Great Tang Dynasty Record of the Western Regions*, translated by Li Rongxi. Moraga, CA: BDK America, 1996.

Yang, Bin. *Between Winds and Clouds: The Making of Yunnan (Second Century BCE to Twentieth Century CE).* New York: Columbia University Press, 2008.

Yang, Juping. "The Relations between China and India and the Opening of the Southern Silk Road during the Han Dynasty." *The Silk Road* 11 (2013): 82–92.

Yang, Lien-sheng. "Historical Notes on the Chinese World Order." In *The Chinese World Order: Traditional China's Foreign Relations*, edited by John K. Fairbank, 20–33. Cambridge, MA: Harvard University Press, 1968.

Yang, Shao-Yun. *The Way of the Barbarians: Redrawing Ethnic Boundaries in Tang and Song China.* Seattle: University of Washington Press, 2019.

Yoshinobu, Shiba. "Sung Foreign Trade: Its Scope and Organization." In *China among Equals: The Middle Kingdom and Its Neighbours, 10th–14th Centuries*, edited by Morris Rossabi, 89–115. Berkeley: University of California Press, 1983.

Yu, Taishan. "China and the Ancient Mediterranean World: A Survey of Ancient Chinese Sources." *Sino-Platonic Papers* 242 (2013).

Yü, Ying-Shin. *Trade and Expansion in Han China: A Study in the Structure of Sino-Barbarian Economic Relations*. Berkeley: University of California Press, 1967.

———. "Han Foreign Relations." In *The Cambridge History of China*, vol. 1, *The Ch'in and Han Empires 221 BC–AD 220*, 377–462. Cambridge: Cambridge University Press, 1986.

Zack, Naomi, ed. *The Oxford Handbook of Philosophy and Race*. Oxford: Oxford University Press, 2017.

Zhao, Tingyang. *Redefining a Philosophy for World Governance*, translated by Liqing Tao. Singapore: Springer Nature Pte Ltd., 2019.

———. *All under Heaven: The Tianxia System for a Possible World Order*. translated by Joseph E. Harroff. Berkeley: University of California Press, 2021.

Zheng, Yangwen. *China on the Sea: How the Maritime World Shaped Modern China*. Leiden: Brill, 2012.

Zhuangzi Zhuangzi and Burton Watson. *Chuang Tzu: Basic Writings*. New York: Columbia University Press, 1964.

Ziporyn, Brook. *Ironies of Oneness and Difference: Coherence in Early Chinese Thought; Prolegomena to the Study of Li 理*. Albany: State University of New York Press, 2012.

———. *Emptiness and Omnipresence: The Lotus Sutra and Tiantai Buddhism*. Bloomington: Indiana University Press, 2016.

———, trans. *Zhuangzi: The Complete Writings*. Indianapolis: Hackett Publishing, 2020.

Chinese Sources

Ban, Gu 班固. *Hanshu* 汉书. *The Complete Eleven Volumes* 全十一册. Beijing: Zhonghua Shuju 中华书局, 1962.

Chen, Guying 陈鼓应. *Zhuangzi Jinzhu Jinshi* 庄子今注今译. Beijing: Shangwu Yinshuguan 商务印书馆, 2016.

Chen, Shou 陈寿. *Sanguo Zhi* 三国志. Beijing: Zhonghua Shuju 中华书局, 1982.

Chen, Tongsheng 陈桐生. *Guoyu* 国语. Beijing: Zhonghua Shuju 中华书局, 2013.

Cheng, Hao 程颢, and Cheng Yi 程颐. *Er Cheng Ji* 二程集. 2 vols. 全二册. Beijing: Zhonghua Shuju 中华书局, 1981.

Dai, De 戴德. *Da Dai Liji Jinzhu Jinyi* 大戴礼记今注今译. Taibei: Taiwan Shangwu Yinshuguan, 1978.

Duan, Yucai 段玉裁. *Shuowen Jiezizhu shang* 说文解字注上. Nanjing: Fenghuang Chubanshe 凤凰出版社, 2015.

Fan, Ye 范晔. *Hou Han Shu* 后汉书. Beijing: Zhonghua Shuju 中华书局, 1965.

Fang, Xuanling 房玄龄. *Jin Shu* 晋书. Beijing: Zhonghua Shuju 中华书局, 1974.

Fang, Shiming 方诗铭, and Wang Xiuling 王修龄. *Guben Zhushujinian Jizheng*. Shanghai: Shanghai Guji Chubanshe, 2005.

Fu, Yashu 傅亚庶. *Kongcongzi Jiaoshi* 孔丛子校释. Beijing: Zhonghua Shuju 中华书局, 2011.

Gao, Ming 高明. 1978. *Dadailiji jinzhu jinyi* 大戴礼记今注今译. Taibei: Taiwan Shangwu Yinshuguan.

Hua, Tao 华涛. "'Silk Road' in the Medieval Chinese and Arabic-Persian Sources." 中文和阿拉伯—波斯文古籍中的"一带一路" 新世纪图书馆 *New Century Library* 11 (2016): 9–14.

Liang, Qichao 梁启超. *Lishishang Zhongguo Minzu zhi Guancha* 历史上中国民族之观察历史上中国民族之观察. Beijing: Zhonghua Shuju 中华书局, 2015.

Liu, Yihong 刘一虹. "Dialogue between Islam and Confucianism—A Study of Chinese Islamic Philosophy in the Ming and Qing Dynasties" 回儒对话——明清时期中国伊斯兰哲学思想研究. *Philosophical Research* 哲学研究 9 (2005): 42–47.

Liu, Xiang 刘向. *Shuoyuan Jiaozheng* 说苑校证. Beijing: Zhonghua Shuju 中华书局, 1987.

Liu, Xu 刘昫. *Jiu Tang Shu* 旧唐书. Beijing: Zhonghua Shuju 中华书局, 1975.

Liu, Zhou 刘昼. *Liuzi Jiaoshi* 刘子校释. Beijing: Zhonghua Shuju 中华书局, 1998.

Ma, Duanlin 马端临. *Wenxian Tongkao* 文献通考. Beijing: Zhonghua Shuju 中华书局, 2011.

Ouyang, Xiu 欧阳修, and Qi Song 宋祁. *Xin Tang Shu* 新唐书. Beijing: Zhonghua Shuju 中华书局, 1975.

Ruan, Yuan 阮元. *Shisanjing Zhushu* 十三经注疏. Beijing: Zhonghua Shuju 中华书局, 2009.

Shen, Yue 沈约. *Song Shu* 宋书. Beijing: Zhonghua Shuju 中华书局, 1974.

Sima, Qian 司马迁. *Shiji* 史记. Commentaries by Han Zhaoqi 韩兆琦. Beijing: Zhonghua Shuju 中华书局, 2010.

Tuo, Tuo 脱脱. *Song Shi* 宋史. Beijing: Zhonghua Shuju 中华书局, 1985.

Wang, Pingzhen 王聘珍. *Da Dai Liji Jiegu* 大戴礼记解诂. Beijing: Zhonghua Shuju 中华书局, 1983.

Wang, Shishun 王世舜, and Cuiye Wang 王翠叶. *Shangshu* 尚书. Beijing: Zhonghua Shuju 中华书局, 2012.

Wang, Shouren 王守仁. *Wang Yangming Quanji* 王阳明全集. 3 vols. 全三册. Shanghai: Shanghai Guji Chubanshe, 2011.

Wang, Wenjin 王文锦. *Liji Yijie* 礼记译解. Beijing: Zhonghua Shuju 中华书局, 2016.

Wei, Shou 魏收. *Wei Shu* 魏书. Beijing: Zhonghua Shuju 中华书局, 1974.

Xie, Liangzuo 谢良佐. *Shangcai Yulu Juanshang* 上蔡语录·卷上. Shanghai: Huadong Shifan Daxue Chubanshe 华东师范大学出版社, 2010.

Xun, Yue 荀悦. *Han Ji* 汉纪. Beijing: Zhonghua Shuju 中华书局, 2002.

Yan, Fuling 阎福玲. *Han Tang Biansaishi Yanjiu* 汉唐边塞诗研究. Beijing: Zhonghua Shuju 中华书局, 2014.

Yao, Silian 姚思廉. *Liang Shu* 梁书. Beijing: Zhonghua Shuju 中华书局, 1973.

Zhai, Jiangyue 翟江月. *Records on the Warring States Period* 战国策. Guilin: Guangxi Normal University Press 广西师范大学出版社, 2008.

Zhang, Tingyu 张廷玉. *Ming Shi* 明史. Beijing: Zhonghua Shuju 中华书局, 1974.

Zhang, Zai 张载. *Zhang Zai Ji* 张载集. Beijing: Zhonghua Shuju 中华书局, 1978.

Zhao, Rukuo 赵汝适. *Zhu Fan Zhi Jiaoshi* 诸蕃志校释. Beijing: Zhonghua Shuju 中华书局, 2000.

Zhou, Weizhou 周伟洲. "tang dai guan zhong min zu de fen bu ji rong he" 唐代关中民族的分布及融合. *Journal of Chinese Historical Geography* 中国历史地理论丛 年3期 (1991): 117–36.

Zhu, Xi 朱熹. *Zhuzi Yulei* 朱子语类. Beijing: Zhonghua Shuju 中华书局, 1986.

INDEX

academics. *See* Sinologists and Western academics

acculturation: becoming human and, 55, 57, 60, 88, 104; Chinese identity and, 49, 52–53, 57; commensurability between peoples and, 107; impossible for barbarian, 72. *See also* assimilation

African-Americans, guilt projected onto, 20

African population: enslaved and halved by Europeans, 1, 20, 201, 202; reason-passion dualism and, 78

agency, human, 59–62; Aristotle on nature and, 142; of female womb, 149; metaphysical determinism and, 115

Age of Discovery, 1, 4, 38, 117, 129, 130, 134, 200, 205, 223n21

Albright, Madeleine, 203

Alcoff, Linda Martin, 15

Algeria, French massacres in, 202

Allan, Sarah, 226n24

Alopen, 68–69

Alvarez Chanca, Diego, 223n4

Amerindians encountered by Europeans: beyond moral concern, 99–100; cannibalism attributed to, 78, 219n4; colonialism as holy war and, 3, 82; European civilization and, 8; ideology of racism and, 4; literary narrative of captivity and, 220n9; myth of vacant land and, 139–40, 142; near-annihilation of, 1, 7–8, 22, 25–26, 117, 126, 144, 147, 201; Puritan fear of mortality and, 124; reason-passion dualism and, 78, 124; in Spanish conquest, 3, 7–8,

78, 104–5, 117, 120, 121, 223n4; as threat to conception of order, 126–27; viewed as natural slaves, 99, 104–5, 120

Ames, Roger, 150, 156

Amoghavajra, 67

Anderson, E. N., 221n6

animals: biblical passages about, 170, 227n6; Chinese attitudes toward, 85–86, 89–90, 169–74; Chinese linguistic descriptions of, 90–91; composite images of, 164; in continuum with humans, 88, 100–101, 170, 173, 222n11; Daoist attitude toward, 172, 221n6; giraffe presented to emperor, 109, 111; Greco-biblical difference between man and, 83–84, 221n13; in Greek tradition, 98, 100–101, 109, 145–46, 171–72; moral distinction of humans from, 102–3, 222n13; as natural kind in Greco-Western tradition, 88; opossum encountered by Europeans, 109, 110; state of Qin analogized with, 103, 222n13

An Lushan, 67

anomalous phenomena: Chinese attitude toward, 91–93, 106, 112; order in white metaphysics and, 125

anthropocentrism, 188, 189

Antichrist, 76, 80

anti-representationalism, 90–91, 154–55, 159, 192

anti-Semitism, 56, 79–80, 211n23, 222n16

Appiah, Anthony, 192

Aquinas, Thomas, 118, 119

Arendt, Hannah, 202

A NOTE ON THE TYPE

This book has been composed in Arno, an Old-style serif typeface in the classic Venetian tradition, designed by Robert Slimbach at Adobe.